GRADE

COMPLETE YEAR **1**

Weekly Learning Activities

Thinking Kids™
Carson-Dellosa Publishing LLC
Greensboro, North Carolina

Thinking Kids™
An imprint of Carson-Dellosa Publishing LLC
P.O. Box 35665
Greensboro, NC 27425 USA

Printed in the USA • All rights reserved.   ISBN 978-1-4838-0191-9
02-209147784

Table of Contents

Table of Contents

Table of Contents

Introduction to *Complete Year: Grade 1*

The *Complete Year* series has been designed by educators to provide an entire school year's worth of practice pages, teaching suggestions, and multi-sensory activities to support your child's learning at home. Handy organizers are included to help students and parents stay on track and to let you see at a glance the important skills for each quarter and each week of the academic year.

A variety of resources are included to help you provide high-quality learning experiences during this important year of your child's development.

Suggested Calendar (Page 7)
Use this recommended timetable to plan learning activities for your child during all 36 weeks of the school year.

A Guide to School Skills and Subject Areas for First Grade: Basic Skills, Reading and Language Arts, Math, Gross and Fine Motor Skills, Science, and Social Studies (Page 8)
Refer to this useful guide for information about what your child will be learning this school year, what to expect from your first grader, and how to help your child develop skills in each subject area.

Quarter Introductions (Pages 14, 108, 202, 296)
Four brief introductions outline the skills covered in practice pages for each nine-week grading period of the school year. In addition, they include a variety of ideas for multi-sensory learning activities in each subject area. These active, hands-on projects are fun for parents and children to do together and emphasize real-world applications for school skills.

Weekly Skill Summaries (Example: Page 17)
Thirty-six handy charts precede the practice pages for each week and give a snapshot of the skills covered. In addition, they provide ideas for fun, multi-sensory learning activities for each subject area.

Practice Pages (Example: Page 18)
Nine practice pages are provided each week for a total of over 300 skill-building activities to help your child succeed this year.

Quarter Check-Ups (Pages 107, 201, 295, 389)
Four informal assessment pages allow students to do a quick self-check of the important skills emphasized during the previous nine weeks. Parents can use these pages to see at a glance the skills their children have mastered.

Suggested *Complete Year* Calendar*

First Quarter: Weeks 1–9
(First nine-week grading period of the school year, usually August–October)

Second Quarter: Weeks 10–18
(Second nine-week grading period of the school year, usually October–December)

Third Quarter: Weeks 19–27
(Third nine-week grading period of the school year, usually January–March)

Fourth Quarter: Weeks 28–36
(Fourth nine-week grading period of the school year, usually April–June)

During Each Nine-Week Quarter:

- Read the **Quarter Introduction** to get an overview of the skills and subject areas emphasized. Choose several multi-sensory learning activities you plan to do with your child this quarter.

- Each week, glance at the **Weekly Skill Summary** to see targeted skills. Make a quick plan for the practice pages and multi-sensory learning activities your child will complete.

- Choose **Practice Pages** that emphasize skills your child needs to work on. Each page should take 10 minutes or less to complete.

- Ask your child to check the boxes on the **Quarter Check-Up** to show what skills he or she has mastered. Praise your child's progress and take note of what he or she still needs to work on.

* This calendar provides a schedule for using *Complete Year* during a typical nine-month academic calendar. If your child attends a year-round school or a school with a different schedule, you can easily adapt this calendar by counting the weeks your child attends school and dividing by four.

A Guide to School Skills for First Grade

This guide provides background information about the skills and subject areas that are important for success in first grade. Tips are provided for helping your child develop in each curricular area.

Complete Year supports skills included in the Grade 1 Common Core State Standards for English Language Arts and Mathematics, which have been adopted by most U.S. states. A complete guide to these standards may be found at www.corestandards.org.

In addition, activities in *Complete Year* support gross motor development and fine motor development, which are essential to a young child's ability to complete schoolwork and regulate behavior.

 **Basic Skills**

- Classifying
  Organizing objects into categories can be done in many ways. For example, have your child group a set of objects by color, size, pattern, purpose, or other attribute.

- Critical Thinking
  Young children love riddles, jokes, and tongue twisters. Use these word games to develop your child's thinking skills. Critical thinking can be encouraged in many ways. Try asking your child to create a new ending to a common story or have him or her be the "teacher" and ask you questions about a story you read together.

- Compare and Contrast
  Help foster your child's ability to observe similarities and differences among objects. Begin with obvious similarities and differences in color, size, and shape, and advance to more subtle similarities and differences in pattern, texture, purpose, etc.

 Reading and Language Arts

Reading
Teach reading with books that fit your child's ability and interests, using a variety of books. Before asking your child to read a book

independently, activate your child's prior knowledge of the book's subject. Then, read the book aloud and discuss the story elements. For example, discuss the stages of a butterfly's life cycle and what caterpillars eat before reading Eric Carle's *The Very Hungry Caterpillar*. Provide books that your child can read independently the first time, while also reading books aloud that are at a higher level than your child's independent reading level.

- Word Recognition
  When encountering a new word, encourage your child to use three different cues: think about the context (meaning), analyze the sense of the sentence (syntax), and/or sound the word out phonetically. After reading a book, make flash cards of words that your child needs to practice. Maintain a word bank of words that your child is learning. Keep a separate bank of learned words to be reviewed periodically.

- Phonics
  Look for opportunities to teach the following skills in context: beginning, middle, and ending sounds; blends and digraphs, like **tr**ain or **sh**ip; rhyming words; and vowel sound families. Make charts to hang around the room for each vowel sound, and add words as your child encounters them in the books he or she reads. He or she will also study syllables and how to recognize the number of syllables when words are spoken aloud.

- Reading Comprehension
  Read to and with your child every day. Build a love of reading through positive experiences with books. A child who loves reading will be a more successful reader. Read a variety of books aloud, and let your child choose books that interest him or her to read independently. See page 394 for a list of books that may appeal to first graders.

  The goal of reading is to acquire meaning from text. After reading a book, ask your child a variety of questions to test comprehension, such as "Explain what the character meant by ..." or "Make a timeline of events in the story." Ask questions related to context clues to test your child's comprehension of information that is not overtly given and must be inferred.

Language Skills

Language skills are often taught in the context of reading. Your child may be asked to apply knowledge gained from reading to the study of words, sentences, and texts. When reading aloud to your child, take the opportunity to point to individual words, sentences, and punctuation marks on the page and talk about them. This will give your child a deeper understanding of how language works.

- Vocabulary Development
  Have your child write stories, in his or her own words, to be used as his or her reading text. This low-risk writing experience builds proficiency with language, and it helps him or her make the connection between the spoken and written word. Because this writing is in your child's own words, he or she will feel successful in reading at a very early stage. That confidence will help him or her be a successful reader of other printed materials.

- Types of Words and Sentences
  This year, your child will learn to recognize the distinguishing features of a sentence, such as capitalization, commas, and ending punctuation to indicate statements and questions.

  Your child will build upon his or her knowledge of nouns, verbs, and adjectives by diving into proper nouns, pronouns, plural nouns, and present- and past-tense verbs. He or she will also study contractions, like **don't** or **I'm**; compound words, like **mailbox** or **backpack**; possessives; and common prefixes and word endings.

Writing

In first grade, your child's writing will progress into full paragraphs of complete thoughts and conclusions. He or she will write to tell stories and share information. Learning to write is a process developed much like learning to speak. Provide your child with modeling and reasons to write, and applaud his or her attempts. First, emphasize fluency in your child's writing, then move toward accuracy. Emphasize one writing skill per writing piece so that your child will not be discouraged by negative feedback. Keep a folder of your child's writing. From time to time, encourage your child to improve an old story or look over the year's work to check for improvement.

- Handwriting
  Practice pages in this book will help your child print uppercase and lowercase letters correctly (see pages 18–20).

- **Story Telling**

  Your child will learn to write fiction and nonfiction stories based on his or her experiences or imagination (see pages 381–383). Encourage your child to describe two or more events written in the correct sequential order, including words such as **then**, **next**, or **finally**.

- **Informative Writing**

  In this type of writing, your child will name a topic, supply some facts or details about the topic, and then provide a conclusion (see page 384).

Speaking and Listening

Good speaking and listening skills are essential to school success. By paying careful attention to what is being said, your child will not only learn more but will develop the skill of being a good conversationalist as well. Make sure to provide ample opportunities for your child to listen to songs, poetry, and stories.

Math

To teach math to your first grader, use hands-on activities and concrete objects to explain new concepts. It is important that your child understand the concept underlying a problem and not just how to solve it. During his or her first-grade year, your child should learn the basic facts through 20 and work to memorize them. He or she should also learn to solve two-digit problems and column addition, which involves adding three or more numbers together in one problem. Also covered this year will be place value, ordinal numbers, fractions, measurement, telling time, identifying and counting money, and graphing information.

- **Addition and Subtraction**

  Your child will focus on adding and subtracting within 20. He or she will be able to solve word problems involving situations of adding to, taking from, putting together, or taking apart. You can help your child relate math skills to daily living activities by creating situations and encouraging him or her to solve the problems.

  Addition is the combining of sets into a new whole. Provide opportunities for your child to discover that by creating and combining meaningful sets, a new set is created. While an eventual goal is memorization, it is essential that your child understand the concept of the part-part-whole relationships of addition and subtraction. It is valuable to be able to visualize that the number 5 is the same as 4 and 1, 3 and 2, 1 and 4, and 2 and 3. Addition as a mathematical process takes on more meaning for your child if there is a need for it.

Use manipulatives to introduce subtraction in the context of stories that your child needs to solve. Working with manipulatives also helps your child grasp the relationship between addition and subtraction. Provide a variety of practice so your child will have a firm understanding of subtraction and its uses.

• Place Value
In first grade, your child will continue working with place value of tens and ones. When your child understands that the number 36 means 3 tens 6 ones, he or she is working with the concept of place value. To understand place value, your child must learn to see a group of ten objects as "one ten," a unit. This is a difficult concept that is built up with hands-on experience grouping a variety of manipulatives and repeated counting of objects by ones as well as by tens and ones.

• Counting
There is a difference between rote counting and understanding the meaning of counting. Help your child develop an understanding of numbers through a variety of concrete counting experiences. Have your child practice counting sets of actual objects, rearranging them, and counting again. Activities such as these will help develop your child's understanding of one-to-one correspondence.

This year, your child will practice skip-counting by tens and fives (5, 10, 15, 20 and 10, 20, 30, 40). This is early practice for multiplication, which your child will begin to learn in the second grade.

• Patterns
Patterns form the basis of mathematics and enhance problem-solving skills. Teach your child to recognize a pattern by modeling rhythmic and visual patterns. Have your child look for the pattern that is repeated in the sequence, then join in the rhythm or have your child complete the visual pattern.

 ## Gross and Fine Motor Skills

Developing motor skills is important to your child's physical development. Many people—both adults and children—learn by doing. What may seem like "play" may help your child internalize a concept or skill.

The movement of the large muscle groups is considered gross motor activity. Running, jumping, climbing, throwing a ball, and other similar activities use the body's large muscles. Your child develops large-muscle maturity through active play. Control of the large muscles helps your child move smoothly and control his or her actions.

Many school activities require your child to use the body's small muscle groups to accomplish tasks such as tracing, cutting, writing, folding, and using blocks. These are fine motor skills. Encourage your child to keep working on these skills. As the small muscles develop, both of you will see improvement in your child's skill level.

 ## Science

During this school year, your child's science learning should focus on living things, plants and animals, the human body, the five senses, seasons and weather, the solar system, and simple machines. To find more information on the topics covered or ideas for experiments, consult the following resources, if available in your area: the local library for videos, informational books and books containing experiments; a science center or museum of natural history; a garden center or botanical garden; the park system or forest service; nature stores; and magazines such as *Ranger Rick* and *National Geographic Kids*.

Social Studies

The concepts taught in social studies will give your child a basic understanding of him or herself, social skills, the community, famous Americans, maps, and places of the world. Provide your child with experiences that will help make the concepts as real to him or her as possible. When studying early America, for example, try going to an antique store or museum. Find the different locations you study on a map and help your child figure out how far they are from your hometown. Seek out people from your community who have visited or lived in other parts of the world and are willing to share their experiences, pictures, etc., with your child. In addition, make use of videos from the library showing places you are unable to visit.

First Quarter Introduction

The early weeks of first grade can be an adjustment for some students. The first grade classroom is a more structured and academic setting than what many children have previously experienced. Help your child get off to a good start with the school year by establishing good routines and study skills. These good habits will remain with your child and benefit him or her throughout the school years ahead.

First Quarter Skills
Practice pages in this book for Weeks 1–9 will help your child improve the following skills.

Basic Skills
- Identify and review colors red, yellow, blue, green, orange, brown, white, black, pink, and purple

Reading and Language Arts
- Write uppercase and lowercase letters **Aa–Zz**
- Match uppercase letters with their lowercase letters
- Recognize short and long vowel sounds
- Recognize the sounds made by the consonants **b, c, d, f, g, h, j, k, l, m, n, p, q, r, s, t, v, w, y, z**

Math
- Recognize squares, circles, triangles, rectangles, ovals, and rhombuses
- Classify shapes as same and different
- Understand shape patterns

Multi-Sensory Learning Activities
Try these fun activities for enhancing your child's learning and development during the first quarter of the school year. Be sure to choose activities that include speaking, listening, touching, and active movement.

Basic Skills

Write color words on index cards and have your child place the cards on objects of the given color. Point to colors around the room and have your child spell the color word on a piece of paper.

Have your child look in the mirror and answer questions about him or herself. What do you see? What color is your hair? Is it curly or straight? What color are your eyes? Have your child draw a picture of him or herself and write a description.

Reading and Language Arts

Write your child's name in uppercase letters vertically down the left side of a page. Have your child write a word or draw a simple picture of an object that begins with each of the letters in his or her name. Repeat using the names of family members.

Have your child look through magazines for pictures beginning with each letter of the alphabet. He or she should cut out and glue each picture onto a sheet of paper with the letter written on it. Hang your child's alphabet letters on a clothesline in alphabetical order.

Dictate a list of three-letter words to your child. Have your child write each word and underline the ending consonant.

Make bread dough letters with your child. Mix the ingredients listed below and divide into 26 pieces.
$3\frac{3}{4}$ cups whole wheat flour
2 cups buttermilk
$\frac{1}{4}$ cup wheat germ
2 teaspoons baking soda
1 cup molasses
On waxed paper, have your child roll out each piece of dough like a snake, then form each piece into a letter of the alphabet. Place the letters on greased cookie sheets and bake at 375° for 20 minutes or until they are golden brown. Use the letters to form simple three-letter words. Ask your child to identify the vowel sound he or she hears in each word.

Math

Play a game in which you describe a shape and have your child identify the shape. Then, name two shapes and discuss characteristics between the two that are the same and different.

Draw one shape on a large sheet of paper. Have your child list or draw things in the room that contain or have that shape. Repeat with other shapes.

Have your child make five paper chains, using patterns of three to five colors on each chain.

Cut a 6-inch circle pattern from tagboard for your child to trace several times onto different colors of construction paper. Have your child write the titles of books he or she has read on the circles. On one circle, have your child draw a caterpillar face. Hang the circles on the wall, building a pattern of colors. Watch as the circles form a caterpillar that can grow around the room as your child continues to read books throughout the year.

First Quarter Introduction, cont.

 Fine Motor Skills

Make a bird feeder. First, take a pipe cleaner and bend one end into an L-shape. Then, ask your child to thread some Cheerios onto the pipe cleaner. When the pipe cleaner is full, twist the ends together and tie a string around the bird feeder to hang outside.

Have your child look at the headlines in a newspaper. Help your child cut out a word that begins with each letter of the alphabet and arrange the words in alphabetical order. He or she can then glue the words on a sheet of paper.

Gross Motor Skills

Play "Broom Hockey." Find some small round objects, such as bottle caps, and line them up on the ground outside. Using a small broom like a hockey stick, encourage your child to hit the bottle caps.

Use sidewalk chalk to make a special hopscotch grid using letters in your child's name. Draw a square for each letter, and a big box at the end to write his or her full name. Encourage your child to practice hopping from one square to the next as he or she spells her name aloud.

Social Studies

Give your child clues about a worker in the community until your child can guess the occupation. For example, you might say, "This worker cuts and packages food. This worker wears a white apron. This worker may work at a grocery store. This person works with something that rhymes with **feet**." Your child would answer, "Butcher."

Discuss a couple of famous Americans, such as George Washington, Martin Luther King, Jr., or Sally Ride. Have your child choose one person to read about. Talk to your child about what he or she learned.

Seasonal Fun

Read *We're Going on a Leaf Hunt* by Steve Metzger. Then, help your child make leaf rubbings. Have your child put a leaf under a thin piece of paper and rub over the paper with the side of a crayon. On the bottom of the page, write "This leaf is _____" and have your child complete the sentence.

Help your child carve a pumpkin. Scoop the pulp onto a newspaper or large mat. Ask your child to count the seeds by putting them in groups of 10.

Week 1 Skills

Subject	Skill	Multi-Sensory Learning Activities
Reading and Language Arts	Write the letters **Aa–Zz**.	• Complete Practice Pages 18–20. • Ask your child to trace each letter on the Practice Pages with his or her finger.
	Recognize upper- and lowercase letters.	• Complete Practice Pages 21 and 22. • Make a set of upper- and lowercase alphabet cards. Scramble both sets and ask your child to identify a given letter, such as uppercase **B** or lowercase **d**. • Read *Chicka Chicka Boom Boom* by Bill Martin, Jr. Clap your hands when you read each letter in the rhyme.
Basic Skills	Work with the colors red, yellow, blue, green, orange, brown, white, black, pink, and purple.	• Complete Practice Pages 23–25. • Make a list of descriptive words that tell about what you see around you. Ask your child to point out objects that have the same color.
Bonus: Math		• Write the numerals 1–10 on index cards, one per card. Using small familiar objects, ask your child to place the number of objects called for on each card.
Bonus: Fine Motor Skills		• Hide small objects, such as coins or beads, in a ball of soft clay. Then, have your child pinch and stretch the clay to find the objects. Show your child how to use the thumb and index finger together to make a pinching motion.

Alphabet

Practice writing the letters.

Alphabet

Practice writing the letters.

Jj

Kk

Ll

Mm

Nn

Oo

Pp

Qq

Rr

Alphabet

Practice writing the letters.

S s -

T t -

U u -

V v -

W w -

X x -

Y y -

Z z -

Letter Recognition

In each set, match the lowercase letter to the uppercase letter.

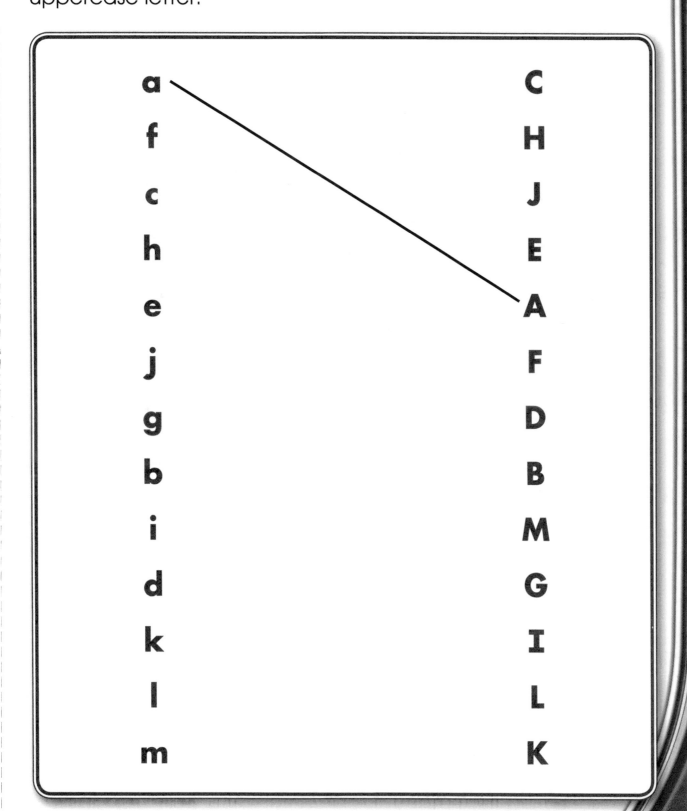

Letter Recognition

In each set, match the lowercase letter to the uppercase letter.

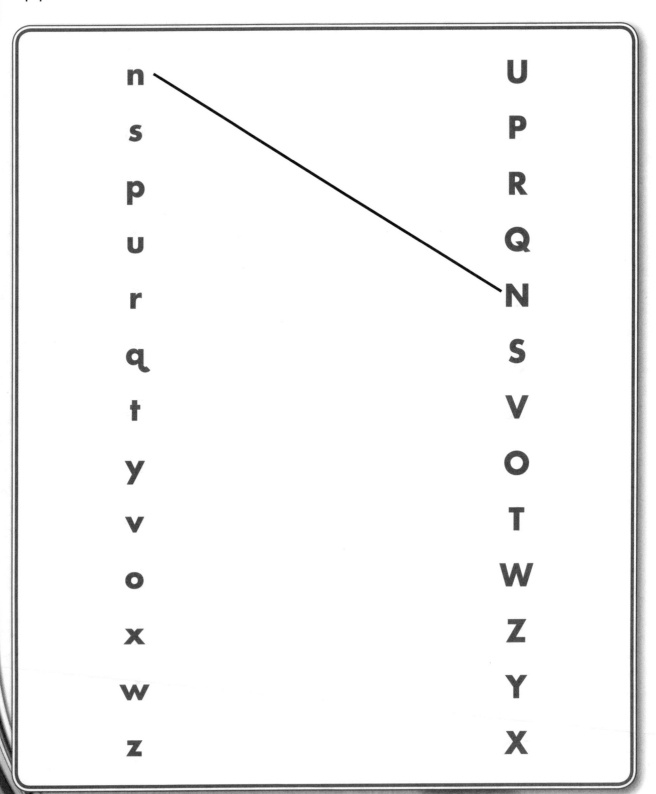

Twinkling Starlights

Stars change as they get older. They start out big and then shrink. As they shrink, they change color. Color the stars the correct color.

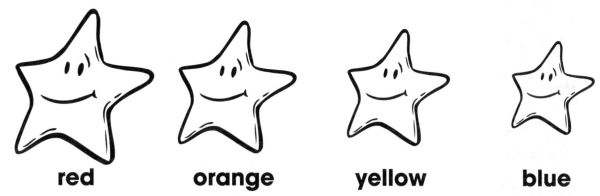

red   **orange**   **yellow**   **blue**

Look at the stars below. Color each star the correct color. Then, draw a circle around the youngest stars and a box around the oldest ones.

Naturally Colorful Canvas

Use the code to color the picture.

1-brown
2-white
3-blue
4-black
5-pink
6-green
7-yellow
8-red
9-orange
10-purple

Use the picture to write the missing color words on the lines.

The _____ cub is eating a

_____ berry. A _____

caterpillar is creeping under a flower. One

_____ duck and one _____

fish are swimming in the _____ pond.

A little _____ bird is resting on a rock. A

_____ butterfly will land on the

_____ flower.

The Four Seasons

Cut out and glue the season words in the correct boxes below.

Color the clothes for:

Fall-blue   **Winter**-red   **Spring**-green   **Summer**-yellow

| Spring | Summer | Fall | Winter |

Week 2 Skills

Subject	Skill	Multi-Sensory Learning Activities
Reading and Language Arts	Identify the **short a** and **long a** vowel sounds.	• Complete Practice Pages 28–32. • Slowly say several words that begin with vowels, such as **ant**, **axe**, and **animal**. Tell your child to clap his or her hands when you say a word that begins with **short a**. • Cut out each of the 26 letters of the alphabet from a sheet of construction paper. Use the letters to form **long a** words like **cake**, **ape**, and **wave**.
Basic Skills	Work with the colors red, black, purple, green, yellow, orange, pink, blue, and brown.	• Complete Practice Pages 33–36. • Have your child sort small objects like buttons or hard candies into piles based on color. Ask your child to name something that these objects have in common.
Bonus: Math		• Introduce the number words **one** through **ten**. Make number word cards with the corresponding number of stickers on each. Give your child a number word card and ask him or her to hop a given number of times.
Bonus: Gross Motor Skills		• Give directional clues that lead your child to a hidden object. For example, say, "Take three steps forward. Turn left and hop forward twice. Then, take two giant side steps to the right."

Words With a

Each train has a group of pictures. Write the word that names the pictures. Read your rhyming words.

These trains use the **short a** sound like in the word **cat**:

These trains use the **long a** sound like in the word **lake**:

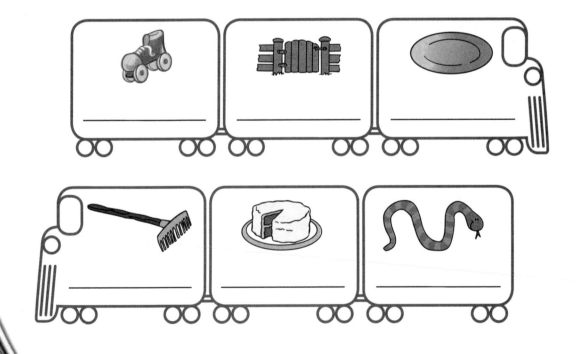

Short and Long Aa

Say the name of each picture. If it has the **short a** sound, color it red. If it has the **long a** sound, color it yellow.

ă   ā

Short a

Write **a** on each line. Draw a line from each word to the correct picture. Then, color the pictures.

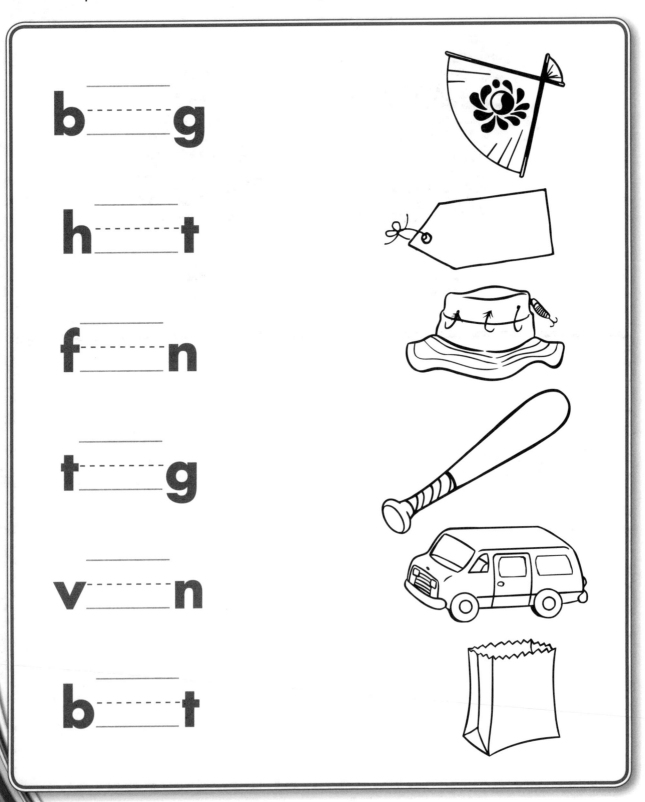

b _____ g

h _____ t

f _____ n

t _____ g

v _____ n

b _____ t

COMPLETE YEAR GRADE 1

Rocket Raccoon

Write the word that names each picture.

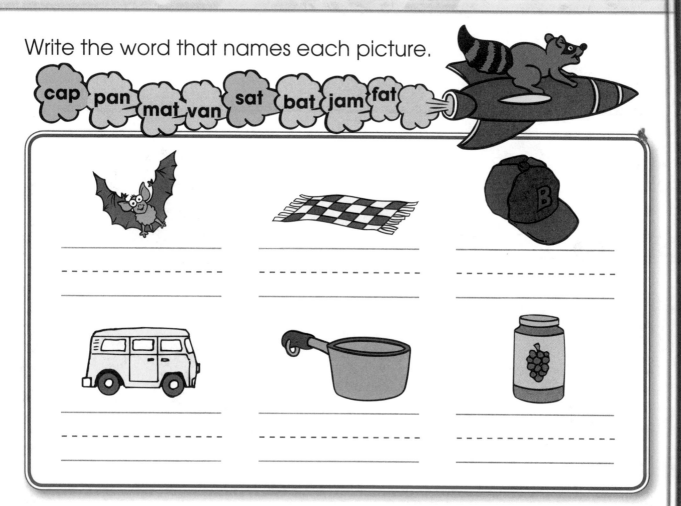

cap pan mat van sat bat jam fat

Write the words that rhyme with the pictures.

Short Vowel Aa

Write the letter **a** to complete each word below. Draw a line to match the word with its picture.

p __ n

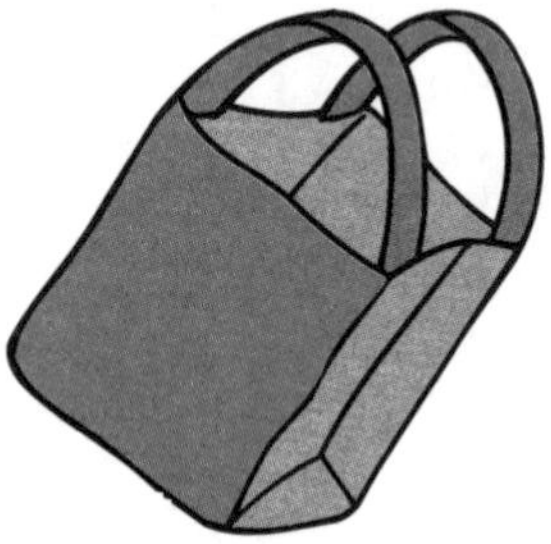

m __ n

b __ g

v __ n

Colors

In each row, color two things that are the same color.

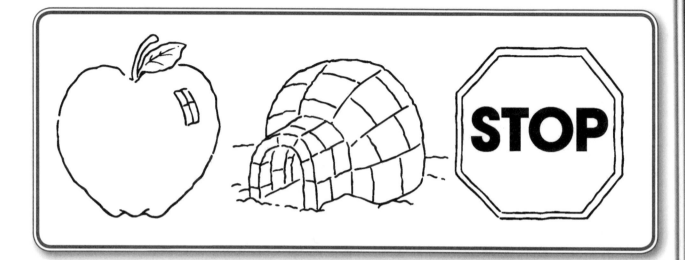

Colors

In each row, color two things that are the same color.

Colors

In each row, color two things that are the same color.

Colors

Draw a line to match each picture to the crayon with the same color.

Week 3 Skills

Subject	Skill	Multi-Sensory Learning Activities
Reading and Language Arts	Identify the **short e** and **long e** vowel sounds.	• Complete Practice Pages 38–42. • Ask your child to spell the following **short e** words aloud: **pet**, **jet**, **tent**, and **wet**. Does your child notice any patterns with the vowel sound he or she hears? • Ask your child to tell a story about a queen. What words in the story have the **long e** sound? Tell your child to illustrate those words.
Math	Recognize and draw squares, circles, and triangles.	• Complete Practice Pages 43–46. • Give step-by-step directions to create a drawing of a house. For example, say, "Draw a square. Draw a triangle on top of the square. Inside the square, draw a circle on the left and a circle on the right." • Out of construction paper, cut several triangles, circles, and squares of varying sizes and colors. Label each shape. Help your child identify shapes and their attributes through sorting and comparing.
Bonus: Fine Motor Skills		• Use a sugar cookie recipe to bake cookies in the shape of gingerbread men. Have your child use frosting and candies to decorate the cookies.

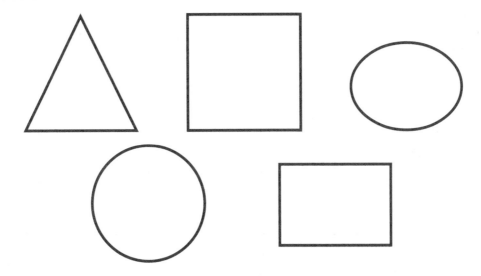

Words With e

Short e sounds like the **e** in **hen**. Long e sounds like the **e** in **bee**. Look at the pictures. If the word has a **short e** sound, draw a line to the hen with your red crayon. If the word has a **long e** sound, draw a line to the bee with your green crayon.

Short and Long Ee

Say the name of each picture. Circle the pictures which have the **short e** sound. Draw a triangle around the pictures which have the **long e** sound.

ĕ   ē

Short e

Say each picture name. If the picture has the sound of **short e**, color the shape blue.

Sneak a Peek!

Write the words where they belong.

bee	**keep**	**see**	**he**
me	**feel**	**we**	**peek**

Nouns or Naming Words

Verbs or Action Words

Circle the misspelled words. Then, write the sentence correctly on the lines.

1. Will ha pek inside?

2. Kep that baa away!

Get On Track

best wet set tent
jet leg nest pet

Write the words in ABC order.

1. _____   4. _____   7. _____

2. _____   5. _____   8. _____

3. _____   6. _____

Read each sentence. Write the missing word in the boxes.

1. Ned fell and cut his ___ .

2. The hen is in the ___ .

3. Please help me ___ the table.

4. Do you have a ___ rabbit?

5. Ted did his ___ .

6. We will go on a trip in a ___ .

7. Dad said, "Yes, you may play in the ___ ."

8. The hat got ___ when it fell in the pond.

Shapes: Square

A **square** is a figure with four corners and four sides of the same length. This is a square ☐ .

Find the squares and put a circle around them.

Trace the word. Write the word.

square

Shapes: Circle

A **circle** is a figure that is round. This is a circle ◯ .

Find the circles and put a square around them.

Trace the word. Write the word.

circle

Shapes: Square and Circle

Practice drawing squares. Trace the samples and make four of your own.

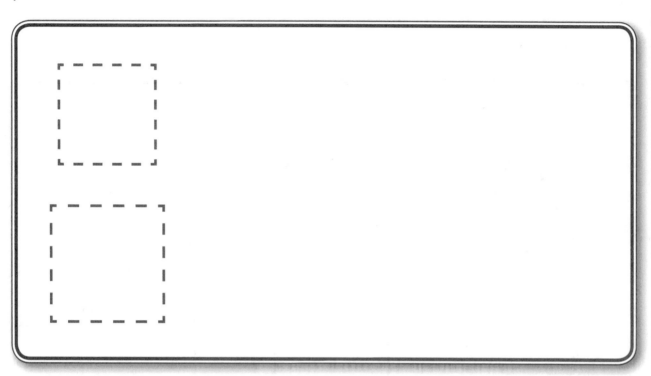

Practice drawing circles. Trace the samples and make four of your own.

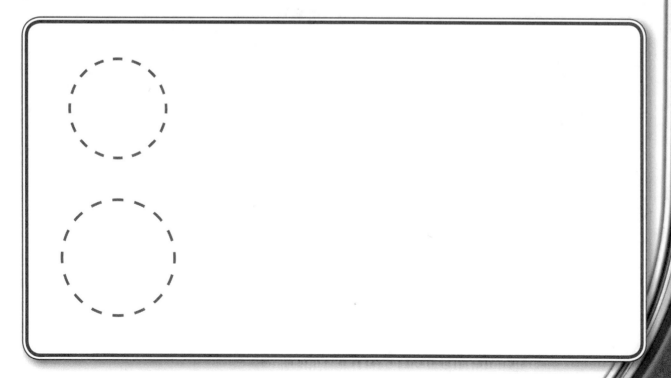

Shapes: Triangle

A **triangle** is a figure with three corners and three sides. This is a triangle △ .

Find the triangles and put a circle around them.

Trace the word. Write the word.

triangle

Week 4 Skills

Subject	Skill	Multi-Sensory Learning Activities
Reading and Language Arts	Identify the **short i** and **long i** vowel sounds.	• Complete Practice Pages 48–52. • Make a word search puzzle using **short i** words, such as **pin**, **ink**, **sing**, **pig**, **lid**, and **fin**. Encourage your child to find and circle all the **short i** words. • Make a booklet for your child featuring **long i** words. On each page, write a phrase using **long i** words, such as "Mike likes to ride a bike," "Violet flies a lilac kite," and "The white tiger smiled." Ask your child to draw a picture to illustrate each sentence.
Math	Recognize and draw rectangles; review triangles.	• Complete Practice Pages 53–56. • Help your child gain experience with wedges. Explain that a wedge is a triangle-shaped tool often used for cutting, and can be found on a knife, axe, screwdriver, or it may hold open a door. Supervise your child while he or she looks for wedges in the kitchen and among the garden tools. • Have your child identify shapes, listing as many descriptors as possible. For example, say, "A triangle has three points, three sides, and no rounded edges."
Bonus: Gross Motor Skills		• Encourage your child to get some daily exercise. Design a clearly marked pathway for running in circles or a straight path from a wall to a soft place to flop down.

Words With i

Short i sounds like the **i** in **pig**. **Long i** sounds like the **i** in **kite**. Draw a circle around the words with the **short i** sound. Draw an **X** on the words with the **long i** sound.

pin

five

pig

slide

kite

lid

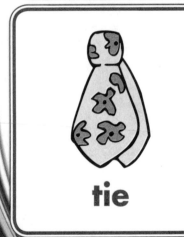

tie

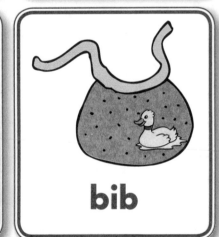

bib

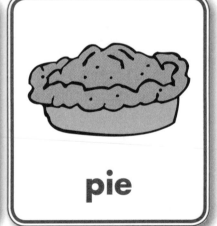

pie

Short and Long Ii

Say the name of each picture. If it has the **short i** sound, color it yellow. If it has the **long i** sound, color it red.

ĭ

ī

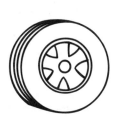

6

5

Short i

Write **i** on each line. Color the correct picture for each word.

p___g

l___d

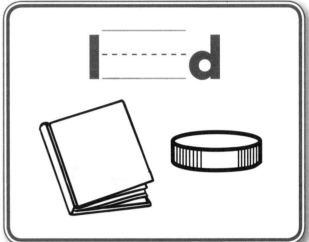

s___x

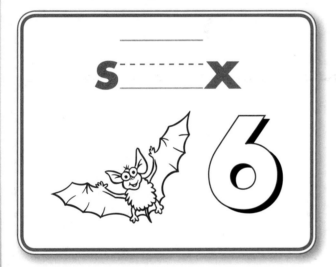

m___lk

w___g

g___ft

Picky Pigs

Write the missing word in each sentence.

pig   sit   pin   fin   dig   win   hit   lid

1. The dog can _____ a hole.

2. Put the _____ on the pan.

3. He will _____ on the bench.

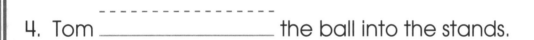

4. Tom _____ the ball into the stands.

5. The _____ sits in the mud.

6. A _____ helps a fish swim.

7. Will he _____ the prize?

8. Mom can _____ the diaper on the baby.

Shining Stars

Write the words in ABC order.

Stars: bite, side, dive, wipe, line, I, tie, hide

1. _____

2. _____

3. _____

4. _____

5. _____

6. _____

7. _____

8. _____

Use the words to complete the puzzle.

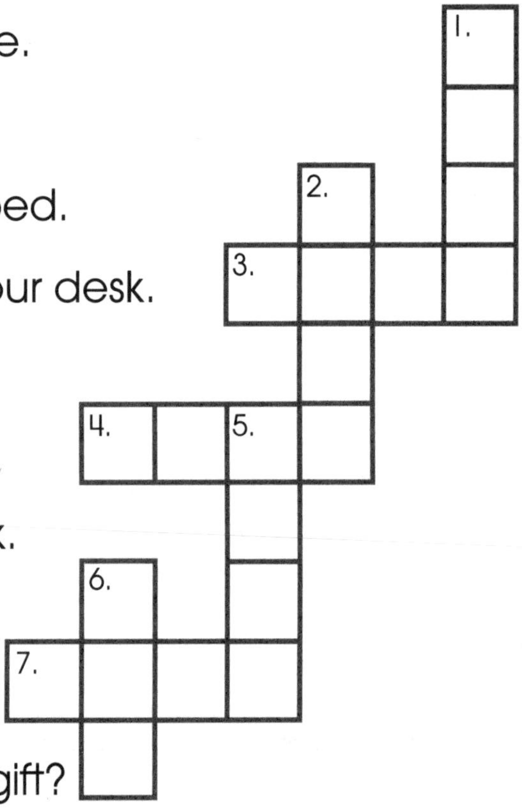

Across

3. The kitten likes to ___ under the bed.

4. Put the book on the left ___ of your desk.

7. Please ___ up the spilled milk.

Down

1. There was a long ___ at the bank.

2. Did the puppy ___ the slipper?

5. The seals will ___ of the rocks.

6. Can you ___ a ribbon on the gift?

Shapes: Rectangle

A **rectangle** is a figure with four corners and four sides. Sides opposite each other are the same length. This is a rectangle ☐.

Find the rectangles and put a circle around them.

Trace the word. Write the word.

rectangle

Shapes: Triangle and Rectangle

Practice drawing triangles. Trace the samples and make four of your own.

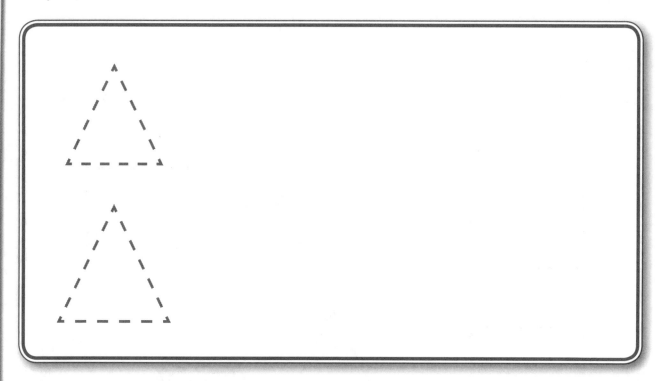

Practice drawing rectangles. Trace the samples and make four of your own.

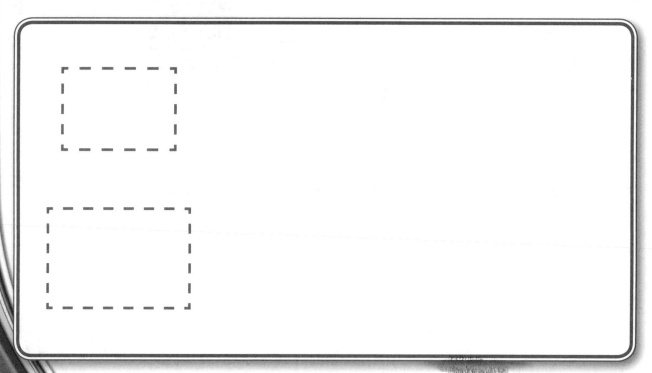

Patterns: Rectangles

In each picture, there is more than one rectangle. Trace each rectangle with a different color crayon. Under each picture, write how many rectangles you found.

_____ rectangles

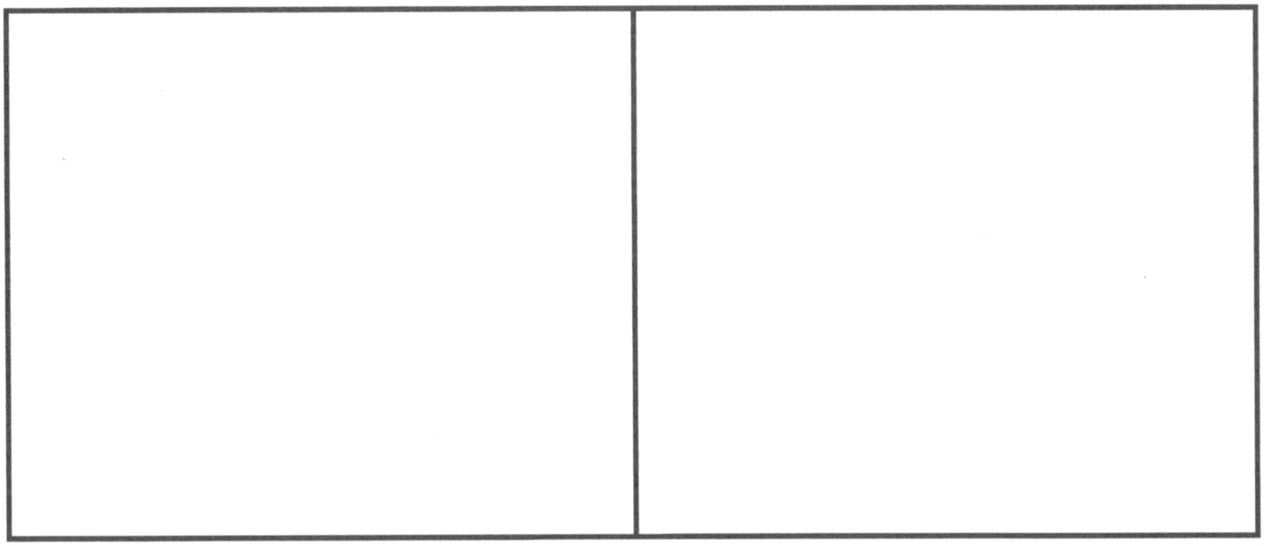

_____ rectangles

Patterns: Triangles

In each picture, there is more than one triangle. Trace each triangle with a different color crayon. Under each picture, write how many triangles you found.

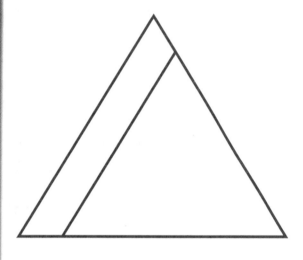

_____ triangles

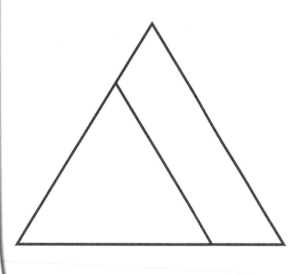

_____ triangles

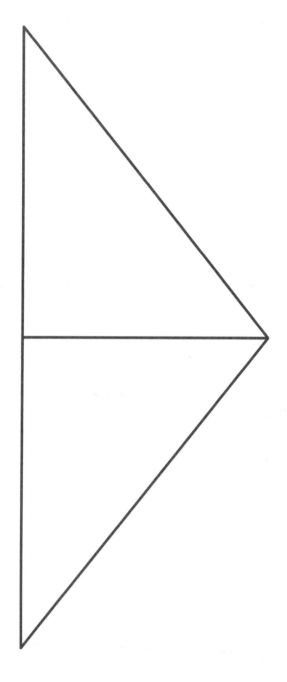

_____ triangles

Week 5 Skills

Subject	Skill	Multi-Sensory Learning Activities
Reading and Language Arts	Identify the **short o** and **long o** vowel sounds.	• Complete Practice Pages 58–61. • Name several **short o** words, such as **top**, **cot**, **drop**, and **long**. Let your child use dried beans, macaroni, or cereal to form the letters of **short o** words. • Read *Hop on Pop* by Dr. Seuss. Tell your child to hop every time he or she hears a **short o** word. • Send your child on a **long o** scavenger hunt! Give him or her a list of **long o** words that can be found around your home, such as **bows**, **clothes**, **oats**, and **phone**. For an added challenge, see if your child can find all of the objects in a set amount of time.
Math	Recognize and draw ovals and rhombuses; review shapes.	• Complete Practice Pages 62–66. • Draw an oval on a piece of paper. Ask your child to turn the oval into a spider, or anything else he or she imagines. • Ask your child to describe a rhombus, using attributes such as number of sides, number of edges, straight or curved lines, etc. Using these attributes, are rhombuses similar to any other shape? • Create flash cards of shapes. Include different sizes and colors of shapes. See how many shapes your child can correctly name in 30 seconds.

Words With o

The **short o** sounds like the **o** in **dog**. **Long o** sounds like the **o** in **rope**. Draw a line from the picture to the word that names it. Draw a circle around the word if it has a **short o** sound.

hot dog

fox

blocks

rose

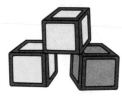

boat

Short and Long Oo

Say the name of each picture. If the picture has the **long o** sound, write a green **L** on the blank. If the picture has the **short o** sound, write a red **S** on the blank.

_____
- - - - - - -
_____

_____
- - - - - - -
_____

_____
- - - - - - -
_____

_____
- - - - - - -
_____

_____
- - - - - - -
_____

_____
- - - - - - -
_____

_____
- - - - - - -
_____

_____
- - - - - - -
_____

_____
- - - - - - -
_____

Short o

Write **o** on each line. Color the sock the correct color.

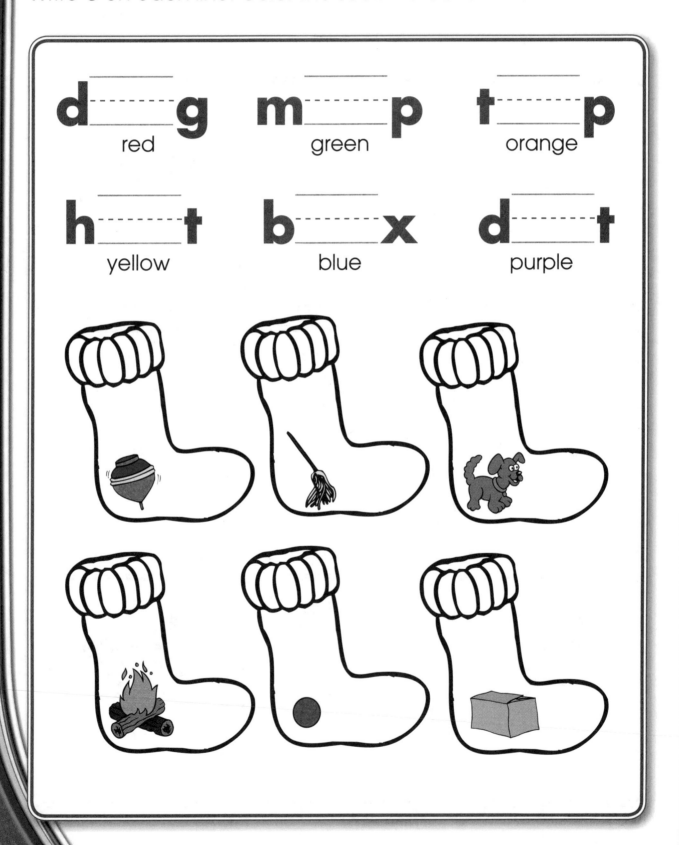

d___g
red

m___p
green

t___p
orange

h___t
yellow

b___x
blue

d___t
purple

Following the Flock

Write the missing word in each sentence.

mom   hop   got   hot   on   not   mop   lot

1. Put it _____ top of the box.

2. Will his _____ let us play?

3. Bob _____ a rock in his sock.

4. That pot is very _____ .

5. A rabbit will _____ on top of the log.

6. We had a _____ of fun at the pond.

7. Rob will _____ up the spilled milk.

8. Ronda did _____ stop at the shop.

Tracking: Straight Lines

Draw a straight line from A to B. Use a different color crayon for each line.

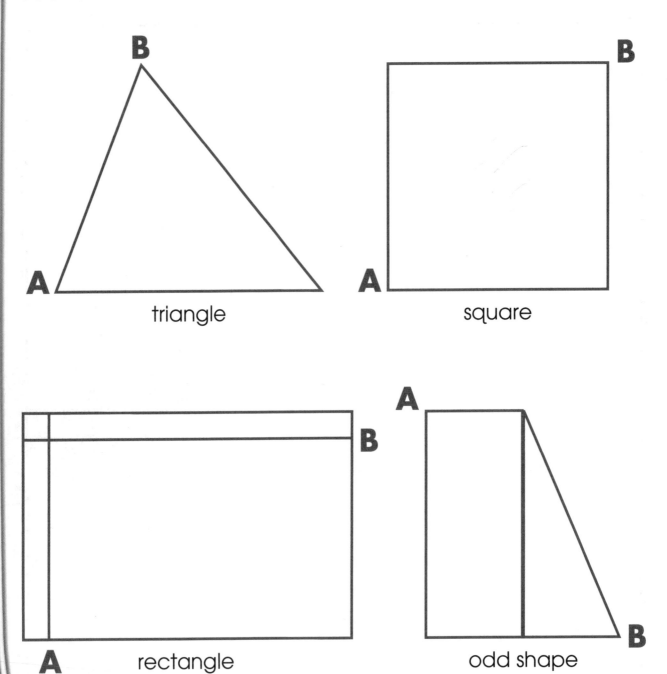

triangle

square

rectangle

odd shape

What shapes do you see hidden in these shapes?

_____

COMPLETE YEAR GRADE 1

Tracking: Different Paths

Trace three paths from A to B.

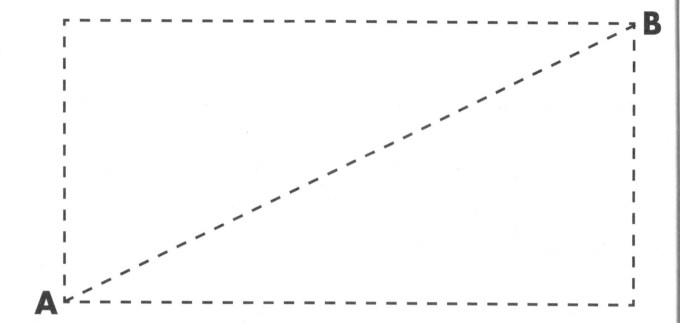

Trace the path from A to B.

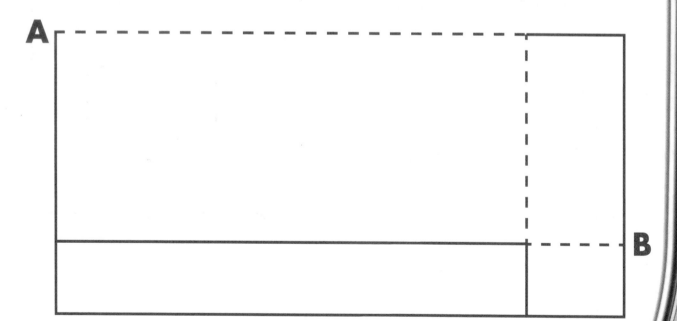

How many corners did you turn? _____

Shapes: Oval and Rhombus

An **oval** is an egg-shaped figure. A **rhombus** is a figure with four sides of the same length. Its corners form points at the top, sides, and bottom. This is an oval ⬭ . This is a rhombus ◇ .

Color the ovals red. Color the rhombuses blue.

Trace the words. Write the words.

oval

rhombus

Shapes: Oval and Rhombus

Practice drawing ovals. Trace the samples and make four of your own.

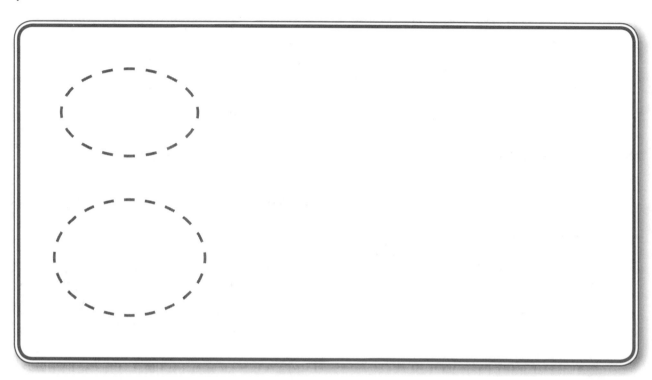

Practice drawing rhombuses. Trace the samples and make four of your own.

Following Directions: Shapes and Colors

Color the squares ☐ purple.

Color the heart ♡ blue.

Color the rhombuses ◇ yellow.

Color the star ☆ red.

Week 6 Skills

Subject	Skill	Multi-Sensory Learning Activities
Reading and Language Arts	Identify the **short u** and **long u** vowel sounds.	• Complete Practice Pages 68–71. • Read a series of four words to your child, making sure only one of which contains the **short u** sound. Ask your child to jump when he or she hears the word with the **short u** sound. • Put some **short u** objects in a tub, such as gum, buns, a mug, and a toy duck. Ask your child to pull out each object, say its name, and then name the vowel sound he or she hears. • Say several **long u** words aloud, asking your child to write the words with his or her finger in a pan of sand, shaving cream, or pudding.
Math	Recognize stars; review and classify shapes.	• Complete Practice Pages 73–76. • Draw several shapes on a piece of paper. Ask your child to count the squares, triangles, circles, etc. • Teach the song "Catch a Falling Star" to your child. Go outside at night and look for stars. Can you see any?
Bonus: Science		• Study a picture of the solar system. Help your child become familiar with the names of the planets. Work together to develop a mnemonic sentence, such as "My Very Eager Mother Just Served Us Nachos," to help your child remember the names of the planets in order.

Words With u

The **short u** sounds like the **u** in **bug**. The **long u** sounds like the **u** in **blue**. Draw a circle around the words with the **short u** sound. Draw an **X** on the words with the **long u** sound.

rug

cup

music

tub

suit

glue

bug

puppy

gum

Short and Long Uu

Say the name of each picture. If it has the **long u** sound, write a **u** in the unicorn column. If it has the **short u** sound, write a **u** in the umbrella column.

Short u

Say each picture name. If the picture has the sound of **short u**, color it yellow.

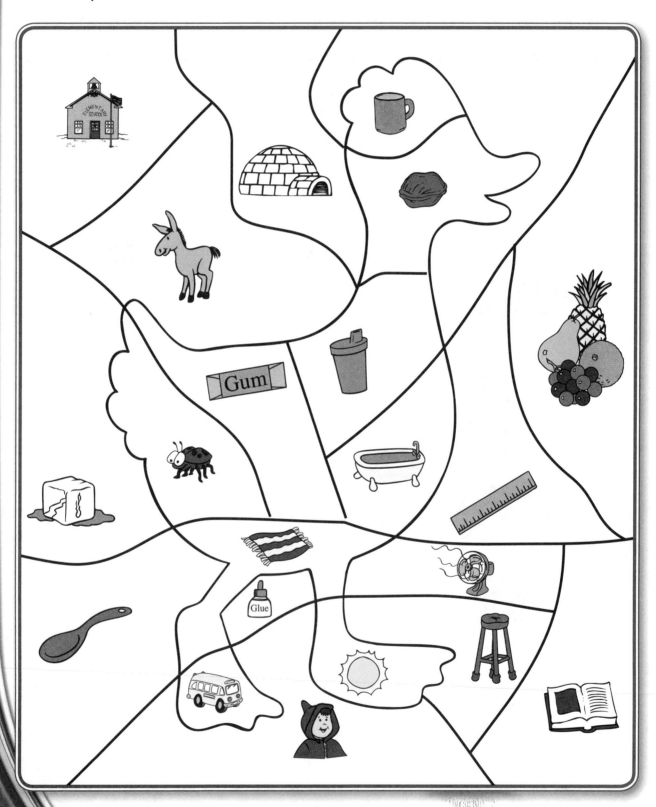

Short Vowel Uu

Cut out the wheels. Put the little wheel on top of the big wheel. Push a toothpick through the center. Turn the little wheel. How many words can you make?

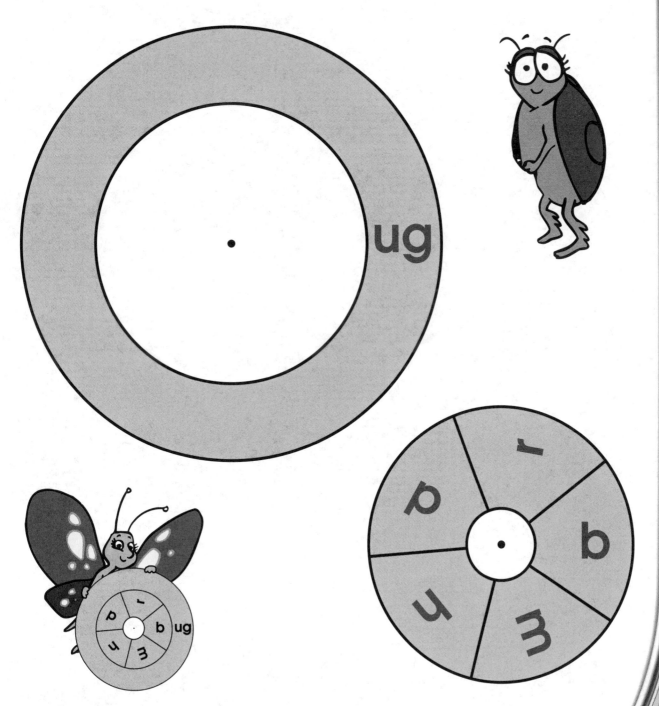

Your finished wheel will look like this.

Shape Review

Color the shapes in the picture as shown.

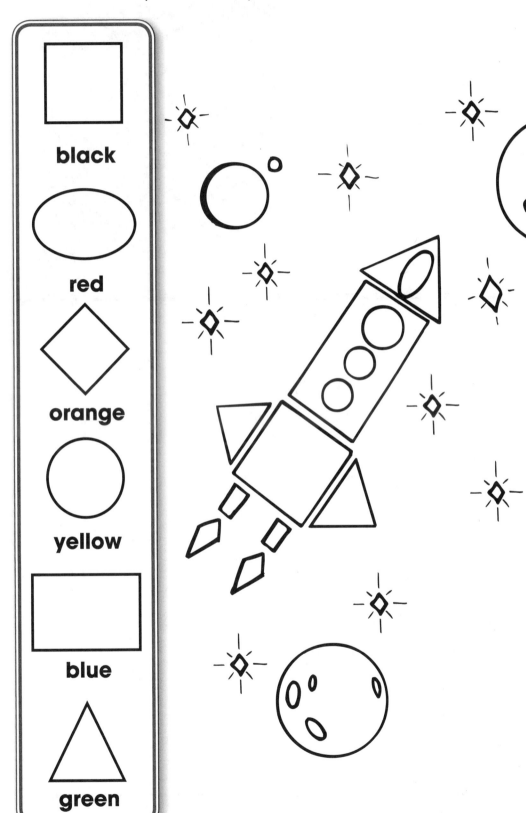

black

red

orange

yellow

blue

green

Shape Review

Trace the circles in red.

Trace the squares in blue.

Trace the rectangles in yellow.

Trace the triangles in green.

Trace the ovals in purple.

Trace the rhombuses in orange.

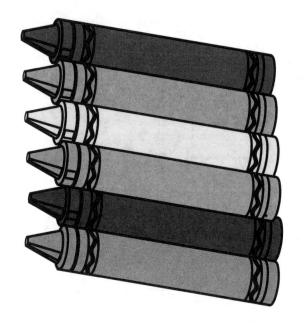

Classifying: Stars

Help Bob find the stars. Color all the stars blue.

How many stars did you and Bob find? _____

Classifying: Shapes

Mary and Rudy are taking a trip into space. Help them find the stars, moons, circles and diamonds.

Color the shapes. Use yellow for the ☆s. Use red for the ◯s. Use blue for the ☾s. Use purple for the ◇s.

How many stars? _____   How many moons? _____

How many circles? _____   How many rhombuses? _____

Week 7 Skills

Subject	Skill	Multi-Sensory Learning Activities
Reading and Language Arts	Review short vowel sounds.	• Complete Practice Pages 78 and 79. • Ask your child to make a list of as many short vowel words as he or she can think of. Once the list is complete, choose several rhyming words and use them to write a silly poem together.
	Review long vowel sounds; understand the super silent **e** as a way to change short vowel words into long vowel words.	• Complete Practice Pages 80–82. • Write **e** on a special sticker or on a star shape cut from paper. Have your child write three-letter words such as **cap**, **fin**, and **cut**, then add the super silent **e** to the end to make new words with long vowel sounds.
Basic Skills	Classify shapes as same and different.	• Complete Practice Pages 83–86. • Choose two books off of your bookshelf and show them to your child. Are the shapes the same or different? • Gather a collection of small objects of varying shapes. Ask your child to sort and classify the items in different ways. Choose one way of sorting the items and make a chart to show the categories and the number of items in each.
Bonus: Social Studies		• Read and discuss a book about a specific career. Discuss what is involved in that job and ask your child whether he or she would like it. Why or why not?

Short Vowels

Vowels are the letters **a**, **e**, **i**, **o** and **u**. **Short a** is the sound you hear in **ant**. **Short e** is the sound you hear in **elephant**. **Short i** is the sound you hear in **igloo**. **Short o** is the sound you hear in **octopus**. **Short u** is the sound you hear in **umbrella**.

Say the short vowel sound at the beginning of each row. Say the name of each picture. Then, color the pictures which have the same short vowel sounds as that letter.

Short Vowel Sounds

In each box are three pictures. The words that name the pictures have missing letters. Write **a**, **e**, **i**, **o** or **u** to finish the words.

p___n

p___n

p___n

b___g

b___g

b___g

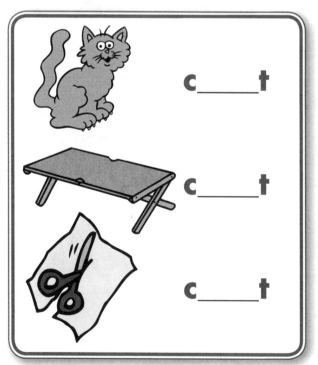

c___t

c___t

c___t

h___t

h___t

h___t

Long Vowels

Vowels are the letters **a**, **e**, **i**, **o** and **u**. Long vowel sounds say their own names. **Long a** is the sound you hear in **hay**. **Long e** is the sound you hear in **me**. **Long i** is the sound you hear in **pie**. **Long o** is the sound you hear in **no**. **Long u** is the sound you hear in **cute**.

Say the long vowel sound at the beginning of each row. Say the name of each picture. Then, color the pictures which have the same long vowel sounds as that letter.

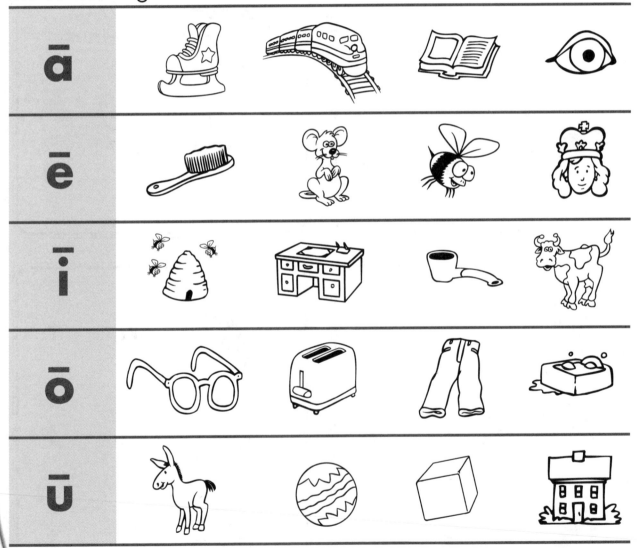

Long Vowel Sounds

Write **a**, **e**, **i**, **o** or **u** in each blank to finish the word. Draw a line from the word to the picture.

c___ke

r___se

k___te

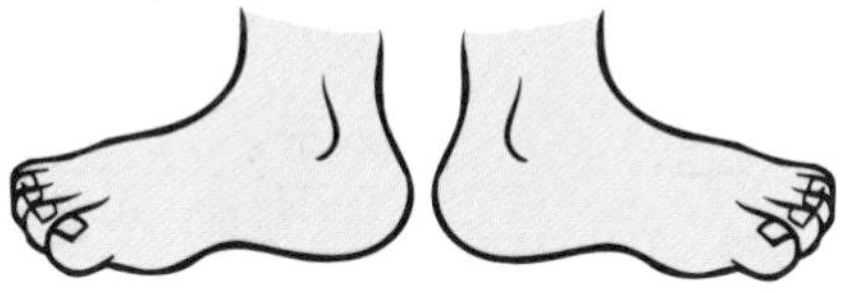

f___t

m___le

Super Silent E

When you add an **e** to the end of some words, the vowel changes from a short vowel sound to a long vowel sound. The **e** is silent.

Say the word under the first picture in each pair. Then, add an **e** to the word under the next picture. Say the new word.

pet _____

tub _____

man _____

kit _____

pin _____

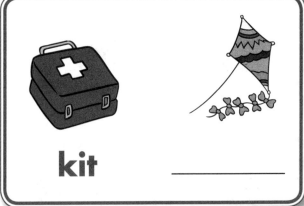

cap _____

Classifying: Shapes

Look at the shapes. Answer the questions.

1. How many all-white shapes? _____

2. How many all-blue shapes? _____

3. How many half-white shapes? _____

4. How many all-blue stars? _____

5. How many all-white circles? _____

6. How many half-blue shapes? _____

Same and Different: Shapes

Color the shape that looks the same as the first shape in each row.

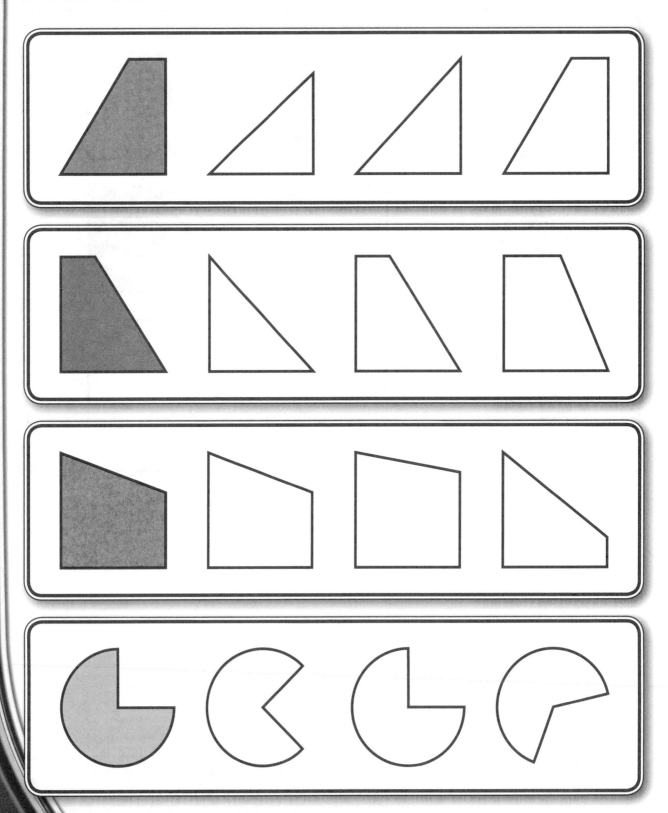

Same and Different: Shapes

Draw an **X** on the shapes in each row that do not match the first shape.

Copying: Shapes and Colors

Color your circle to look the same.

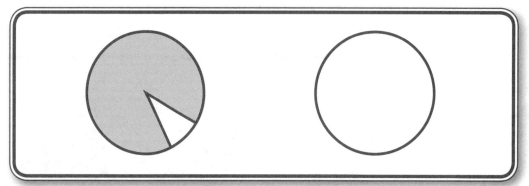

Color your square to look the same.

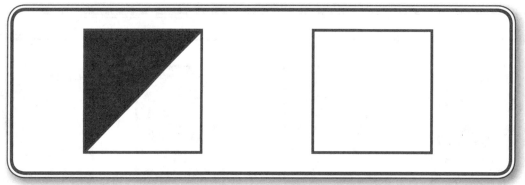

Trace the triangle. Color it to look the same.

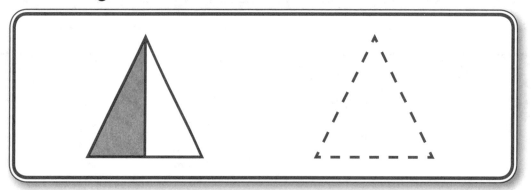

Trace the star. Color it to look the same.

Week 8 Skills

Subject	Skill	Multi-Sensory Learning Activities
Reading and Language Arts	Associate beginning sounds with their corresponding letters.	• Complete Practice Pages 88–92. • Provide samples of food that start with different letter sounds. Then, have your child write the beginning sound for each food and draw a picture of him- or herself eating that food. • Go for a "word walk." Have your child identify things seen on your walk and tell the beginning sound. Have your child dictate a story describing your word walk. Then, your child can copy the story and draw an illustration.
Math	Review shapes.	• Complete Practice Pages 93 and 95. • Draw more shapes for your child to add to the figure he or she created from the activity on Page 93. How many shapes are there total?
Bonus: Fine Motor Skills		• Give your child two plastic cups. Help him or her pierce a hole in each one with scissors. Have your child cut a piece of fishing line about 10 feet long. Instruct him or her to put one end of line through the hole of one cup from its bottom side and to tie the line to a paper clip inside the cup. Then, have your child do the same with the other end of the line to the other cup. The line must be pulled tightly between two people. One person speaks into a cup while the other person listens from the other cup.

Beginning Sounds

Say each picture name. Circle the beginning sound for each picture. Color the pictures.

b t c s

b t c s

b t c s

b t c s

b t c s

b t c s

b t c s

b t c s

b t c s

Beginning Sounds

Say each picture name. Write the beginning sound for each picture. Color the pictures.

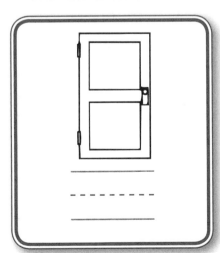

Beginning Sounds

Draw a line from each picture to the pictures that begin with that sound. Color the pictures.

Beginning Sounds

Say each picture name. Write the beginning sound for each picture. Color the pictures.

Beginning Sounds

Say each picture name. Circle the beginning sound for each picture. Color the pictures.

l q y z

l q y z

l q y z

l q y z

l q y z

l q y z

l q y z

l q y z

l q y z

Shapely Figures

Color and cut out the shapes below. Glue them on another sheet of paper to make a picture. Add details using crayons.

Mayflower Shipshape

1. Color the ship and the sails.
2. Cut out and glue the shapes correctly on the ship below.

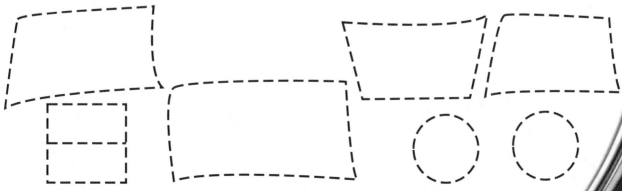

Week 9 Skills

Subject	Skill	Multi-Sensory Learning Activities
Reading and Language Arts	Associate beginning sounds with their corresponding letters.	• Complete Practice Pages 98–102. • Play with magnetic letters or letter tiles from a word game. Give six to each player. Who can use the tiles to spell and say a word the fastest? Players who can't make a word may draw another letter from a bag. • Write each letter of the alphabet on a large index card. Choose four to eight of the alphabet cards and lay them out on a table. Say a word that begins with one of the letters and have your child identify the beginning sound.
Math	Work with shape patterns.	• Complete Practice Pages 103–106. • Use foods such as small cereal pieces, crackers, or dry pasta to create a pattern. Repeat the pattern twice before your child continues it. Have your child glue the patterns onto paper. • Go for a "pattern walk" outside or around the house. Discuss patterns your child sees in familiar objects such as fabrics, furniture, wallpaper, tiles, and landscaping.
Bonus: Basic Skills		• Put 10 objects on a tray. Let your child look at it for a minute. Tell your child to close his or her eyes. Remove one object. Have your child open his or her eyes and tell what is missing.

How Do I Begin?

Say the name of each picture. Write the beginning sound for each picture.

 ___at

 ___oat

 ___ite

 ___am

 ___acks

 ___ate

 ___ey

 ___appy

Write each word next to its beginning sound.

g ---------------------

g ---------------------

h ---------------------

h ---------------------

j ---------------------

j ---------------------

k ---------------------

k ---------------------

How Do I Begin?

Say each letter sound. Color the pictures in each row that begin with that sound.

Say the name of each picture. Write the beginning sound for each picture.

Hidden Picture

Say the name of each picture. Write the beginning sound for each picture. Then, color the picture.

__itten __encil __ut __ollipop

__eaf

__ask

__itt

__amp

__ilk

__ock

__oon

__ouse

9

__ine

__ot

__et

__opcorn __ig

__ie

__est

__op

__ug

__ote

Start Your Engine!

Say the name of each picture. Then, write the beginning sound for each picture.

____acket

____oat

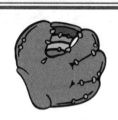
____og

____itt

____ipper

____ock

____icket

____an

____opcorn

____et

____arn

____uilt

____ot dog

____at

____ug

____ock

Beginning Sounds

Write the food names that answer the questions.

| egg | milk | ice cream | apple | cookie | cake |

1. Which food words start with the same sounds as the pictures?

_____   _____

_____

2. Which food word ends with the same sound as the picture?

_____

3. Which food words have two letters together that are the same?

_____   _____   _____

Find the Shapes

Find each shape. Then, color the picture using the code.

red   green   blue   orange   yellow

Patterns: Shapes

Draw a line from the box on the left to the box on the right with the same shape and color pattern.

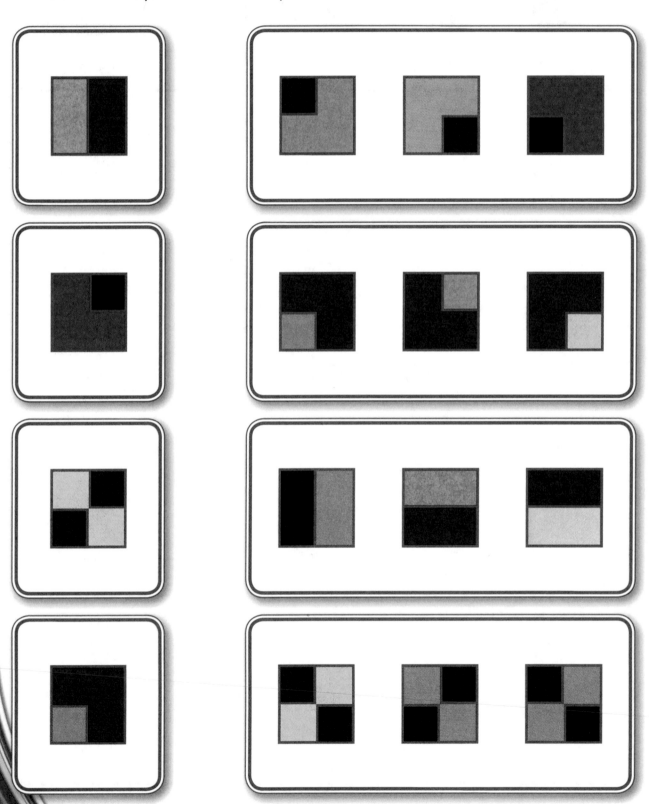

Patterns: Shapes

Draw a line from the box on the left to the box on the right with the same shape and color pattern.

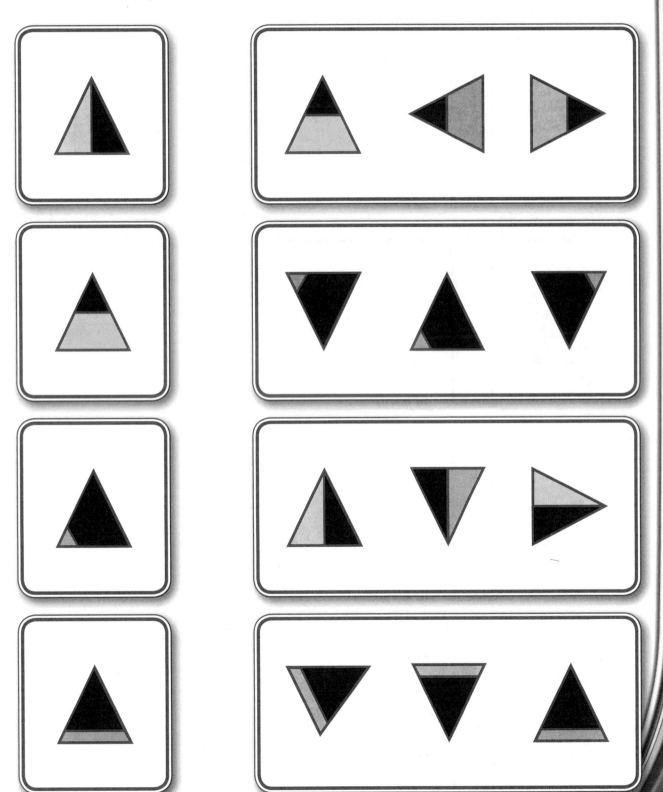

Patterns: Find and Copy

Circle the shape in the middle box that matches the one on the left. Draw another shape with the same pattern in the box on the right.

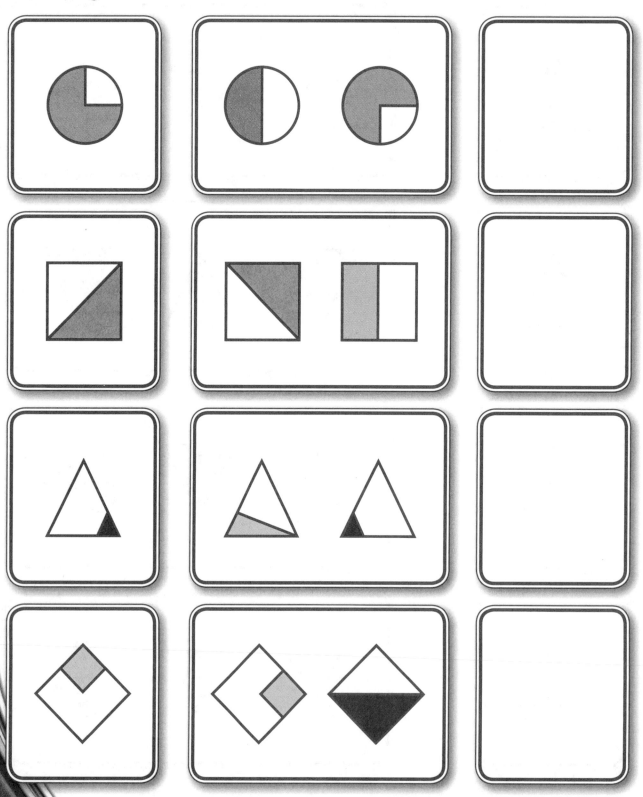

First Quarter Check-Up

Basic Skills

☐ I know these colors: red, yellow, blue, green, orange, brown, white, black, pink, and purple.

Reading and Language Arts

☐ I can write uppercase and lowercase letters **Aa-Zz**.

☐ I can match uppercase letters with their lowercase letters.

☐ I know the **short a** and **long a** sounds.

☐ I know the **short e** and **long e** sounds.

☐ I know the **short i** and **long i** sounds.

☐ I know the **short o** and **long o** sounds.

☐ I know the **short u** and **long u** sounds.

☐ I know the sounds made by these consonant letters: **b**, **c**, **d**, **f**, **g**, **h**, **j**, **k**, **l**, **m**, **n**, **p**, **q**, **r**, **s**, **t**, **v**, **w**, **y**, **z**.

Math

☐ I recognize squares, circles, triangles, rectangles, ovals, and rhombuses.

☐ I can classify shapes as same and different.

☐ I can work with and understand shape patterns.

Final Project

Read *Brown Bear, Brown Bear* by Bill Martin, Jr. Look at the beginning sounds of the words in the book. Then, look at the pattern of *Brown Bear, Brown Bear* and write your own book using the same pattern. Use familiar objects in your story. For example, you could write, "Orange cat, orange cat, what do you see? I see a yellow mouse looking at me." Then, draw pictures to illustrate your book.

Second Quarter Introduction

During the second quarter of the school year, many children are settled into routines at home and at school. Make sure your family's routines include time for playing, eating and talking together, and reading aloud. Supporting your child's learning and development will build his or her confidence in all areas.

Second Quarter Skills

Practice pages in this book for Weeks 10–18 will help your child improve the following skills.

Reading and Language Arts
- Recognize ending consonant sounds
- Identify vowel sounds
- Know the sounds of consonant blends
- Understand digraphs
- Recognize nouns, proper nouns, pronouns, present- and past-tense verbs, and adjectives

Math
- Work with patterns of shapes, colors, numbers, and letters
- Recognize numbers and count from 1–10
- Read number words **one** through **twelve**
- Provide the missing number in a sequence
- Skip-count by tens and fives
- Understand less than and greater than
- Understand place value of tens and ones
- Solve addition problems

Multi-Sensory Learning Activities

Try these fun activities for enhancing your child's learning and development during the second quarter of the school year. Be sure to choose activities that include speaking, listening, touching, and active movement.

 Reading and Language Arts

On a chart, label two columns **One Syllable** and **Two Syllables**. Have your child listen as you say some one- and two-syllable words. Tell your child to repeat each word and clap the number of syllables in it. Under your child's direction, list words in the appropriate column of the chart.

Write words on index cards and cut the digraph off each. Mix up the cards and have your child match the parts to spell the words.

Have your child draw a picture of some special places he or she has visited. Write the name of the place above your child's drawing and point out the capital letter.

COMPLETE YEAR GRADE 1

Throw a ball to your child. Tell your child to catch it. Then, write **I throw the ball. You catch it.** Tell your child to underline the verbs.

Brainstorm some adjectives that describe size and shape. Ask your child to point out round objects, flat objects, small objects, and other objects of different sizes and shapes.

Review nouns, adjectives, and verbs with your child. Have your child look in books he or she has read for 10 nouns, 10 adjectives, and 10 verbs. Have your child sort and label the categories and then write three sentences using some of the found words.

Play "Twenty Questions." Have your child think of an object (noun) and tell you if it is a person, place, or thing. Ask up to 20 questions that will help you figure out what the object is. Once you guess the object, reverse roles and play again.

Read *King Bidgood's in the Bathtub* by Audrey Wood. Choose one picture from the book with a lot of detail. Have your child write a list of nouns found in the picture and an adjective for each one. Then, encourage your child to practice reading the words and using them in written sentences.

 **Math**

Have your child practice counting sets of objects, then rearranging them and counting again. Emphasize that there is always the same number of objects no matter what order they are in.

Make number cards from 1–10, one number per card. Show your child a number card and ask him or her to hop that many times.

Provide your child with practice grouping tens into one hundred. Use a different manipulative each time or make it a game so your child doesn't tire of the activity.

In each of several jars, place between 15 and 99 small objects, such as paper clips, cotton balls, dried beans, etc. Have your child estimate the number of objects before counting them. Encourage your child to place the objects in groups of ten to make counting easier.

Place several addition flash cards in a grid pattern on the floor. Have your child toss a beanbag onto a problem. Ask your child to say the correct answer to the problem aloud before tossing the beanbag again.

Second Quarter Introduction, cont.

 Basic Skills

Play a short audiobook for your child. Ask him or her to recall details from the story. Have your child turn his or her back to you while you make noises with a variety of familiar things. Operate a hair dryer, tear paper, turn the pages of a book, or open a drawer. Ask your child to identify each sound.

 Fine Motor Skills

Spread some baking soda on a cookie sheet. Then, pour some white vinegar into three small dishes and add some food coloring to each. Give your child different types of droppers, such as an old medicine syringe or a turkey baster. Ask your child to fill the droppers with vinegar and squirt it onto the baking soda, encouraging your child to be creative with designs and colors.

Give your child a long strip of white paper. Teach your child to fold the paper like an accordion. Have your child make an animal's head and back end out of construction paper and glue them to either end of the accordion.

 **Science**

Encourage your child to decorate a foam cup with a face. Have your child fill the cup with dirt and plant several grass seeds about $\frac{3}{4}$ inch under the soil. Your child should water the plant as needed and keep it in a sunny spot. Allow your child to watch and observe as the "hair" grows taller and taller.

 Seasonal Fun

Make beaded candy cane ornaments with your child. First, twist a knot at the end of a pipe cleaner. Then, have your child stack red and white beads on the pipe cleaner. Repeat the pattern with your child as he or she stacks. When finished, twist the end again so the beads stay on, and bend the pipe cleaner to form a candy cane shape.

Make a dreidel to celebrate Hanukkah. First, wash and clean a small milk carton and dry it completely. Re-seal the top so that it forms a box shape, using glue if needed to seal it tightly. Have your child paint the sides of the carton using the colors closely associated with Hanukkah: blue, silver, and white. When the paint dries, carefully write the Hebrew letters **nun**, **gimel**, **hay**, and **shin** on each side of the carton. Then, carefully poke a sharpened pencil from the bottom of the carton through to the other side, and your homemade dreidel is complete.

Week 10 Skills

Subject	Skill	Multi-Sensory Learning Activities
Reading and Language Arts	Associate ending sounds with their corresponding letters.	• Complete Practice Pages 112–115. • Write a list of easy three-letter words and read the list to your child as you point to each word. On the second reading, have your child listen for the ending sound of each word. Emphasize the last letter with your voice and by pointing to it. Have your child name the ending sound.
	Associate middle sounds with their corresponding vowels.	• Complete Practice Page 116. • Say a single-syllable word, such as **map**, **bell**, **hot**, or **tune**. Use the word in a sentence. Then, say the word again. Have your child listen for the middle sound and identify the vowel.
Math	Work with shape, color, and number patterns.	• Complete Practice Pages 117–120. • Give your child several types of small objects, like coins, cotton balls, and candies. Ask your child to make several different patterns using the objects. • Write a number pattern using different colored markers, making sure all **1**s are the same color, all **2**s are the same color, etc. Ask your child to complete the pattern with the correct number and the correct color.

Final Sounds

Write the sound you hear at the end of each word.
Color the pictures.

- - - - - - - -

_____

- - - - - - - -

_____

- - - - - - - -

_____

- - - - - - - -

_____

- - - - - - - -

_____

- - - - - - - -

_____

- - - - - - - -

_____

- - - - - - - -

_____

- - - - - - - -

_____

Final Sounds

Draw a line from each letter to the pictures that end with that sound. Color the pictures.

Final Sounds

Say each picture name. Write the ending sound for each picture.

 tu____

 pai____

 pa____

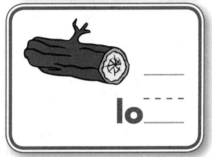 lo____

 hoo____

 mu____

 boo____

 ha____

 shel____

 lea____

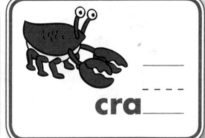 cra____

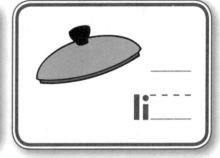 li____

 gir____

 bea____

 broo____

Final Sounds

Say each picture name. Write the ending sound for each picture.

fla___

boo___

bo___

we___

mo___

ca___

ga___

ha___

lea___

pi___

be___

duc___

ca___

si___

dru___

roo___

Middle Sounds

Say each picture name. Write the missing vowel **a**, **e**, **i**, **o** or **u** in the puzzle.

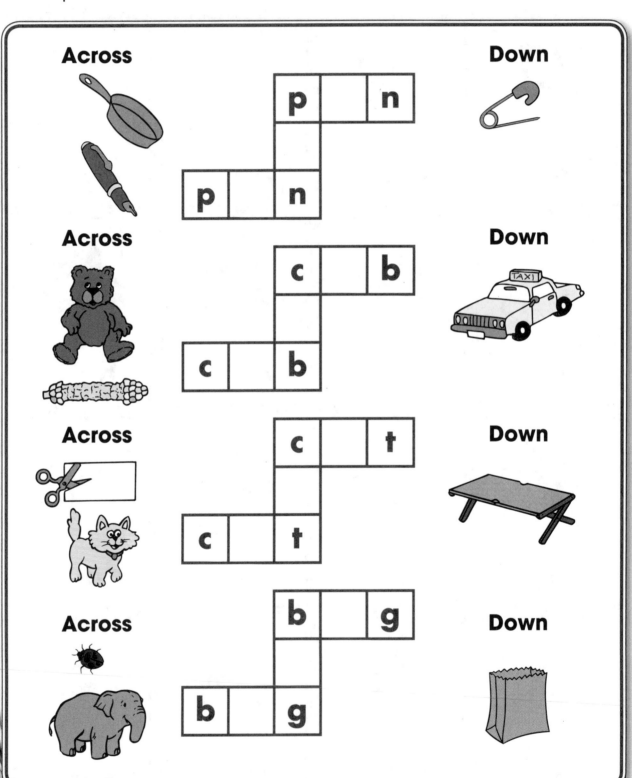

COMPLETE YEAR GRADE 1

Patterns

Draw what comes next in each pattern. The first one is done for you.

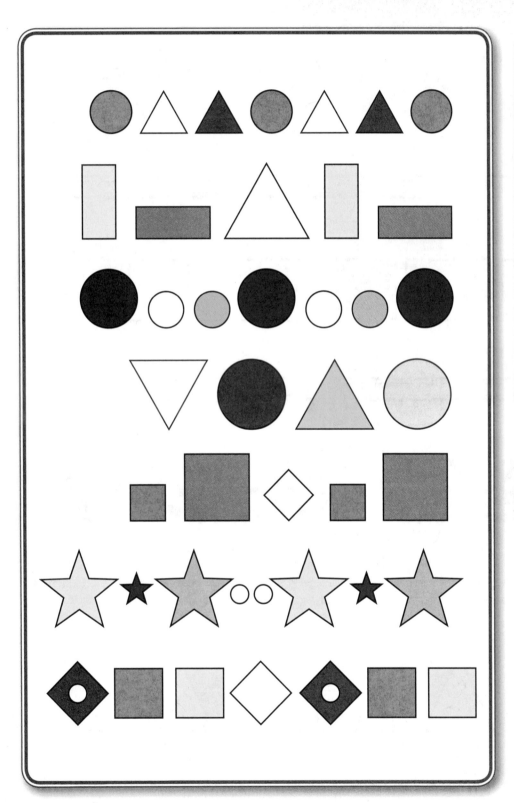

Patterns

Fill in the missing shape in each row. Then, color it.

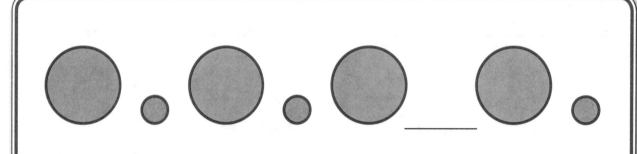

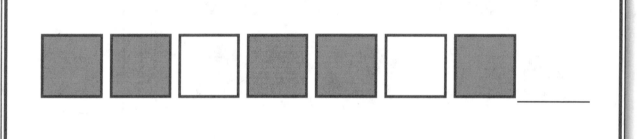

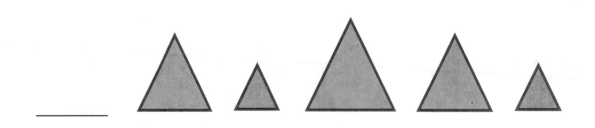

Patterns

Color to complete the patterns.

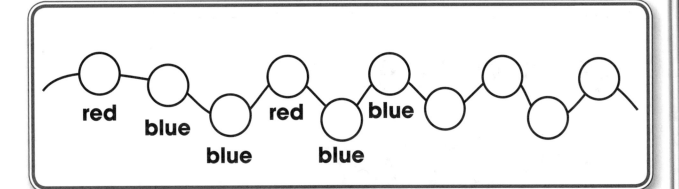

red   blue   blue   red   blue   blue

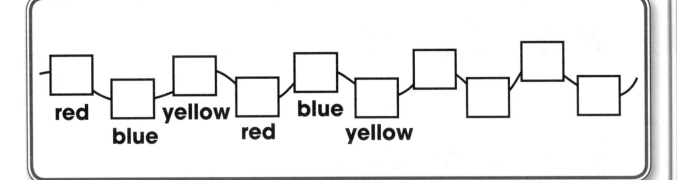

red   blue   yellow   red   blue   yellow

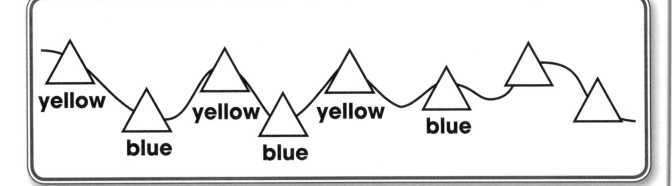

yellow   blue   yellow   blue   yellow   blue

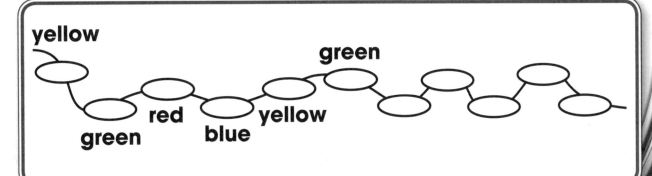

yellow   green   red   blue   yellow   green

Plenty of Patterns

Continue each pattern below.

_____ _____ _____ _____

_____ _____ _____ _____

_____ _____ _____ _____

_____ _____ _____ _____

1 5 2 5 1 5 2 _____ _____ _____ _____

5 4 6 5 4 6 5 _____ _____ _____ _____

9 9 8 9 9 8 9 _____ _____ _____ _____

1 3 5 7 9 1 3 _____ _____ _____ _____

Week 11 Skills

Subject	Skill	Multi-Sensory Learning Activities
Reading and Language Arts	Recognize beginning consonant blends and the sounds the two consonants make when paired together.	• Complete Practice Pages 122–126. • Write these letter pairs on cards or slips of paper and put them in a bag: **bl**, **br**, **fl**, **gr**, **gl**, **sm**. Ask your child to draw one from the bag and say a word that includes that blend. • Create learning tubs for blends. Mark the outside of small tubs with a consonant blend and then fill the containers with small toys or objects that contain that blend. For example, if creating a **br** tub, include objects representing **bread**, **brown**, **braid**, and **brush**.
Math	Work with shape and letter patterns.	• Complete Practice Pages 127–130. • Play a game of "Tic-Tac-Toe" with your child. Can he or she spot any letter patterns in the grid? • Have your child listen to and copy several auditory patterns (snap, clap, snap, clap, etc.). Then, do other patterns, such as varying the volume of claps (soft, loud, soft). Ask your child to create his or her own pattern for you to follow along.
Bonus: Fine Motor Skills		• Use objects such as construction paper, paint, and toothpicks to make prints with your child. Drop some paint on the paper and ask your child to use the toothpicks to draw a picture in the paint.

Consonant Blends

Consonant blends are two or more consonant sounds together in a word. The blend is made by combining the consonant sounds. **Example: fl**oor

The name of each picture begins with a blend. Circle the beginning blend for each picture.

bl   fl   cl

cl   fl   gl

fl   bl   pl

fl   cl   gl

pl   gl   cl

gl   fl   sl

gl   fl   cl

sl   fl   cl

cl   gl   sl

Consonant Blends

The beginning blend for each word is missing. Fill in the correct blend to finish the word. Draw a line from the word to the picture.

_ _ _ _ _ **ain**

_ _ _ _ _ **og**

_ _ _ _ _ **ab**

_ _ _ _ _ **um**

_ _ _ _ _ **ush**

_ _ _ _ _ **esent**

Consonant Blends

Draw a line from the picture to the blend that begins its word.

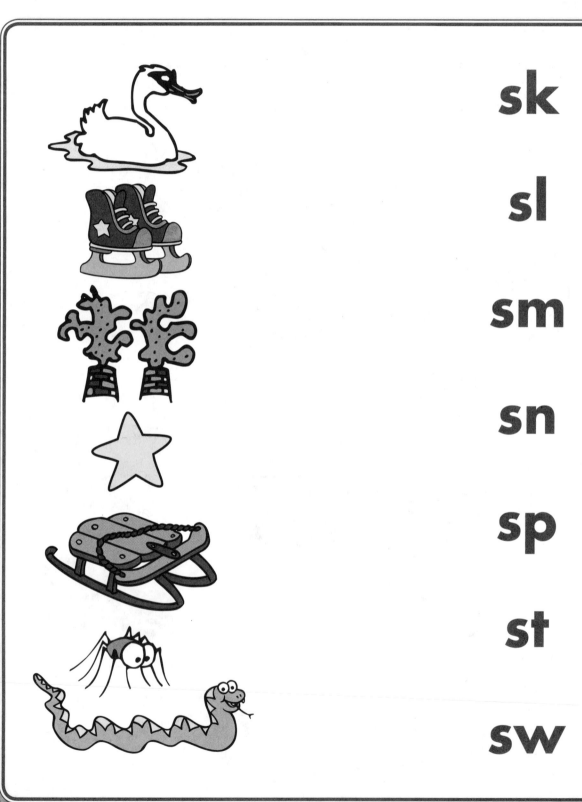

sk

sl

sm

sn

sp

st

sw

Consonant Blends

Look at the first picture in each row. Circle the pictures in that row that begin with the same sound.

chair

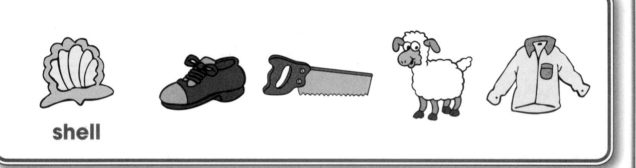

shell

thumb

wheel

Beginning Blends

Say the blend for each word as you search for it.

```
b  l  o  s  l  e  d  a  b  f  t  k  a  i  n
l  b  r  e  a  d  x  s  t  o  p  i  x  a  p
o  l  g  u  f  e  n  p  s  p  i  d  e  r  i
c  l  o  w  n  a  w  l  p  z  j  c  r  a  b
k  t  c  e  n  t  h  s  t  e  g  l  q  c  r
d  h  b  r  e  a  e  j  w  k  x  o  w  h  y
h  u  s  n  a  k  e  m  d  j  l  c  m  a  j
v  m  i  u  k  l  l  s  k  u  n  k  c  i  f
i  b  g  l  o  b  e  m  h  n  o  q  t  r  r
b  f  l  j  x  s  y  a  z  s  l  e  g  o  o
s  h  e  l  l  w  k  l  f  s  s  v  u  p  g
h  a  r  l  c  a  d  l  l  v  w  k  z  s  n
o  z  y  q  s  n  l  t  a  h  n  r  u  m  q
e  f  l  o  w  e  r  a  g  l  o  v  e  e  r
w  g  m  b  c  e  n  m  o  p  d  o  f  l  g
p  r  e  s  e  n  t  r  a  i  n  b  p  l  i
```

Words to find:

block	frog	globe	crab
clock	glove	present	flower
train	flag	skunk	snake
swan	small	smell	spider
bread	sled	chair	shell
stop	wheel	shoe	
thumb		clown	

COMPLETE YEAR GRADE 1

Shape Patterns

Draw and color the shape that comes next in each pattern.

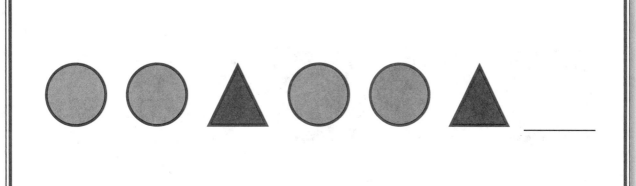

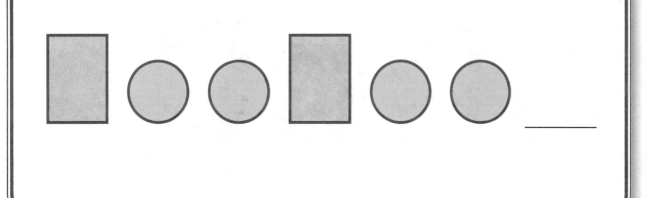

Patterns

Draw and color the shape that comes next in each pattern.

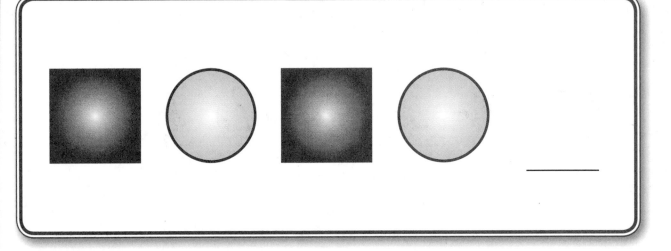

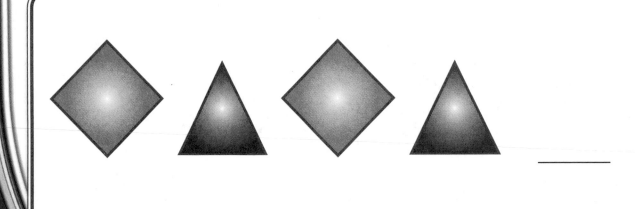

COMPLETE YEAR GRADE 1

Patterns

Draw and color the shape that comes next in each pattern.

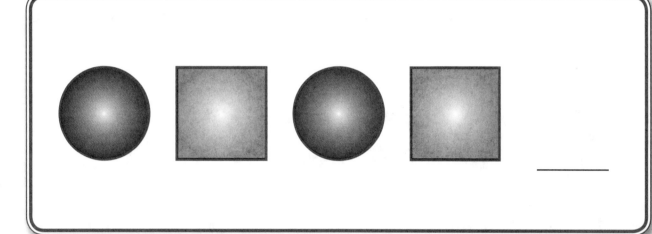

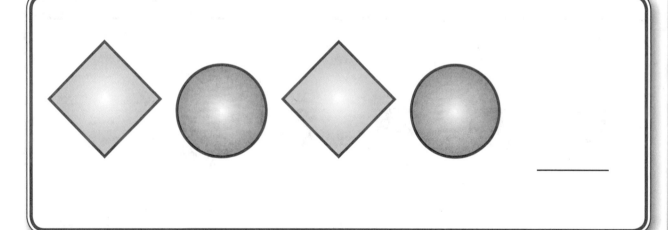

Patterns

Complete the letter patterns. At the end of the row, write the letter that comes next.

C O C O C ___

B P B P B ___

M N M N M ___

Week 12 Skills

Subject	Skill	Multi-Sensory Learning Activities
Reading and Language Arts	Recognize ending consonant blends and the sounds the two consonants make when paired together.	• Complete Practice Pages 132–135. • Create riddles with clues to words with ending consonant blends and see if your child can solve them. For example, say, "It ends like **ramp**. It is what you do with a rope on the playground. What is it?" Your child would answer, "**Jump**."
Math	Recognize numerals **1–10**.	• Complete Practice Pages 136 and 139. • Make a bingo grid for your child, repeating numbers **1–10** as necessary. Write each number on a small card and put them all in a larger container. Draw a number from the container and have your child cover the number(s) on his or her card with a penny or dried bean.
	Count from 1–10.	• Complete Practice Pages 137 and 138. • Pour some paint on a sturdy paper or plastic plate, adding some water to dilute it if necessary. Have your child put his or her hands, palms down, in the paint and make handprints on a sheet of paper. Then, ask your child to count the finger- and thumbprints.

Ending Consonant Blends

Write **lt** or **ft** to complete the words.

be_____

ra_____

sa_____

qui_____

le_____

Ending Consonant Blends

Draw a line from the picture to the blend that ends the word.

lf

lk

sk

st

Ending Consonant Blends

Every juke box has a word ending and a list of letters. Add each of the letters to the word ending to make rhyming words.

___ and

b _____
h _____
l _____
s _____

___ ent

b _____
d _____
t _____
w _____

___ ump

b _____
d _____
j _____
p _____

___ ink

p _____
s _____
l _____
th _____

___ ing

r _____
s _____
st _____
k _____

___ ank

b _____
r _____
s _____
t _____

Ending Consonant Blends

Say the blend for each word as you search for it.

```
b  e  l  t  l  e  m  m  i  l  k  r  p
b  r  l  z  m  a  a  i  u  v  r  i  n
r  r  d  u  m  p  s  h  n  x  i  t  a
i  b  p  i  n  g  k  p  i  b  n  g  w
n  m  k  i  q  i  w  e  n  t  g  d  s
g  t  h  i  n  k  n  c  e  s  i  r  h
e  e  i  k  i  f  h  r  c  d  x  e  e
t  c  s  j  b  c  l  a  s  p  n  m  l
e  r  i  e  l  o  m  n  i  y  e  p  f
n  b  n  b  a  n  d  k  g  o  s  f  k
t  a  g  l  n  a  l  a  n  d  t  e  d
e  d  c  o  k  u  z  j  e  l  u  m  p
r  a  f  t  b  r  h  s  h  r  i  n  k
```

Words to find:

belt	raft	milk	shelf
mask	clasp	nest	band
think	went	lump	crank
ring	blank	shrink	land
bring	tent	dump	sing

Number Recognition

Count the number of objects in each group. Draw a line to the correct number.

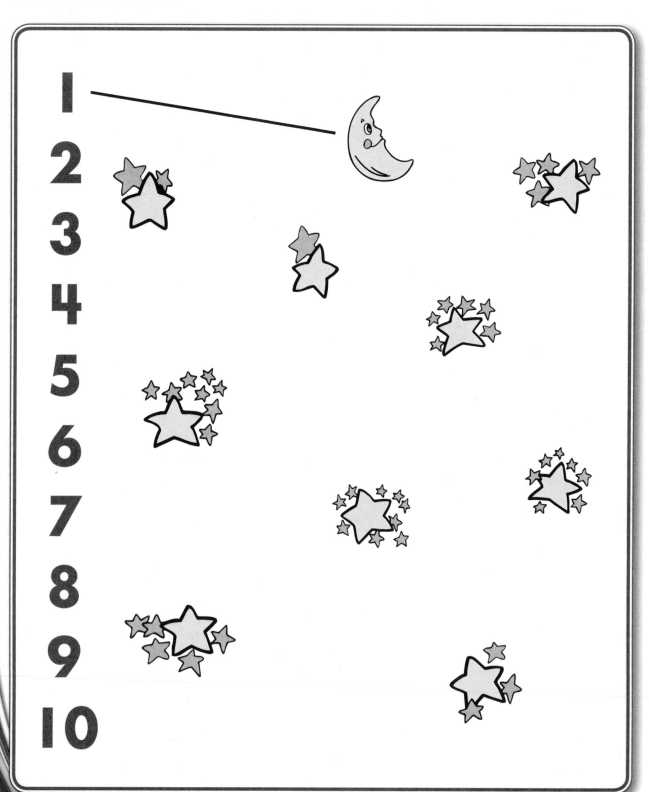

Counting

How many are there of each picture? Write the answers in the boxes. The first one is done for you.

Counting

How many are there of each picture? Write the answers in the boxes. The first one is done for you.

Number Recognition

Cut out the pieces. Mix them up and match the number with the picture.

Week 13 Skills

Subject	Skill	Multi-Sensory Learning Activities
Reading and Language Arts	Review digraphs /**sh**/, /**ch**/, /**wh**/, /**th**/; review ending consonant blends.	• Complete Practice Pages 142–146. • Write these letter pairs on cards or slips of paper and put them in a bag: **bl**, **br**, **ch**, **fl**, **gr**, **pl**, **sh**, **sm**, **th**, **wh**. Ask your child to draw one and say a word that includes that blend or digraph. • Read *Sheep on a Ship* by Nancy Shaw. Emphasize the sound of the /**sh**/ digraph as you read. With your child, brainstorm a list of other /**sh**/ words.
Math	Recognize number words **one** through **twelve**.	• Complete Practice Pages 147–150. • Introduce the number words **one** through **twelve**. Make number word cards and numeral cards up to 12. Give your child a number word card, and have him or her match it with a numeral card. As an added challenge, shuffle both sets of cards and flip them upside down. Play a game of "Memory" with your child to see who can find the most pairs.
Bonus: Basic Skills		• With your child blindfolded in the center of the room, walk to various places in the room and whistle or make another small sound. Have your child point in the direction of the sound.

Consonant Teams

Consonant teams are two or three consonant letters that have a single sound. **Examples: sh** and **tch**

Write each word from the word box next to its picture. Underline the consonant team in each word. Circle the consonant team in each word in the box.

bench	match	shoe	thimble
shell	brush	peach	watch
whale	teeth	chair	wheel

Letter Teams: sh, ch, wh, th

Look at the first picture in each row. Circle the pictures that have the same sound.

whistle

shoe

chin

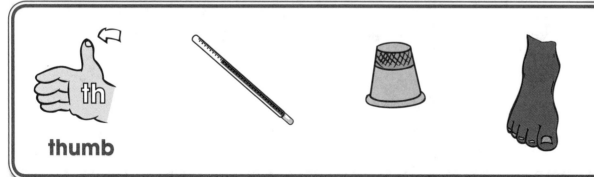

thumb

Letter Teams: sh, ch, wh, th

Look at the pictures and say the words. Write the first two letters of the word on the line below each picture.

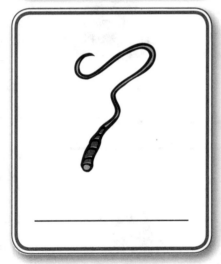

_____

_____

_____

_____

_____

_____

_____

_____

_____

Consonant Teams

Circle the consonant teams in each word in the word box. Write a word from the word box to finish each sentence. Circle the consonant teams in your words.

> trash
> shut
> ship
>
> splash
> chicken
> when
> which
>
> chain
> catch
> patch

1. My _____ won't lay eggs.

2. I put a _____ on my bicycle so nobody can take it.

3. We watched the big _____ dock and let off its passengers.

4. It is my job to take out the _____.

5. I have to wear a _____ over my eye until it is better.

6. The baby likes to _____ in the bathtub.

7. Can you _____ the ball with one hand?

8. Please _____ the windows before it rains.

9. _____ are we going to leave for school?

10. I don't know _____ of these books is mine.

Consonant Teams

Look at the words in the word box. Write all of the words that end with the **ng** sound under the picture of the **ring**. Write all of the words that end with the **nk** sound under the picture of the **sink**. Finish the sentences with words from the word box.

strong	rank	bring	bank	honk	hang	thank
long	hunk	song	stung	bunk	sang	junk

ng _____

_____

_____

_____

_____

_____

_____

nk _____

_____

_____

_____

_____

_____

_____

1. _____ your horn when you get to my house.

2. He was _____ by a bumblebee.

3. We are going to put our money in a _____.

4. I want to _____ you for the birthday present.

5. My brother and I sleep in _____ beds.

Number Word Find

Find the number words hidden in the box.

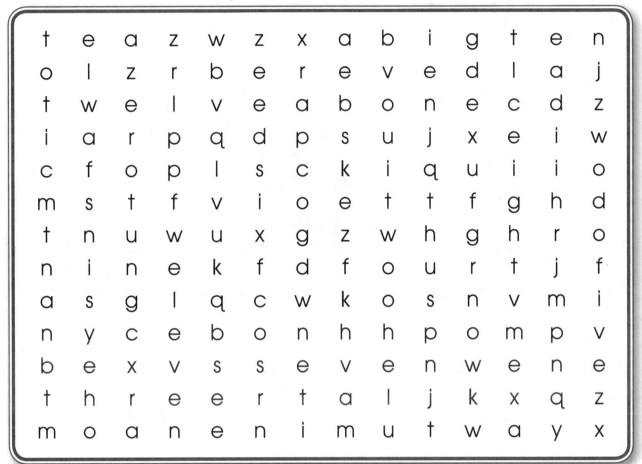

```
t  e  a  z  w  z  x  a  b  i  g  t  e  n
o  l  z  r  b  e  r  e  v  e  d  l  a  j
t  w  e  l  v  e  a  b  o  n  e  c  d  z
i  a  r  p  q  d  p  s  u  j  x  e  i  w
c  f  o  p  l  s  c  k  i  q  u  i  i  o
m  s  t  f  v  i  o  e  t  t  f  g  h  d
t  n  u  w  u  x  g  z  w  h  g  h  r  o
n  i  n  e  k  f  d  f  o  u  r  t  j  f
a  s  g  l  q  c  w  k  o  s  n  v  m  i
n  y  c  e  b  o  n  h  h  p  o  m  p  v
b  e  x  v  s  s  e  v  e  n  w  e  n  e
t  h  r  e  e  r  t  a  l  j  k  x  q  z
m  o  a  n  e  n  i  m  u  t  w  a  y  x
```

Words to find:

zero	four	eight	eleven
one	five	nine	twelve
two	six	ten	
three	seven		

Number Words

Number the buildings from **1** to **6**.

Draw a line from the word to the number.

two   1

five   3

six   5

four   6

one   2

three   4

Number Words

Number the buildings from **5** to **10**.

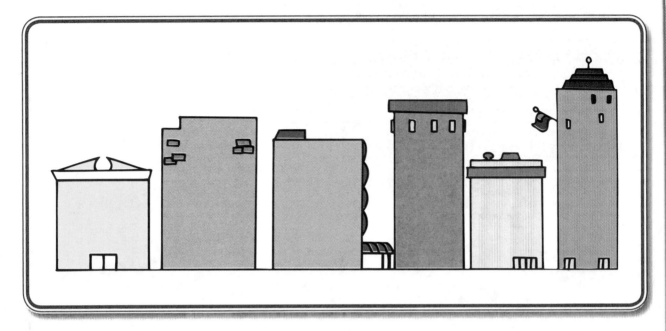

Draw a line from the word to the number.

nine	**8**
seven	**10**
five	**7**
eight	**5**
six	**9**
ten	**6**

Number Recognition Review

Match the correct number of objects with the number. Then, match the number with the word.

1		four
2		ten
3		two
4		six
5		one
6		nine
7		three
8		eight
9		five
10		seven

Week 14 Skills

Subject	Skill	Multi-Sensory Learning Activities
Reading and Language Arts	Review digraphs /sh/ , /ch/ , /wh/ , /th/.	• Complete Practice Pages 152–156. • Give your child a list of words that include a digraph, such as **whistle**, **brush**, **shoe**, **cash**, and **dish**. Ask your child to tell a story that uses all of the words.
Math	Associate number words with a given number of counters.	• Complete Practice Pages 157 and 160. • Create a booklet of numbers and number words with your child. On each page, write a number word **one** through **twelve**. Ask your child to place the appropriate number of stickers on each page.
	Provide the missing number in a sequence of three consecutive numerals.	• Complete Practice Page 159. • Read *One...Two...Three...Sassafras!* by Stuart J. Murphy. Then, ask your child to draw pictures of the people in his or her family. Help your child cut out the drawings and arrange them in order from oldest to youngest or tallest to shortest. • Play a game with your child. Call out two sequential numbers and ask your child to say what comes next.
Bonus: Science		• Brainstorm with your child any words related to plants. Have your child use each word in a sentence.

Digraphs

Circle the correct digraph for each picture. Color the pictures.

sh   ch

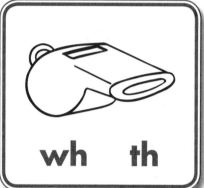

wh   th

ch   sh

wh   th

sh   ch

tch   sh

sh   ch

ch   sh

wh   th

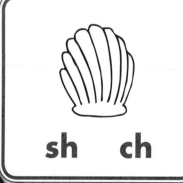

sh   ch

ch   sh

wh   th

Cheer Up!

Say the name of each picture. Write the word that rhymes with it. Read the sentences. Use the words to complete the puzzle.

| chop | chin | cheek | check | chain | children | child | chase |

Across

3. They will use a ___ to pull the car.

5. Many ___ like to go to the circus.

6. Write a ___ mark in the correct box.

Down

1. The baby spilled food on his ___.

2. Only one ___ is on the slide.

4. They like to run and ___ each other.

6. Dad will ___ the stump into logs.

7. The kitten licked the girl's ___.

Shuttling Around

Write the missing words on the lines.

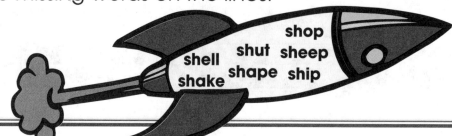

1. A flock of _____ graze on the hillside.

2. The _____ will sail from the dock very soon.

3. We must keep the gate _____ to keep the dog in.

4. Please _____ the bottle of salad dressing.

5. A square is a _____ that has four equal sides.

6. Does she like to _____ at the mall?

7. The clam always stays inside its _____ .

Whistle a Tune

Read each sentence. Write the missing words.

| which whip whale why where when what wheel |

1. _____

   _____ are we going this afternoon?

2. _____

   _____ red dress will Wendy buy?

3. A huge _____

   _____ swam near the shore.

4. _____

   _____ are they going to the basketball game?

5. The shopping cart has a broken _____

   _____ .

6. _____

   _____ will we see at the zoo?

7. The lion sat down when the trainer snapped

   the _____

   _____ .

8. _____

   _____ is Mother Duck taking her ducklings to the pond?

Catch a Fish

Write a word to complete each sentence.

peach wash teach brush rich wish fish dish

1. Don't forget to _____ your hands before lunch.

2. Father dropped the _____ into the paint.

3. I have a pet _____ .

4. My favorite fruit is a _____ .

5. A _____ man bought the big house on the hill.

6. I made a _____ upon a star.

7. Can you _____ me to play that game?

8. My brother dropped a _____ and broke it.

Number Match

Cut out the pictures and number words below. Mix them up and match them.

one		two	eight
		five	
	three		nine
four		seven	
	six		ten

Sequencing Numbers

Write the missing numbers. **Example:** 4, __5__, 6

3, _____, 5   7, _____, 9   8, _____, 10

13, _____, 15   _____, 20, 21   _____, 29, 30

39, 40, _____   _____, 44, 45   _____, 50, 51

_____, 54, 55   _____, 60, 61   62, _____, 64

69, 70, _____   74, 75, _____   77, 78, _____

88, _____, 90   _____, 85, 86   80, _____, 82

90, 91, _____   110, 111, _____   104, _____, 106

99, 100, _____   _____, 101, 102   _____, 119, 120

Number Crossword Puzzle

Write the correct number word in the boxes provided.

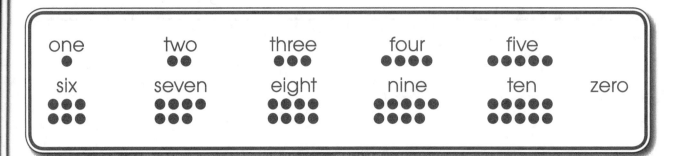

one ●   two ●●   three ●●●   four ●●●●   five ●●●●●

six ●●● ●●●   seven ●●●● ●●●   eight ●●●● ●●●●   nine ●●●●● ●●●●   ten ●●●●● ●●●●●   zero

Across

2. 4

3. 8

5. 2

7. 7

9. 10

Down

1. 0

2. 5

4. 3

6. 1

7. 6

8. 9

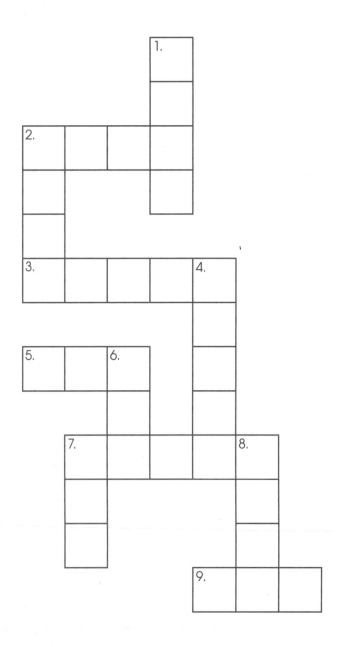

Week 15 Skills

Subject	Skill	Multi-Sensory Learning Activities
Reading and Language Arts	Understand nouns as naming words.	• Complete Practice Pages 162 and 163. • Make three columns on a chart. Write **People** at the top of the first column, **Places** at the top of the second, and **Things** at the top of the third. Have your child name people, places, and things and add them to the columns.
	Understand proper nouns, or words that name a specific person, place, or thing.	• Complete Practice Pages 164 and 165. • List the names of people your child knows. Have your child copy each name correctly, including the capital letter.
	Understand pronouns, or words that take the place of nouns.	• Complete Practice Page 166. • Look for pronouns in the books you and your child read together. Help your child identify to whom each pronoun refers.
Math	Review counting 1–10.	• Complete Practice Pages 167 and 168. • Have your child go around the house, finding various numbers of objects. Have him or her count the objects, then make a booklet entitled *How Many in My House?*
	Understand and practice skip-counting by tens.	• Complete Practice Pages 169 and 170. • Make up a tune to go along with the words as your child counts from 10 to 100 by tens.

Nouns

A **noun** is a word that names a person, place or thing. When you read a sentence, the noun is what the sentence is about.

Complete each sentence with a noun.

The _____ is fat.

My _____ is blue.

The _____ has apples.

The _____ is hot.

Nouns

Write these naming words in the correct box.

store	zoo	child	baby	teacher	table
cat	park	gym	woman	sock	horse

Person

_____   _____

_____   _____

_____   _____

Place

_____   _____

_____   _____

Thing

_____   _____

_____   _____

Proper Nouns

A **proper noun** is a special name for a person, place or thing. It always begins with a capital letter. Write a proper noun to name each person and pet. Use the word box.

| Rover | Sarah | Pedro | Jack and Jill | Piggy | Fluffy |

Proper Nouns

Proper nouns are the names of specific people, places and pets. Proper nouns begin with a capital letter.

Write the proper nouns on the lines below. Use a capital letter at the beginning of each word.

logan, utah

mike smith

lynn cramer

buster

fluffy

chicago, illinois

Pronouns

A **pronoun** is a word that can take the place of a noun in a sentence.

Example: My dad is a pilot. **He** flies airplanes.
My dad loves to fly. **He** is a good pilot.

Circle the pronoun that can take the place of the bold words.

1. **My mother** is a pilot, too.   a. They   b. She

2. **Mom and Dad** own a small plane.   a. We   b. They

3. **My brother and I** have flown   a. We   b. They
   with them.

4. **My brother** wants to be a pilot.   a. It   b. He

5. **Mother** says flying is fun.   a. She   b. He

6. **Dad** loves to fly.   a. They   b. He

7. **My brother** is older than I am.   a. He   b. We

Number Review

Count the objects and write the number word.

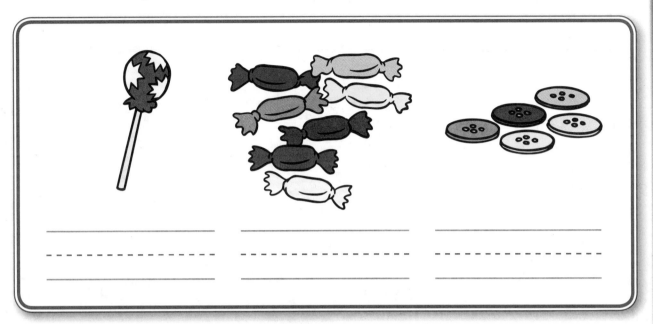

_____

- - - - - - - - - - - - - - -

_____

Match the number to the word.

two   1

four   9

seven   2

three   3

one   4

nine   7

Sheepish Shepherd

Count the sheep on each hill. Then, write that number on each tree.

Counting by Tens

Count by tens to draw the path the boy takes to the store.

Counting by Tens

Use the groups of 10s to count to 100.

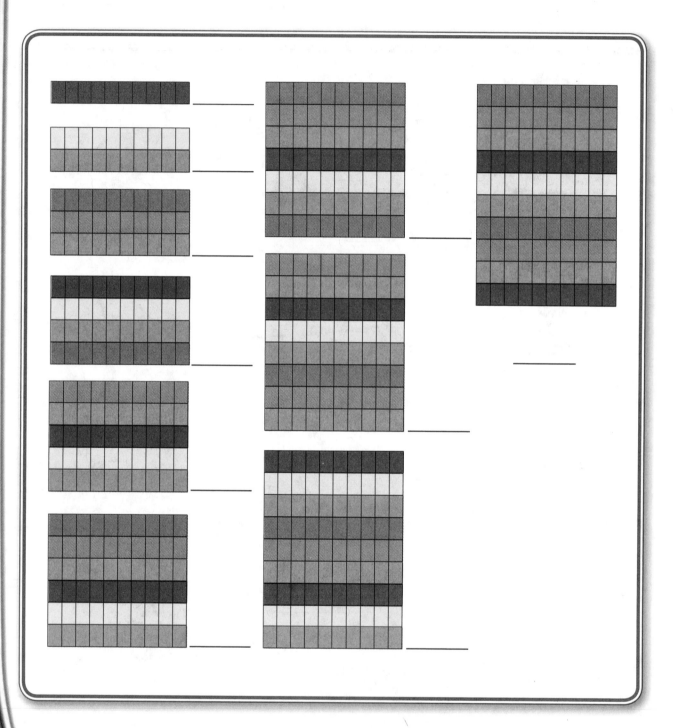

Week 16 Skills

Subject	Skill	Multi-Sensory Learning Activities
Reading and Language Arts	Understand present-tense verbs, or action words that take place now.	• Complete Practice Pages 172–175. • Write several verbs on a piece of paper, such as **hop**, **wave**, **smile**, and **bend**. Ask your child to act out some of the verbs. • Write two or three simple sentences. Omit the verb in each one. Have your child read each sentence fragment and supply his or her own verb. For example: The pig _____ in the dirt. (rolls); A man _____ the house. (paints); The wind _____ loud noises. (makes)
	Understand past-tense verbs, or action words that happened in the past.	• Complete Practice Page 176. • Ask your child to write a sentence about something he or she did yesterday. Circle the verbs, explaining that the verbs are past tense because they already happened.
Math	Count by fives and tens.	• Complete Practice Pages 177–179. • Tape a nickel to a wall chart. Under the nickel, write **5 cents** and explain that a nickel is worth 5 cents. Have your child lay out some nickels in a row, count them, and tell how many nickels there are and the total value.
	Understand greater than and less than.	• Complete Practice Page 180. • Play a game to reinforce the concepts of greater than/less than. For example, say, "I am thinking of a number that is greater than 4 and less than 6. What is it?"

Verbs

Look at the picture and read the words. Write an action word in each sentence below.

swing rings kick run talk

1. The two boys like to _____ together.

2. The children _____ the soccer ball.

3. Some children like to _____ on the swing.

4. The girl can _____ very fast.

5. The teacher _____ the bell.

Present-Tense Verbs

A **present-tense verb** tells about action that is happening now. **Example:** Dad **works**. The children **help**.

Write a verb that tells about what is happening now to complete each sentence.

rakes	waters	weeds	mows	plants	pick

1. The kids _____ .

2. Dave _____ .

3. Suzie _____ .

4. Troy _____ .

5. Mother _____ .

6. Jane _____ .

Verbs

A **verb** tells what a person, animal or thing does. **Examples: play**, **sing**, **stand**. Write a verb under each picture. Use the word box.

| runs | cheers | chases | hits | catches | throws |

Verbs

A **verb** tells what a person, animal or thing does. Color the spaces with verbs yellow. Color the other spaces green.

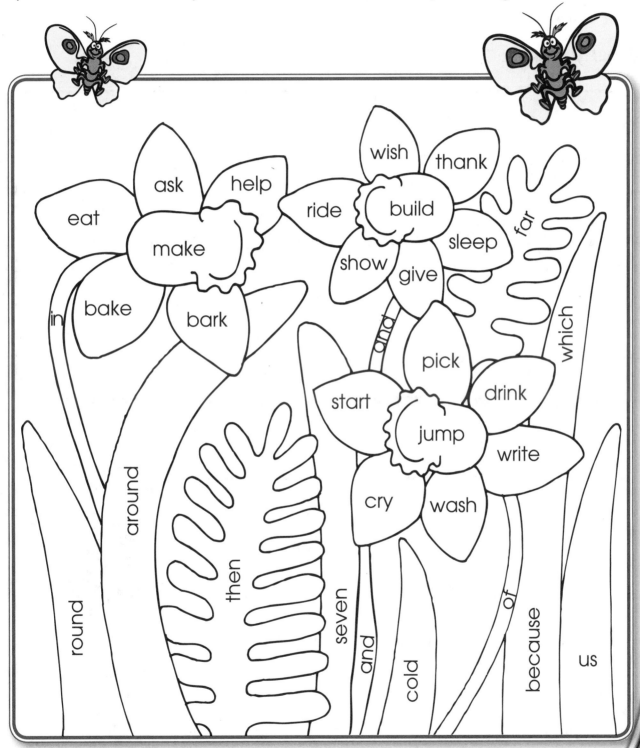

Past-Tense Verbs

A **past-tense verb** tells about something that has already happened. Add **ed** to most verbs to show the past tense. Write the past tense of each verb.

Examples: pass**ed**   play**ed**   walk**ed**   crawl**ed**

1. push _____

2. want _____

3. help _____

4. heat _____

5. color _____

6. pull _____

Write the past tense of each verb on the blank.

1. I _____ Mom a gift.
   (hand)

2. She _____ it quickly.
   (open)

3. Mom _____ surprised.
   (look)

Counting by Fives

Count by fives to draw the path to the playground.

Counting by Fives

Use tally marks to count by fives. Write the number next to the tallies. **Example:** A tally mark stands for one = 1. Five tally marks look like this = 卌.

卌 _____

卌 卌 _____

卌 卌
卌 _____

卌 卌
卌 卌 _____

卌 卌 卌
卌 卌 _____

卌 卌 卌
卌 卌 卌 _____

卌 卌 卌
卌 卌
卌 卌 _____

卌 卌 卌
卌 卌 卌
卌 卌 _____

卌 卌 卌
卌 卌 卌
卌 卌 卌 _____

卌 卌 卌
卌 卌 卌
卌 卌 卌
卌 _____

Caterpillar Count

Count by 5s. Draw triangles around each number in the box.

1	2	3	4	5	6	7	8	9	10
11	12	13	14	15	16	17	18	19	20
21	22	23	24	25	26	27	28	29	30
31	32	33	34	35	36	37	38	39	40
41	42	43	44	45	46	47	48	49	50

Count by 5s.

_____ _____ _____ _____ _____

_____ _____ _____ _____ _____

Count by 10s. Draw boxes around each number in the box.

1	2	3	4	5	6	7	8	9	10
11	12	13	14	15	16	17	18	19	20
21	22	23	24	25	26	27	28	29	30
31	32	33	34	35	36	37	38	39	40
41	42	43	44	45	46	47	48	49	50

Count by 10s.

_____ _____ _____ _____ _____

Less Than, Greater Than

The open mouth points to the larger number. The small point goes to the smaller number. Draw the symbol **<** or **>** to the correct number.

Example: 5 (>) 3   This means that 5 is greater than 3, and 3 is less than 5.

12 ◯ 2   16 ◯ 6

16 ◯ 15   1 ◯ 2

7 ◯ 1   19 ◯ 5

9 ◯ 6   11 ◯ 13

COMPLETE YEAR GRADE 1

Week 17 Skills

Subject	Skill	Multi-Sensory Learning Activities
Reading and Language Arts	Understand past-tense verbs as action words that happened in the past.	• Complete Practice Pages 182 and 183. • Play a matching game. Write past- and present-tense verbs on individual index cards. Your child can mix and match cards or play a game of "Memory."
	Review nouns and verbs.	• Complete Practice Pages 184–186. • On index cards, write ten singular nouns and ten present-tense verbs. Have your child determine how to sort the words into two groups (nouns and verbs).
Math	Understand the place value of double-digit numbers.	• Complete Practice Pages 187–190. • Have your child count and group into tens several sets of objects (toothpicks, uncooked macaroni, dried beans, cubes, etc.). When ten objects are grouped, call the group a "ten." • Make a place value board. Divide a large piece of paper or board into two columns. Label one column "tens" and one column "ones." Provide your child with about 25 toothpicks. As your child counts them aloud, have him or her place them on the ones side of the place-value board. Have your child count them again, but this time when he or she counts 10, have him or her wrap all 10 in a rubber band and put them on the tens side.

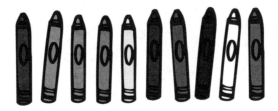

Past-Tense Verbs

Some verbs tell what happened in the past. Verbs that end with **ed** tell about the past. **Examples:** Jill bak**ed** a cake for the bake sale. It tast**ed** delicious.

Write the verb that tells what happened in the past. Write it in the blank.

1. First, Jill _____ the flour.
   (measured, measures)

2. She _____ some baking powder and salt.
   (adds, added)

3. Next, she _____ the sugar and the butter.
   (mixed, mixes)

4. She _____ an egg into the bowl.
   (cracked, cracks)

5. She _____ in a little milk and vanilla.
   (pours, poured)

6. Jill _____ the batter into a cake pan.
   (spooned, spoons)

7. She _____ it for 35 minutes.
   (bakes, baked)

Past-Tense Verbs

A **past-tense verb** tells about action that has already happened. Add **ed** to most verbs to show the past tense. **Example:** We paint**ed** in art class yesterday. I finish**ed** my picture on time.

Write the past tense of the verb in the blank.

1. Ms. Lewis _____ out the papers.
   (passes, passed)

2. I _____ my name.
   (printed, print)

3. We _____ to the directions.
   (listen, listened)

4. We _____ water to the paint.
   (added, add)

5. I _____ yellow and blue.
   (mixed, mix)

6. I _____ a stem.
   (painted, paint)

7. I _____ my brush.
   (clean, cleaned)

Circus Action

Circle the verb in each sentence below.

1. The bear climbs a ladder.

2. Two tiny dogs dance.

3. A boy eats popcorn.

4. A woman swings on a trapeze.

5. The clown falls down.

6. A tiger jumps through a ring.

COMPLETE YEAR GRADE 1

Nouns and Verbs

A **noun** is a person or thing a sentence tells about. A verb tells what the person or thing does.

Circle the noun in each sentence. Underline the verb.
Example: The (cat) sleeps.

1. Jill plays a game on the computer.

2. Children swim in the pool.

3. The car raced around the track.

4. Mike throws the ball to his friend.

5. Monkeys swing in the trees.

6. Terry laughed at the clown.

Review

Read the sentences below. Draw a red circle around the nouns. Draw a blue line under the verbs.

1. The boy runs fast.

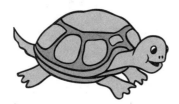

2. The turtle eats leaves.

3. The fish swim in the tank.

4. The girl hits the ball.

Place Value

Write the value of each number below.

35 _____ tens _____ ones

19 _____ ten _____ ones

8 _____ tens _____ ones

26 _____ tens _____ ones

49 _____ tens _____ ones

10 _____ ten _____ ones

Write the number below.

4 tens   6 ones   _____   3 tens   2 ones   _____

2 tens   9 ones   _____   4 tens   0 ones   _____

1 ten   4 ones   _____   0 tens   6 ones   _____

2 tens   1 one   _____   4 tens   7 ones   _____

3 tens   3 ones   _____   1 ten   1 one   _____

Place Value: Tens and Ones

The place value of a digit, or numeral, is shown by where it is in the number. For example, in the number **23**, **2** has the place value of tens, and **3** is ones.

Count the groups of ten crayons and write the number by the word **tens**. Count the other crayons and write the number by the word **ones**.

Example: + = __|__ ten + __|__ one

+ = _____ tens + _____ ones

+ = _____ tens + _____ ones

+ = _____ tens + _____ ones

6 tens + 3 ones = _____   5 tens + 1 one   = _____

3 tens + 8 ones = _____   9 tens + 7 ones = _____

4 tens + 5 ones = _____   2 tens + 8 ones = _____

Place Value: Tens and Ones

Count the groups of ten blocks and write the number by the word **tens**. Count the other blocks and write the number by the word **ones**.

Example:

⊞⊞⊞⊞⊞⊞⊞⊞⊞⊞ + ▮▮ = ___1___ ten + ___2___ ones

⊞⊞⊞ + ▮ = _____ tens + _____ ones

⊞⊞⊞⊞⊞ + ▮▮▮▮▮ = _____ tens + _____ ones

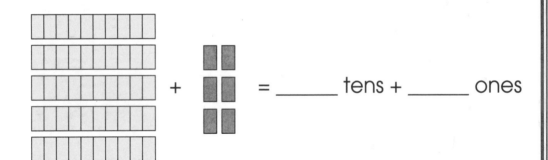 + ▮▮▮▮▮▮ = _____ tens + _____ ones

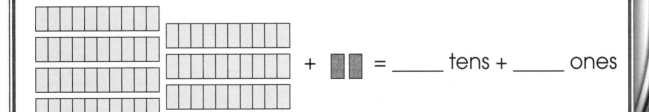 + ▮▮ = _____ tens + _____ ones

Place Value: Tens and Ones

Write the answers in the correct spaces.

		tens	ones		
3 tens, 2 ones		3	2	=	32
3 tens, 7 ones		___	___	=	___
9 tens, 1 one		___	___	=	___
5 tens, 6 ones		___	___	=	___
6 tens, 5 ones		___	___	=	___
6 tens, 8 ones		___	___	=	___
2 tens, 8 ones		___	___	=	___
4 tens, 9 ones		___	___	=	___
1 ten, 4 ones		___	___	=	___
8 tens, 2 ones		___	___	=	___
4 tens, 2 ones		___	___	=	___

28 = ____ tens, ____ ones

64 = ____ tens, ____ ones

56 = ____ tens, ____ ones

72 = ____ tens, ____ ones

38 = ____ tens, ____ ones

17 = ____ ten, ____ ones

63 = ____ tens, ____ ones

Week 18 Skills

Subject	Skill	Multi-Sensory Learning Activities
Reading and Language Arts	Understand adjectives, or describing words.	• Complete Practice Pages 192–196. • Plan a tasting activity. Prepare foods of varying tastes and textures, including fruits, vegetables, peanut butter, dressings, meat, and chips. Have your child describe how each food tastes. As an added challenge, blindfold your child so that he or she can concentrate only on taste. Make a list of the adjectives your child uses to describe the tastes. • Have your child draw an outline of him or herself and divide it into sections. Have your child write a word or phrase in each section that describes him or her.
Math	Work with addition equations.	• Complete Practice Pages 197 and 198. • Provide several addition equations for your child to solve with the help of cards that show various numbers of dots. Periodically replace dot cards with number cards until your child is solving problems without the aid of the dot card.
	Determine the missing addend when given one addend and the sum of an addition problem.	• Complete Practice Pages 199 and 200. • Using masking tape, make a number line to 9 on the floor. Have your child stand at zero on the number line and toss two beanbags—the bag that lands on the smaller number is an addend, and the bag that lands on the larger number is the sum. If one landed on 4 and another landed on 5, your child would say "4 + 1 = 5."

Words That Describe

Describing words tell us more about a person, place or thing.

Read the words in the box. Choose the word that describes the picture. Write it next to the picture.

happy	round	sick	cold	long

Words That Describe

Read the words in the box. Choose the word that describes the picture. Write it next to the picture.

wet	round	funny	soft	sad	tall

Words That Describe

Circle the describing word in each sentence. Draw a line from the sentence to the picture.

1. The hungry dog is eating.

2. The tiny bird is flying.

3. Horses have long legs.

4. She is a fast runner.

5. The little boy was lost.

Words That Describe: Colors and Numbers

Colors and numbers can describe nouns.

Underline the describing word in each sentence. Draw a picture to go with each sentence.

A yellow moon was in the sky.

Two worms are on the road.

The tree had red apples.

The girl wore a blue dress.

Animal Adjectives

Write a describing word in each sentence below. Use the word web to help you.

1. A  has a _____ tail.

_____
- - - - - - - - - - - - - - - - -

2. A has _____ legs.

_____
- - - - - - - - - - - - - - - - -

3. The will become a _____ frog.

_____
- - - - - - - - - - - - - - - - -

4. A has _____ teeth.

_____
- - - - - - - - - - - - - - - - -

5. _____ hang by their tails.

_____
- - - - - - - - - - - - - - - - -

6. An has _____ eyes.

How Many?

Add the ones and then the tens in each problem. Then, write the sum on the blank.

Example:

    2 tens   and   6 ones
  + 1 ten   and   3 ones
  _____
    3 tens   and   9 ones = **39**

---

    1 ten   and   4 ones
  + 3 tens   and   3 ones
  _____
    ___ tens   and   ___ ones = ___

---

    1 ten   and   6 ones
  + 2 tens   and   3 ones
  _____
    ___ tens   and   ___ ones = ___

---

    1 ten   and   6 ones
  + 3 tens   and   1 one
  _____
    ___ tens   and   ___ ones = ___

---

    1 ten   and   3 ones
  + 1 ten   and   1 one
  _____
    ___ tens   and   ___ ones = ___

---

    2 tens   and   5 ones
  + 2 tens   and   0 ones
  _____
    ___ tens   and   ___ ones = ___

---

    1 ten   and   5 ones
  + 2 tens   and   4 ones
  _____
    ___ tens   and   ___ ones = ___

---

    2 tens   and   3 ones
  + 2 tens   and   2 ones
  _____
    ___ tens   and   ___ ones = ___

It's All the Same

Count the objects and fill in the blanks. Then, switch the addends and write another addition sentence.

If ___3___ + ___8___ = ___11___ , so does ___8___ + ___3___ .

If _____ + _____ = _____ , so does _____ + _____ .

If _____ + _____ = _____ , so does _____ + _____ .

If _____ + _____ = _____ , so does _____ + _____ .

If _____ + _____ = _____ , so does _____ + _____ .

If _____ + _____ = _____ , so does _____ + _____ .

Bear Necessities

How many more are needed? Draw the missing pictures.
Complete the addition sentences.

1 + _____ = 3

3 + _____ = 5

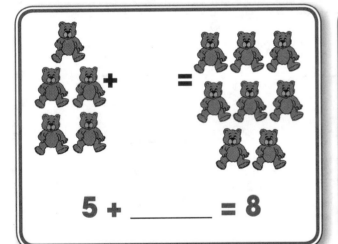

5 + _____ = 8

3 + _____ = 6

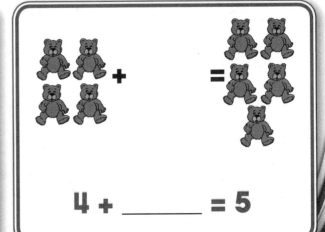

2 + _____ = 7

4 + _____ = 5

Be a Good Detective

Find the missing numbers in the problems below.

$5 +$ ◯ $= 14$ $12 +$ ▢ $= 18$

$4 +$ △ $= 17$ $9 +$ ◯ $= 15$ $7 +$ ▢ $= 13$

$11 +$ ◯ $= 16$ $8 +$ ▢ $= 13$ $6 +$ △ $= 16$

$9 +$ △ $= 17$ ◯ $+ 10 = 14$ ▢ $+ 1 = 12$

◯ $+ 3 = 12$ ▢ $+ 2 = 14$ △ $+ 8 = 15$

▢ $+ 7 = 10$ △ $+ 9 = 18$ ◯ $+ 6 = 11$

Second Quarter Check-Up

Reading and Language Arts

☐ I know the sounds made by these consonant letters at the ends of words: **b, d, f, g, k, l, m, n, p, r, s, t, x**.

☐ I know the sounds vowels make in the middle of words.

☐ I know the sounds of consonant blends at the beginning and ends of words.

☐ I understand digraphs /**sh**/, /**ch**/, /**wh**/, and /**th**/.

☐ I understand nouns, proper nouns, pronouns, present- and past-tense verbs, and adjectives.

Math

☐ I can work with and understand patterns of shapes, colors, numbers, and letters.

☐ I can recognize numbers and count from 1–10.

☐ I know number words **one** through **twelve**.

☐ I can provide the missing number in a sequence.

☐ I can skip-count by tens and fives.

☐ I know the concept of less than and greater than.

☐ I understand place value of tens and ones.

☐ I can work with addition equations and solve addition problems.

Final Project

Go on a counting tour of your home. Choose a household item, such as forks or pillows, and count all of them that you can find. Then, choose another item and count those as well. Which item had the highest number? Look at the group of items with the highest number and write a list of at least five adjectives describing those items.

Third Quarter Introduction

In the weeks after the winter or mid-year break, students are often ready to tackle new learning challenges. In many classrooms, brand-new concepts and skills are introduced during third quarter that may be difficult for your child. You can help at home by encouraging your child and providing positive learning support using resources found in *Complete Year*.

Third Quarter Skills

Practice pages in this book for Weeks 19–27 will help your child improve the following skills.

Basic Skills
- Classify and sort objects into appropriate categories

Reading and Language Arts
- Understand one- and two-syllable words
- Identify synonyms and antonyms
- Work with telling and asking sentences
- Use commas appropriately
- Identify and understand the prefix **re** and suffixes **ing**, **est**, and **ed**

Math
- Practice addition problems through 20
- Add three or more numbers
- Work with the commutative property of addition
- Practice subtraction problems within 15
- Work with ordinal numbers **first** through **tenth**

Multi-Sensory Learning Activities

Try these fun activities for enhancing your child's learning and development during the third quarter of the school year. Be sure to choose activities that include speaking, listening, touching, and active movement.

 Basic Skills

Brainstorm with your child a list of things found on a farm. Have your child sort the list into living and non-living things.

Play a silly game. Take turns naming three things, such as **bread, butter**, and **pencil**. Ask your child to name which one does not belong and tell why.

Discuss and list both good and bad manners. Teach appropriate manners at the dinner table, at a movie theater, and at a restaurant through role-playing.

Have your child paint a rainbow. When the paint dries, ask your child to dictate a sentence about each color of the rainbow. Write each sentence on the arc of its color.

Reading and Language Arts

Help your child make a list of the names of favorite characters from books, movies, and TV shows. Say each name. Underline the letters that make each vowel sound. How many syllables does each name have? Do the number of syllables and vowel sounds match?

Write "The little boy was crying." Under the sentence, write the words **weeping**, **smiling**, and **sitting**. Ask your child to circle the synonym that means about the same thing as the underlined word.

When you read a story with your child, pause when you come to verbs such as **said, ran, laughed,** or **shouted**. For each verb, challenge your child to supply another word with a similar meaning.

At the count of three, make a fist to represent a period or curve your hand in a c-shape with your thumb pointing downward to represent a question mark. Can your child think of a sentence that goes with that punctuation mark? Take turns.

2 8 4 9 6 Math

On index cards, write numbers **1–20** and symbols **+**, **–**, and **=**. Cut the center from another card to make an empty frame. Decorate the frame. Then, form equations with the cards, putting the empty frame in various positions for your child to fill in.

Play with magnetic numbers. Think aloud with your child as you add three numbers. For example, when adding the numbers **4**, **4**, and **2**, say, "I know that four plus four equals eight, and that two more than eight is 10, so the answer must be 10."

Raise a number of fingers greater than five and have your child do the same. Invite your child to lower some of your fingers and transfer the count to his or her fingers to total 10. How many of your fingers remain raised in addition to 10?

Draw an octopus shape with nine arms. Write a number, such as **6**, on its head. On eight arms, write a problem whose answer is 6. On one arm, write a problem with a different answer. Can your child find the false number sentence and cross it out?

Practice ordinal numbers with your child in everyday contexts. For example, ask your child to point to the fifth day of the week on the calendar, the third button on his or her shirt, the eighth tile on the floor, etc.

Read *1, 2, 3 to the Zoo* by Eric Carle. Talk about which animals are first, second, third, and so on. Then, give your child a drawing of a train and ask him or her to glue pictures of animals in the correct position. For example, glue the lions in the fifth car and the tigers in the second car.

Third Quarter Introduction, cont.

Give your child a black and white drawing of a rainbow. Give oral clues using ordinal numbers telling your child how to color the rainbow.

 **Science**

Have your child fill two glasses halfway with water. Then, have your child cover one glass with plastic wrap, place a rubber band around it and set both glasses in a warm spot. Have your child check for changes twice a day for two days. Your child should record observations by drawing the water line each time on a record sheet. After two days, discuss what happened and where the water is.

Gather several household objects. Have your child sort the objects into groups of things he or she thinks will stick to a magnet and those that he or she thinks will not. Record your child's predictions. Have your child touch a magnet to each object and determine the accuracy of his or her predictions.

Set up a "fish pond." Fill a plastic tub or glass baking dish with paper clips, nails, candy, a wire, pieces of paper, a rubber band, a tack, staples, and other small objects. Tie one end of a string onto a stick and the other end onto a magnet to make a fishing pole. Have your child "fish" for the magnetic objects.

 Seasonal Fun

Make a cereal box snowman with your child. Paint an empty cereal box with white paint. Then, paint two small paper cups red. Glue the earmuffs on the sides of the cereal box, with a strip of construction paper connecting them across the top. Use construction paper for the scarf and nose, and black paint to make pieces of coal for the eyes and mouth.

Help your child bring the winter weather inside by making frost. First, fill an empty soup can $\frac{2}{3}$ full with crushed ice. Spread a teaspoon of water on a piece of paper and place underneath the can. Fill the can the rest of the way with salt and mix with the ice until well mixed. Watch as frost starts to appear on the outside of the can.

Week 19 Skills

Subject	Skill	Multi-Sensory Learning Activities
Basic Skills	Classify and sort objects into appropriate categories.	• Complete Practice Pages 206–210. • Make a book of lists. On each page, have your child brainstorm a different list. Encourage your child to add to the lists as opportunities arise. Ideas for lists include: things that are red, friendly animals, words that begin with **z**, friends, relatives, books about cars, toys, and words that are fun to say.
Math	Practice addition problems through 10.	• Complete Practice Pages 211 and 212. • Relate math skills to daily activities by creating problem-solving situations. For example, when preparing for a meal, tell your child five people will be eating, but you only have three plates out. Ask your child how many more plates you need and how he or she will solve the problem.
	Add 3 or more numbers.	• Complete Practice Pages 213 and 214. • Draw three sets of circles on a piece of paper. Count each set, then add all three numbers together and write the total.

What's What?

Write the words from the word box in the correct place.

car	house	boat	plane	cow	window
girl	hen	bird	dog	tree	rocks

Living	**Non-Living**
1. _____	1. _____
2. _____	2. _____
3. _____	3. _____
4. _____	4. _____
5. _____	5. _____
6. _____	6. _____

Food Fun

Read the names of each food in the box. Write the words where they belong.

carrots	cherries	chicken	cheese	fish	ham
cake	lettuce	bagel	oranges	pears	rolls
beans	milk	toast	pie	candy bar	yogurt

GRAINS

VEGETABLE

DAIRY

FRUITS

SWEETS

MEATS

Classifying

Classifying is putting similar things into groups.

Write each word from the word box on the correct line.

baby	donkey	whale	family	fox
uncle	goose	grandfather	kangaroo	policeman

People   ### Animals

_____   _____

_____   _____

_____   _____

_____   _____

_____   _____

Classifying

Read the sentences. Write the words from the word box where they belong.

bush	rocket	cake	thunder	bicycle	Danger
airplane	wind	candy	rain	car	grass
Stop	truck	Poison	flower	pie	bird

1. These things taste sweet.

   _____ _____ _____

2. These things come when it storms.

   _____ _____ _____

3. These things have wheels.

   _____ _____ _____

4. These are words you see on signs.

   _____ _____ _____

5. These things can fly.

   _____ _____ _____

6. These things grow in the ground.

   _____ _____ _____

Classifying

The words in each box form a group. Choose the word from the word box that describes each group and write it on the line.

clothes	animals	colors
fruits	noises	toys
family	coins	flowers

rose
buttercup
tulip
daisy

_____

crash
bang
ring
pop

_____

mother
father
sister
brother

_____

puzzle
wagon
blocks
doll

_____

green
purple
blue
red

_____

grapes
orange
apple
plum

_____

shirt
socks
dress
coat

_____

dime
penny
nickel
quarter

_____

dog
horse
elephant
moose

_____

Addition 1-5

Count the tools in each toolbox. Write your answers in the blanks. Circle the problem that matches your answer.

$$\left(\begin{array}{c} 2 \\ +\ 2 \\ \hline \end{array}\right) \qquad \begin{array}{c} 2 \\ +\ 1 \\ \hline \end{array}$$

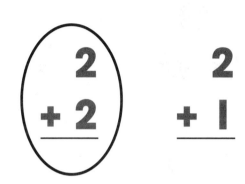

4 ___

$$\begin{array}{c} 5 \\ +\ 0 \\ \hline \end{array} \qquad \begin{array}{c} 4 \\ +\ 2 \\ \hline \end{array}$$

___

$$\begin{array}{c} 6 \\ +\ 2 \\ \hline \end{array} \qquad \begin{array}{c} 4 \\ +\ 3 \\ \hline \end{array}$$

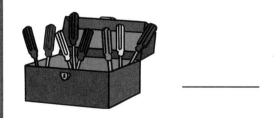

___

$$\begin{array}{c} 3 \\ +\ 1 \\ \hline \end{array} \qquad \begin{array}{c} 2 \\ +\ 3 \\ \hline \end{array}$$

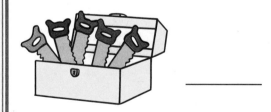

___

Picture Problems: Addition

Solve the number problem under each picture.

$6 + 2 =$ _____

$3 + 1 =$ _____

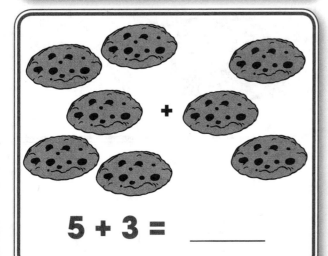

$5 + 3 =$ _____

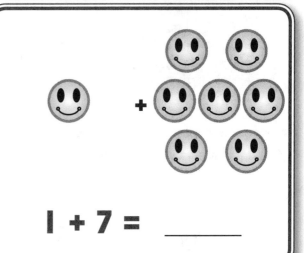

$1 + 7 =$ _____

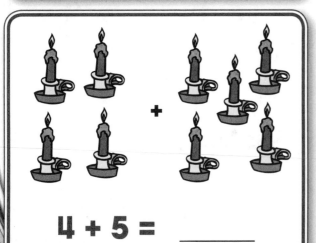

$4 + 5 =$ _____

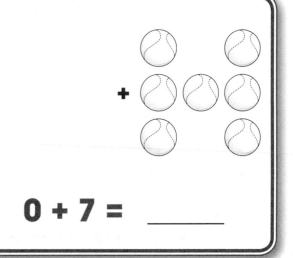

$0 + 7 =$ _____

Tall Number Tales

Read each story. Write the numbers in the box. Then, add to solve the problem.

1. Marty had 3 marbles. Jake had 7 marbles. John had 4 marbles. How many marbles did the boys have all together?

2. The soccer team won! Andrea made 2 goals. Michael made 3 goals. Sam made 3. How many goals did the soccer team make?

3. The first grade ran in three races. Team A scored 5 points. Team B scored 6 points. Team C scored 8 points. How many points did the first grade score?

4. We went to the farm. We saw 6 black pigs. We saw 4 black and white cows. We saw 6 brown hens. How many farm animals did we see at the farm?

5. Mother picked flowers from the garden. She picked 7 pansies, 4 tulips, 4 irises and 3 daffodils. How many flowers did Mother pick?

Adding 3 or More Numbers

Add all the numbers to find the sum. Draw pictures to help or break up the problem into two smaller problems.

Example:

$$
\begin{array}{r}
1 \\
2 \\
+\,3 \\
\hline
6
\end{array}
\quad\bigcirc\;\;\bigcirc\bigcirc\;\;\bigcirc\bigcirc\bigcirc
$$

$$
\begin{array}{r}
2 \\
5 \\
2 \\
+\,4 \\
\end{array}
\;\longrightarrow\; 7 \;\longrightarrow\;
\begin{array}{r}
7 \\
+\,6 \\
\hline
13
\end{array}
$$

$$
\begin{array}{r}
3 \\
6 \\
+\,2 \\
\hline
\end{array}
\qquad
\begin{array}{r}
8 \\
5 \\
+\,4 \\
\hline
\end{array}
\qquad
\begin{array}{r}
3 \\
1 \\
+\,5 \\
\hline
\end{array}
\qquad
\begin{array}{r}
8 \\
2 \\
+\,9 \\
\hline
\end{array}
$$

$$
\begin{array}{r}
2 \\
8 \\
4 \\
+\,3 \\
\hline
\end{array}
\qquad
\begin{array}{r}
3 \\
6 \\
5 \\
+\,2 \\
\hline
\end{array}
\qquad
\begin{array}{r}
4 \\
1 \\
2 \\
+\,5 \\
\hline
\end{array}
\qquad
\begin{array}{r}
6 \\
7 \\
3 \\
+\,1 \\
\hline
\end{array}
$$

Week 20 Skills

Subject	Skill	Multi-Sensory Learning Activities
Basic Skills	Practice classifying and sorting objects into appropriate categories.	• Complete Practice Pages 216–220. • Read *The Button Box* by Margarette S. Reid. Then, give your child a pile of objects to sort, such as buttons, toys, clothes, or food. Ask your child to classify the objects into different categories.
Math	Practice addition problems using counters.	• Complete Practice Pages 221 and 222. • Use two different colors of counters, or small round objects that can be used for counting. Fill several cups with combinations that add up to the same number. For example, in one cup place one blue and three yellow counters and in another cup place two blue and two yellow for the sum four. Do not have any sum go above 10. Have your child dump the contents of one cup and count each group, saying the numbers aloud. Repeat the activity until each combination for that sum has been modeled at least once.
	Review addition problems through 10.	• Complete Practice Pages 223 and 224. • Hold four small counters in one palm and let your child count them. Move some counters to your other hand and close your fists. Open one hand. Can your child tell you what is hidden in your closed fist?

Classifying: Food Groups

Color the meats and eggs brown. Color the fruits and vegetables green. Color the breads tan. Color the dairy foods (milk and cheese) yellow.

fish

bread

apple

cheese

crackers

carrot

orange

eggs

steaks

pear

milk

yogurt

ice cream

chicken

potato

pretzel

Classifying: What Does Not Belong?

Draw an **X** on the picture that does not belong in each group.

fruit

apple   peach   corn   watermelon

wild animals

bear   kitten   gorilla   lion

pets

cat   fish   elephant   dog

flowers

grass   rose   daisy   tulip

Classifying: What Does Not Belong?

Draw an **X** on the word in each row that does not belong.

1.	flashlight	candle	radio	fire
2.	shirt	pants	coat	bat
3.	cow	car	bus	train
4.	beans	hot dog	ball	bread
5.	gloves	hat	book	boots
6.	fork	butter	cup	plate
7.	book	ball	bat	milk
8.	dogs	bees	flies	ants

Classifying: Objects

Write each word in the correct row at the bottom of the page.

| airplane | drum | radio | plate | car | pencil |
| spoon | crayon | chalk | fork | television | boat |

Things we ride in:

_____

- - - - - - - - - - - - - - - - - -

_____

Things we eat with:

_____

- - - - - - - - - - - - - - - - - -

_____

Things we draw with:

_____

- - - - - - - - - - - - - - - - - -

_____

Things we listen to:

_____

- - - - - - - - - - - - - - - - - -

_____

Classifying: Names, Numbers, Animals, Colors

Write the words from the box next to the words they describe.

Joe	Sue	dog	blue	pig	ten
two	cat	green	red	Tim	six

Name Words

- -

- -

Number Words

- -

- -

Animal Words

- -

- -

Color Words

- -

- -

Addition Using Counters

Use counters to add.

Example: 2 + 1 = ___?___

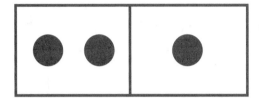

Put in 2.   Put in 1 more.

How many counters are there in all? __3__

2 + 1 = 3. The number that tells how many in all is called the **sum**. The sum of 2 + 1 is 3.

Use counters to find each sum.

2 + 4 = ____

5 + 2 = ____

3 + 3 = ____

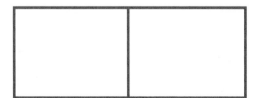

3 + 4 = ____

Cuddly Kitten

Use counters. Trace or draw each group you make. Then, write how many in all.

How many?		How many more?		How many in all?
3	+	2	=	
2	+	1	=	
4	+	3	=	
1	+	6	=	

Think of a story for this picture. Write how many in all.

How many in all?

Pet Picture Problems

Circle the picture that matches the addition sentence.

1 + 2 = 3	3 + 2 = 5
2 + 4 = 6	3 + 3 = 6
3 + 4 = 7	1 + 6 = 7

How Many in All?

Write two addition sentences for each picture story. Find how many in all.

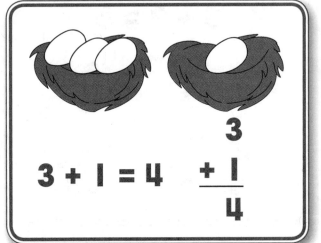

$3 + 1 = 4$

$\begin{array}{r} 3 \\ + 1 \\ \hline 4 \end{array}$

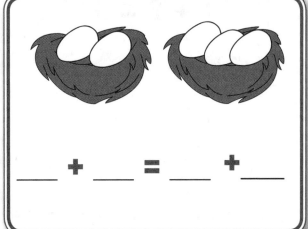

__ + __ = __ + __

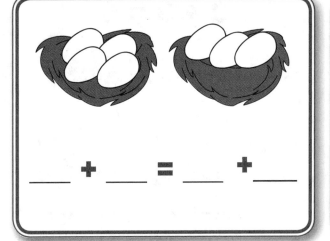

__ + __ = __ + __

__ + __ = __ + __

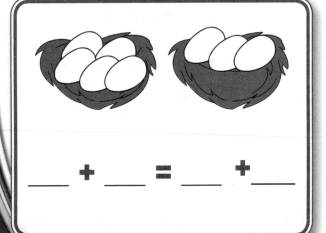

__ + __ = __ + __

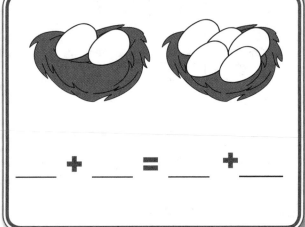

__ + __ = __ + __

Week 21 Skills

Subject	Skill	Multi-Sensory Learning Activities
Reading and Language Arts	Understand one- and two-syllable words.	• Complete Practice Pages 226–229. • Help your child make a list of the names of his or her classmates and friends. Say each name. Underline the letters that make each vowel sound. How many syllables does each name have? Do the number of syllables and vowel sounds match? • Say a one-syllable word, such as **class**. Have your child say a two-syllable word, such as **classroom**. Then, say a three-syllable word. How high can you go? Help your child write the last word given, underlining letters that make the vowel sounds.
Math	Review addition problems through 10.	• Complete Practice Pages 231–234. • Use flash cards to present addition facts in a logical order. The goal is for your child to see the relationship between facts. Build the sense of, "If I know what 2 + 7 is, then I know what 3 + 7 is."
Bonus: Basic Skills		• Have your child march to marching band music, counting and keeping the beat. Play other kinds of music with a strong beat and have your child clap along.

Syllables

When a double consonant is used in the middle of a word, the word can usually be divided between the consonants. Look at the words in the word box. Divide each word into two syllables. Leave space between each syllable. One is done for you.

butter dinner pillow	puppy chatter letter	kitten ladder mitten	yellow happy summer

but ter _____ _____

_____ _____ _____

_____ _____ _____

_____ _____ _____

Many words are divided between two consonants that are not alike. Look at the words in the word box. Divide each word into two syllables. One is done for you.

window mister barber	doctor winter sister	number pencil picture	carpet candle under

win dow _____ _____

_____ _____ _____

_____ _____ _____

_____ _____ _____

Syllables

Write **1** or **2** on the line to tell how many syllables are in each word. If the word has 2 syllables, draw a line between the syllables. **Example: sup|per**

dog _____   timber _____

bedroom _____   cat _____

slipper _____   street _____

tree _____   chalk _____

batter _____   blanket _____

chair _____   marker _____

fish _____   brush _____

master _____   rabbit _____

Syllables

Dividing a word into syllables can help you read a new word. You also might divide syllables when you are writing if you run out of space on a line.

Many words contain two consonants that are next to each other. A word can usually be divided between the consonants.

Divide each word into two syllables. The first one is done for you.

kitten   _kit ten_   harder   _____

lumber   _____   dirty   _____

batter   _____   sister   _____

winter   _____   little   _____

funny   _____   dinner   _____

Take One or Two

Look at the picture on each cookie and read the word on it. Cut out and glue each cookie on the correct jar to show how many syllables are in the word.

1 Syllable

2 Syllables

cut ✂ -

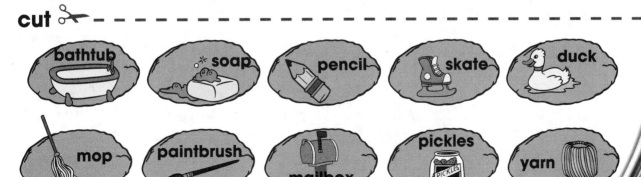

bathtub   soap   pencil   skate   duck

mop   paintbrush   mailbox   pickles   yarn

Alien Problems

Look at the pictures. Complete the addition sentences.

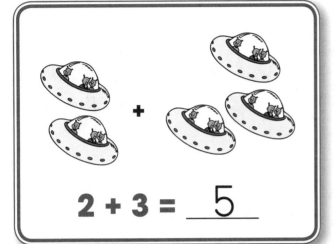

2 + 3 = __5__

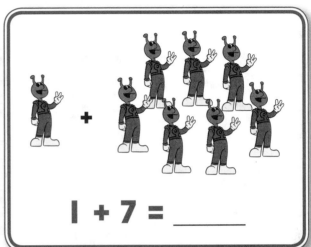

1 + 7 = _____

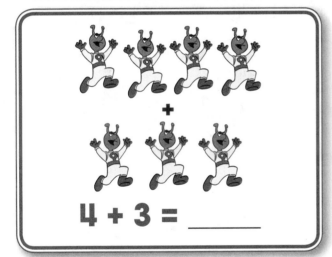

4 + 3 = _____

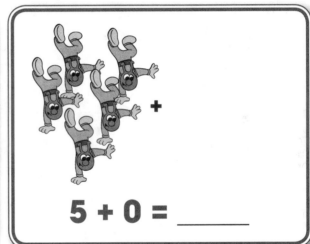

5 + 0 = _____

3 + 3 = _____

4 + 5 = _____

How Many Robots in All?

Look at the pictures. Complete the addition sentences.

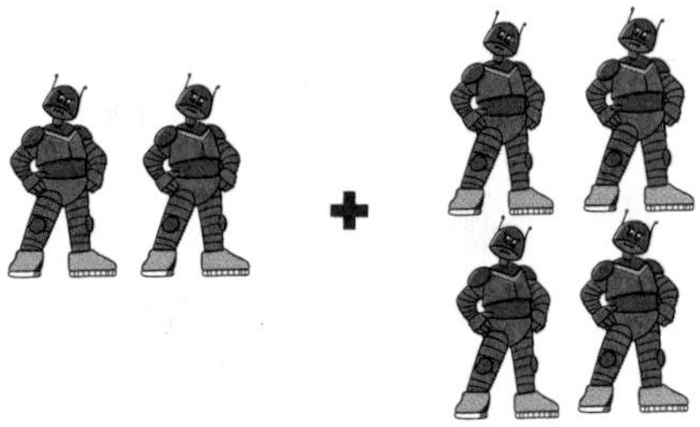

How many s are there in all?

2 + 4 = 6

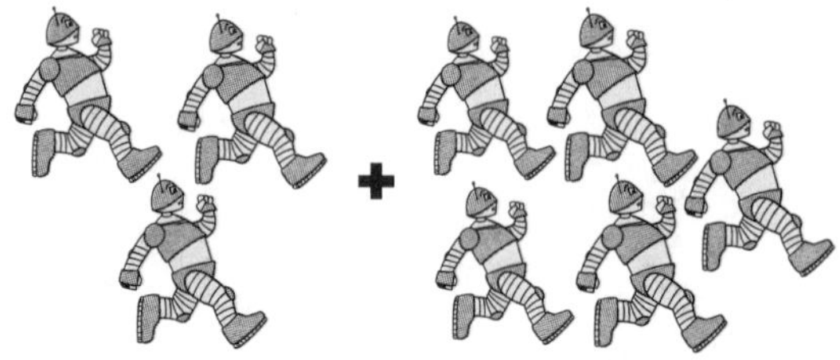

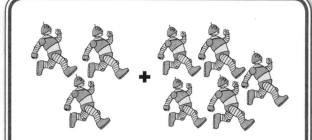

How many s are there in all?

3 + 5 = ______

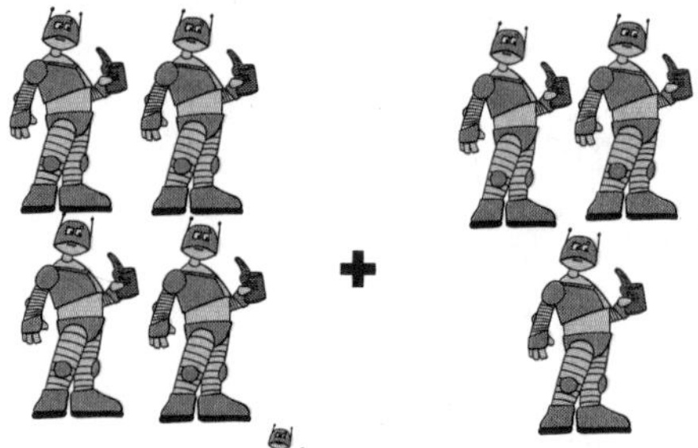

How many s are there in all?

4 + 3 = ______

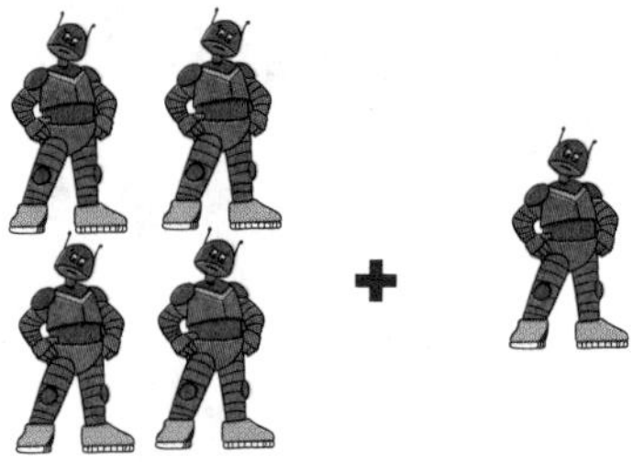

How many s are there in all?

4 + 1 = ______

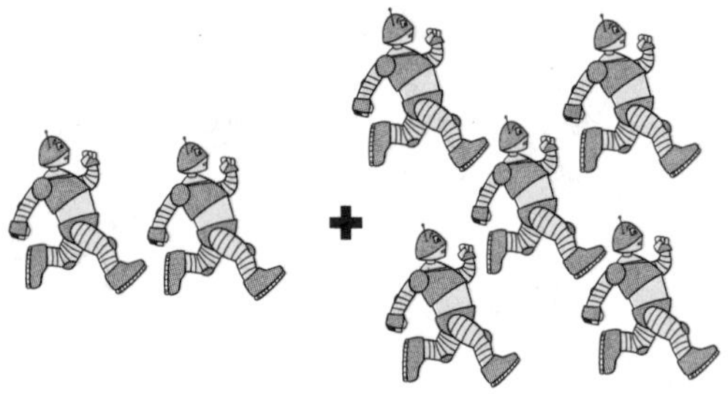

How many s are there in all?

2 + 5 = ______

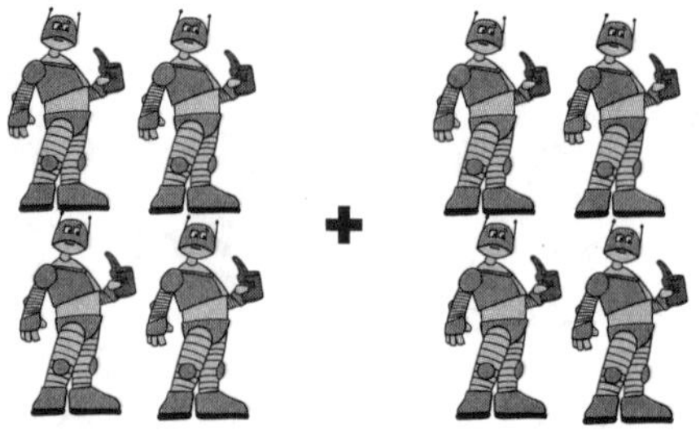

How many s are there in all?

4 + 4 = ______

Creature Count

Add to find the sum. Write each answer on a spaceship.

4 + 6 = 10

1 + 9 =

7 + 1 =

7 + 3 =

5 + 2 =

6 + 1 =

8 + 2 =

3 + 5 =

6 + 3 =

6 + 2 =

Bee Addition

Add to find the sum. Write each answer on a beehive.

1 + 2 = 3

2 + 3 =

3 + 2 =

3 + 1 =

1 + 1 =

2 + 2 =

2 + 1 =

1 + 3 =

Week 22 Skills

Subject	Skill	Multi-Sensory Learning Activities
Reading and Language Arts	Understand and identify synonyms as words that mean the same, or about the same, as another word.	• Complete Practice Pages 236–240. • Write pairs of synonyms on individual index cards—one word per card. Play a memory game, encouraging your child to match the words with similar meanings.
Math	Practice addition problems up to 20.	• Complete Practice Pages 241–243. • Use flash cards to practice "counting on." Teach your child to state the larger number in each problem and count on the other amount. For the fact **8 + 3**, your child should say, "8, 9, 10, 11." It helps to tap while saying "9, 10, 11."
	Work with the commutative property of addition.	• Complete Practice Page 244. • Make rods from construction paper or cardboard. Each rod should be one inch wide. Cut the longest rod 10 inches long and the shortest rod one inch long. Make at least ten 1s, five 2s, three 3s, two 4s, and two of every other number through 10. Color each number a different color. Have your child lay out one rod and experiment with different ways that length rod may be matched using just two other rods. For example, a purple rod (4) matches two reds (2 + 2) or a white and a green (1 + 3).

Similar Meanings

Read the words in the box. Write two words under each picture.

rock	start	road	begin	street	stone
shut	sad	talk	unhappy	speak	closed

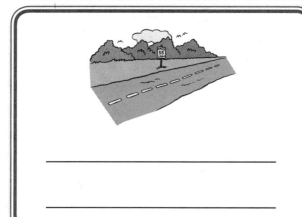

_____

_____

_____

_____

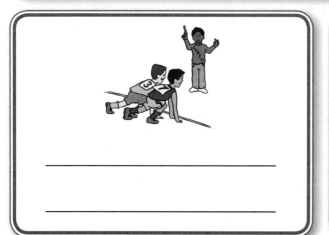

_____

_____

_____

_____

_____

_____

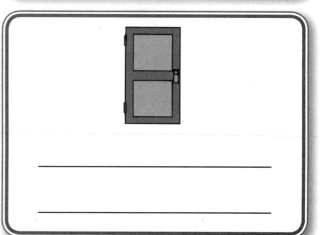

_____

_____

Same or Opposite?

Color the spaces yellow if they have word pairs with opposite meanings. Color the spaces blue if they have word pairs with the same meanings.

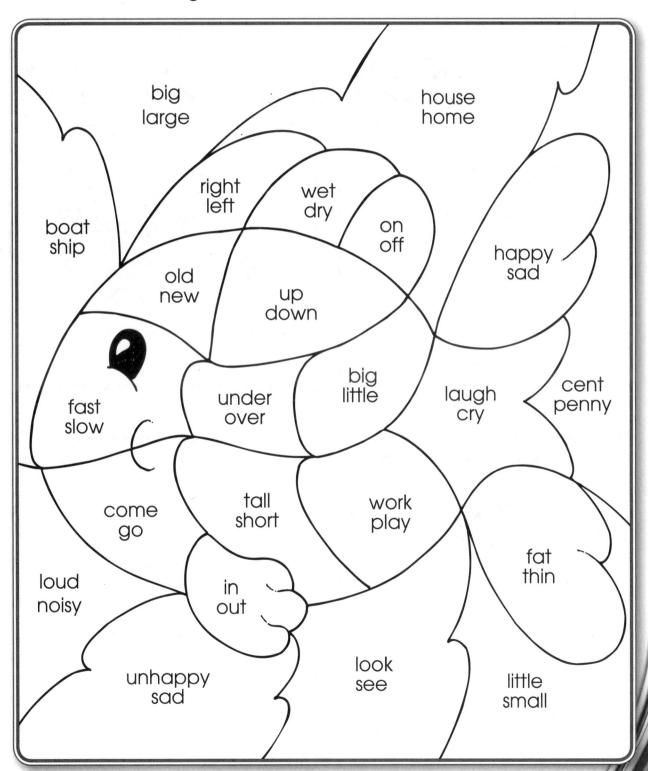

Synonyms

Synonyms are words that mean almost the same thing. **Start** and **begin** are synonyms.

Find the synonyms that describe each picture. Write the words in the boxes below the picture.

small   funny   large   sad   silly   little   big   unhappy

Similarities: Synonyms

Circle the word in each row that is most like the first word in the row.

Example:

grin		(smile)	frown	mad
bag		jar	sack	box
cat		fruit	animal	flower
apple		rot	cookie	fruit
around		circle	square	dot
brown		tan	black	red
bird		dog	cat	duck
bee		fish	ant	snake

Synonyms

Synonyms are words that have the same meaning.

Read each sentence and look at the underlined word. Circle the word that means the same thing. Write the new words.

1. The <u>little</u> dog ran.	tall	funny	small
2. The <u>happy</u> girl smiled.	glad	sad	good
3. The bird is in the <u>big</u> tree.	green	pretty	tall
4. He was <u>nice</u> to me.	kind	mad	bad
5. The baby is <u>tired</u>.	sleepy	sad	little

1. _____

2. _____

3. _____

4. _____

5. _____

How Many in All?

Count the number in each group and write the number on the line. Then, add the groups together and write the sum.

  _____ strawberries

_____ strawberries

How many in all? _____

 _____ cookies

 _____ cookies

How many in all? _____

 _____ shoes

 _____ shoes

How many in all? _____

 _____ balloons

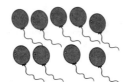 _____ balloons

How many in all? _____

_____ balls

_____ balls

How many in all? _____

 _____ flowers

 _____ flowers

How many in all? _____

 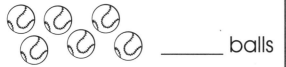 

Addition Grid

Write the sums where the columns and rows meet. The first one shows you what to do.

+	1	2	3	4	5	6	7	8	9
1	2								
2									
3									
4									
5									
6									
7									
8									
9									

Now, on the Count of . . .

Trace each number and write its number word next to it.

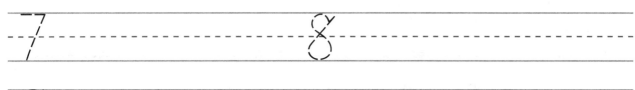

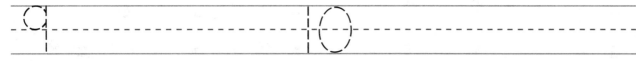

Solve the problems. Write the answers on the lines. Then, write the answers using the correct number words in the puzzle.

Across

1. 3 + 2 = _____

2. 4 + 2 = _____

3. 2 + 1 = _____

4. 1 + 0 = _____

5. 5 + 3 = _____

7. 2 + 7 = _____

Down

1. 2 + 2 = _____

2. 4 + 3 = _____

3. 0 + 2 = _____

6. 4 + 6 = _____

Addition: Commutative Property

The **commutative property of addition** states that even if the order of the numbers is changed in an addition sentence, the sum will stay the same.

Example: 2 + 3 = 5
3 + 2 = 5

Look at the addition sentences below. Complete the addition sentences by writing the missing numerals.

5 + 4 = 9   3 + 1 = 4   2 + 6 = 8
4 + ___ = 9   1 + ___ = 4   6 + ___ = 8

6 + 1 = 7   4 + 3 = 7   1 + 9 = 10
1 + ___ = 7   3 + ___ = 7   9 + ___ = 10

Now try these:

6 + 3 = 9   10 + 2 = 12   8 + 3 = 11
___ + ___ = 9   ___ + ___ = 12   ___ + ___ = 11

Look at these sums. Can you think of two number sentences that would show the commutative property of addition?

___ + ___ = 7   ___ + ___ = 11   ___ + ___ = 9
___ + ___ = 7   ___ + ___ = 11   ___ + ___ = 9

Week 23 Skills

Subject	Skill	Multi-Sensory Learning Activities
Reading and Language Arts	Review synonyms.	• Complete Practice Pages 246–249. • Read *The Napping House* by Audrey Wood. Then, ask your child to write a variation of the story using synonyms. For example, perhaps your child's new story could be called *The Sleeping Home*.
Math	Practice subtraction problems within 10.	• Complete Practice Pages 251–254. • Use masking tape to create a giant number line on the floor. Give subtraction problems and invite your child to walk or jump along the line to find the answer. • Have your child begin to count 10 pennies, moving them one-by-one from one pile to another. At a random time, say, "Stop!" Then, your child must write a subtraction equation based on the current count. For example, if two pennies were moved to the new pile, he or she would write **10 – 2 = 8**.
Bonus: Science		• Read *Frederick* by Leo Lionni and discuss the current season with your child. What types of activities are appropriate for the season? What are the animals doing? What is happening to the plants? Brainstorm with your child any words related to the seasons and use each word in a sentence.

Synonyms

Read each sentence and look at the underlined word. Circle the word that means the same thing. Write the new words.

1. The boy was <u>mad</u>.	happy	angry	pup
2. The <u>dog</u> is brown.	pup	cat	rat
3. I like to <u>scream</u>.	soar	mad	shout
4. The bird can <u>fly</u>.	soar	jog	warm
5. The girl can <u>run</u>.	sleep	jog	shout
6. I am <u>hot</u>.	warm	cold	soar

1. _____

2. _____

3. _____

4. _____

5. _____

6. _____

Similarities: Synonyms

Read each sentence. Read the word after the sentence. Find the word that is most like it in the sentence and circle it.

1. The flowers grew very tall.  plants

2. Jan picked the apple from the tree.   applesauce

3. Juan's van is dirty.  truck

4. A dog makes a sound different from a cat. wolf

5. Dad put up a fence in the yard.  gate

Similarities: Synonyms

Read the story. Write a word on the line that means almost the same as the word under the line.

Dan went to the _____ .
                    store

He wanted to buy _____ .
                        food

He walked very _____ .
                      quickly

The store had what he wanted.

He bought it using _____ .
                          dimes

Instead of walking home, Dan _____ .
                                    jogged

Synonyms

Synonyms are words that mean almost the same thing.

Read the word in the center of each flower. Find a synonym for each word on a bee at the bottom of the page. Cut out and glue each bee on its matching flower.

quick

close

icy

sleepy

cut

shut

fast

cold

tired

Sea Creature Subtraction

Look at the pictures. Complete the subtraction sentences.

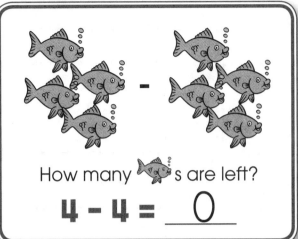

How many s are left?

4 - 4 = __0__

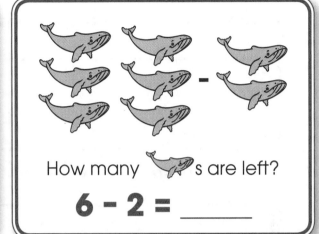

How many s are left?

6 - 2 = _____

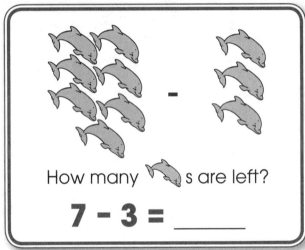

How many s are left?

7 - 3 = _____

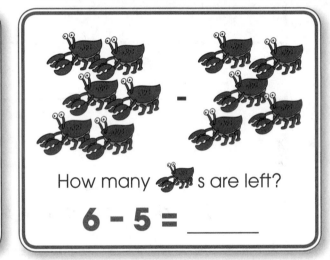

How many s are left?

6 - 5 = _____

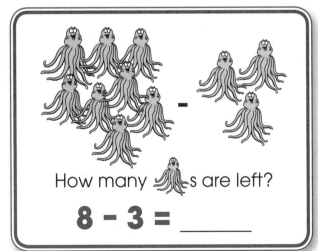

How many s are left?

8 - 3 = _____

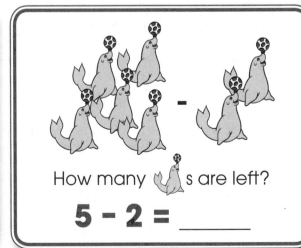

How many s are left?

5 - 2 = _____

Counting Kittens

Use counters. Make a group, then take some away. Write how many are left.

	_____
Put in 4. Take away 1.	**are left**
	_____
Put in 5. Take away 2.	**are left**
	_____
Put in 7. Take away 3.	**are left**

Think of a story for this picture. Write how many are left.

How many are left?

_____

COMPLETE YEAR GRADE 1

Transportation Problems

Circle the picture that matches the subtraction sentence. Then, complete the number sentence.

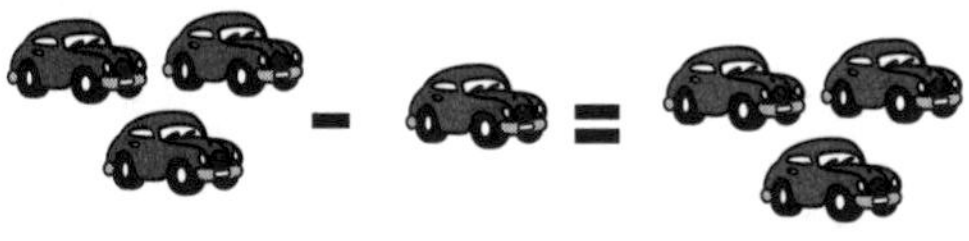

or

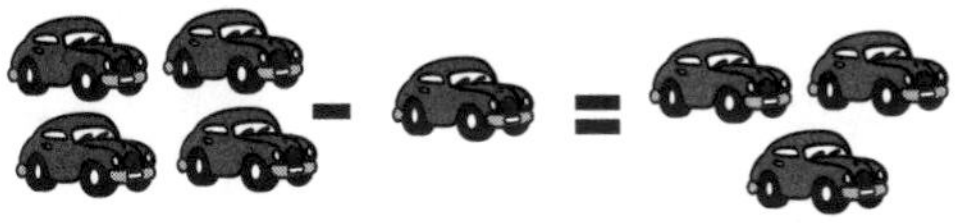

4 - 1 = 3

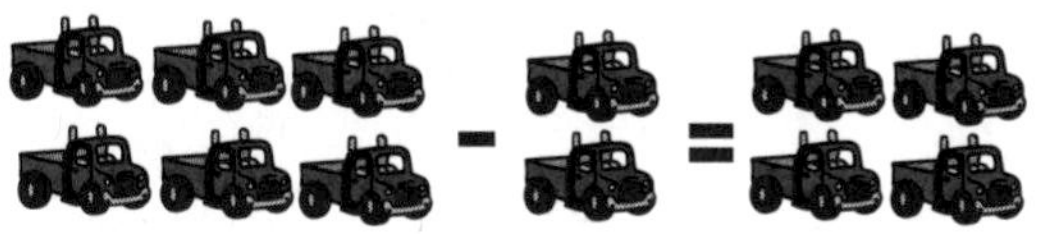

or

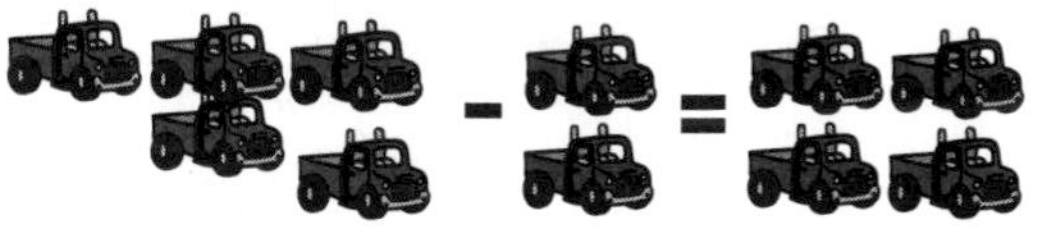

6 - 2 = ______

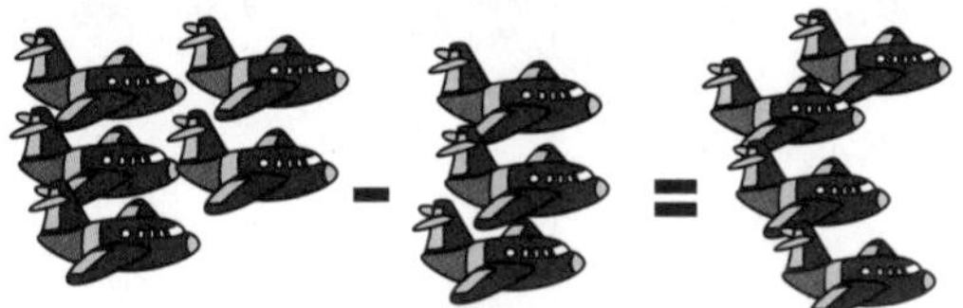

or

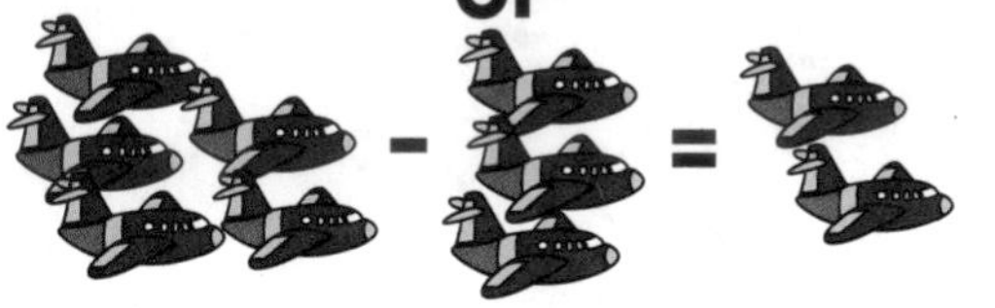

5 - 3 = ______

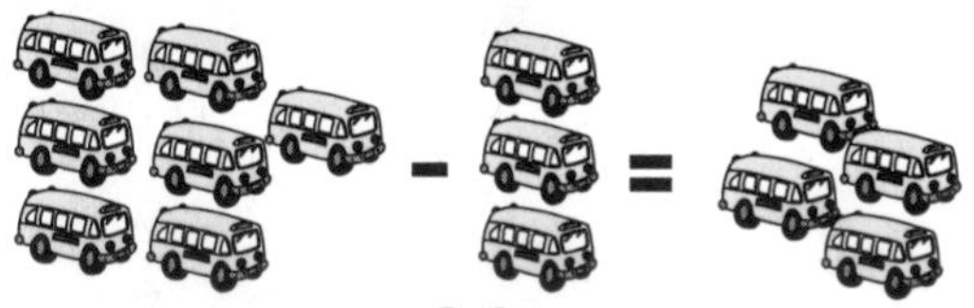

or

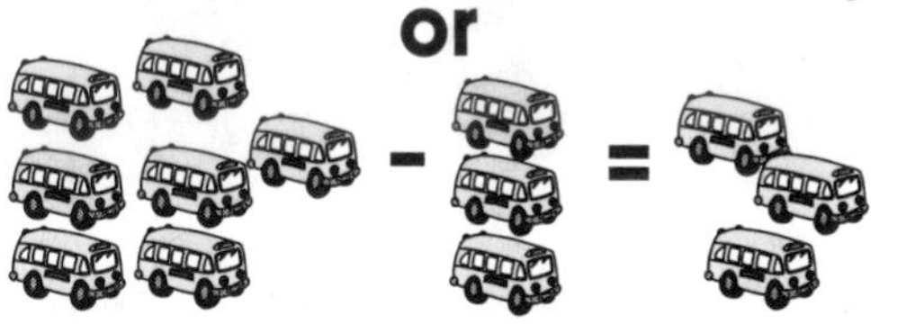

7 - 3 = ______

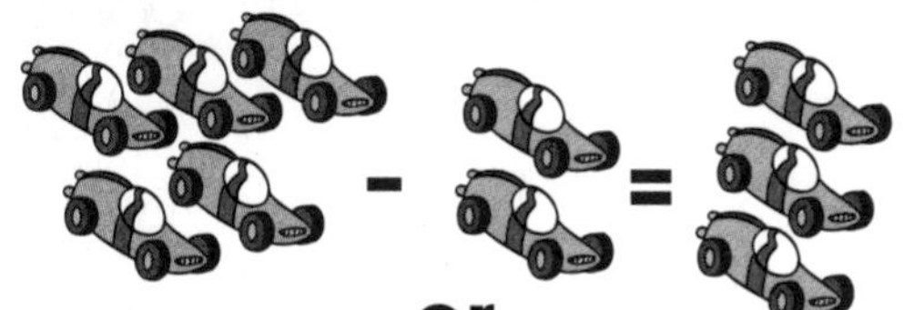

or

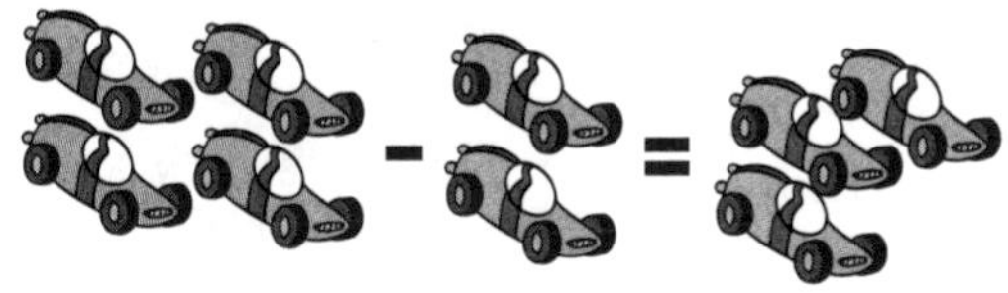

5 - 2 = ______

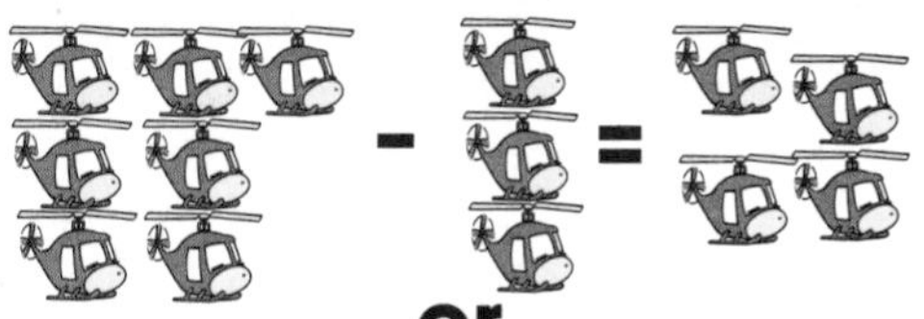

or

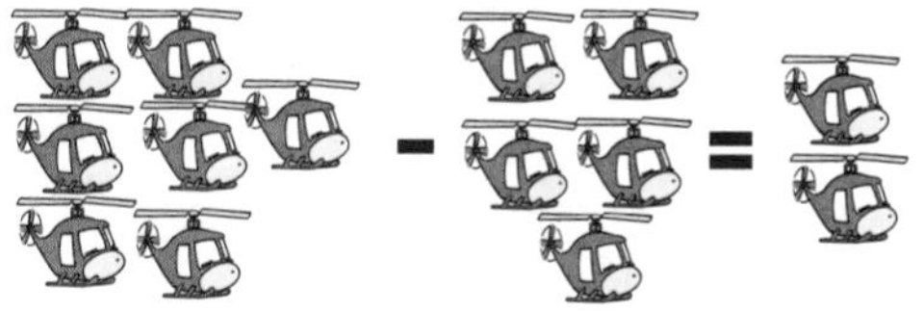

7 - 5 = ______

Sweet Treats

Solve the subtraction problems.

$$9 \atop -1$$

$$8 \atop -2$$

$10 - 1 = \underline{\quad}$

$7 - 1 = \underline{\quad}$

$10 - 4 = \underline{\quad}$

$9 - 2 = \underline{\quad}$

$$8 \atop -1$$

$$8 \atop -2$$

$$9 \atop -4$$

$10 - 3 = \underline{\quad}$

$10 - 4 = \underline{\quad}$

$10 - 1 = \underline{\quad}$

$10 - 4 = \underline{\quad}$

$7 - 2 = \underline{\quad}$

$9 - 1 = \underline{\quad}$

Week 24 Skills

Subject	Skill	Multi-Sensory Learning Activities
Reading and Language Arts	Understand and identify antonyms, or opposites.	• Complete Practice Pages 256–260. • Read *Amazing Grace* by Mary Hoffman. Have your child search through the book for words and their opposites and make a list of antonym pairs. Then, have your child find descriptive words in the book and think of opposites that are not in the book.
Math	Review subtraction problems within 10.	• Complete Practice Pages 261–263. • Divide a deck of cards in half. Flip two cards face up. Ask your child to subtract the smaller number from the larger number, assuming that all face cards are equal to 10.
	Practice subtraction problems within 15.	• Complete Practice Page 264. • Cut out fish-shaped pieces of construction paper, write a number from **1** to **15** on each, and attach a metal paper clip to one end of the fish. Form fishing poles out of wooden craft sticks, strings, and small magnets. Ask your child to go fishing for two fish, then subtract the smaller number from the larger number of the fish he or she catches.

Antonyms

Antonyms are words that are opposites. **Hot** and **cold** are antonyms. Draw a line between the antonyms.

closed

below

full

empty

above

old

new

open

Opposites

Draw lines to connect the words that are opposites.

up   wet

over   down

dry   dirty

clean   under

Opposites

Opposites are things that are different in every way.

Draw a line between the opposites.

day

little

happy

closed

big

night

open

back

front

sad

Opposites

Circle the picture in each row that is the opposite of the first picture.

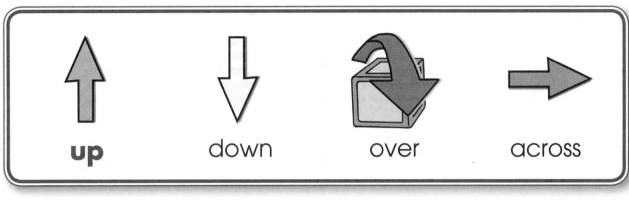

up   down   over   across

cold   frozen   hot   warm

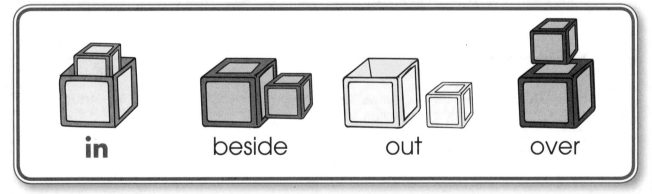

in   beside   out   over

cloud   rain   storm   sun

Antonyms

Write the antonym pairs from each sentence in the boxes.

Example: Many things are bought and sold at the market.

bought	sold

1. I thought I lost my dog, but someone found him.

2. The teacher will ask questions for the students to answer.

3. Airplanes arrive and depart from the airport.

4. The water in the pool was cold compared to the warm water in the whirlpool.

5. The tortoise was slow, but the hare was fast.

Subtraction

Draw the correct number of dots next to the numbers in each problem. Cross out the ones subtracted to find your answer.

Example:

$$5 \quad \bullet \ \bullet \ \bullet$$
$$\underline{-2} \quad \times \times$$
$$3$$

$$2 - 1 = \underline{1}$$
$$\bullet \qquad \times$$

$$4 - 2 = \underline{}$$

$$8$$
$$\underline{-6}$$

$$6$$
$$\underline{-1}$$

$$3 - 1 = \underline{}$$

$$9 - 6 = \underline{}$$

$$4$$
$$\underline{-3}$$

A Whale of a Job!

Put the number of counters needed on the page. Then, take them away by sliding them into the whale's mouth. Count how many counters are left.

$\begin{array}{r} 7 \\ -\ 3 \\ \hline \end{array}$	$\begin{array}{r} 9 \\ -\ 2 \\ \hline \end{array}$	$\begin{array}{r} 6 \\ -\ 4 \\ \hline \end{array}$	$\begin{array}{r} 5 \\ -\ 2 \\ \hline \end{array}$	$\begin{array}{r} 8 \\ -\ 3 \\ \hline \end{array}$
$\begin{array}{r} 9 \\ -\ 3 \\ \hline \end{array}$	$\begin{array}{r} 6 \\ -\ 3 \\ \hline \end{array}$	$\begin{array}{r} 7 \\ -\ 5 \\ \hline \end{array}$	$\begin{array}{r} 8 \\ -\ 2 \\ \hline \end{array}$	$\begin{array}{r} 5 \\ -\ 1 \\ \hline \end{array}$

$8 - 4 =$ _____ $6 - 2 =$ _____ $7 - 4 =$ _____

Hop Along Numbers

Use the number line to count back.

Example: 8, _7_ , _6_ , _5_

0 1 2 3 4 5 6 7 8 9 10

7 - 3 = ___

7, ___ , ___ , ___

6 - 2 = ___

6, ___ , ___

8 - 1 = ___

8, ___

7 - 2 = ___

7, ___ , ___

Crayon Count

Solve the problems on each box. Count the crayons. Write the number on the blank. Circle the problems that equal the answer.

$$
\begin{array}{cc}
12 & 11 \\
-1 & -1 \\
\hline
\end{array}
$$

$13 - 3 =$ _____

$$
\begin{array}{cc}
13 & 15 \\
-1 & -1 \\
\hline
\end{array}
$$

____

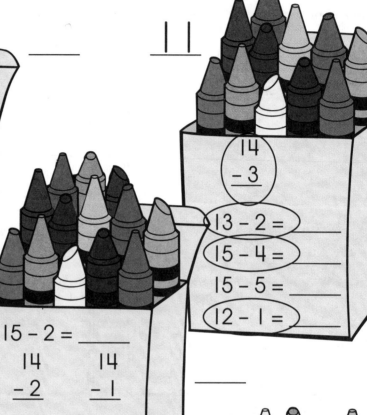

$15 - 2 =$ _____

$$
\begin{array}{cc}
14 & 14 \\
-2 & -1 \\
\hline
\end{array}
$$

$14 - 1 =$ _____

$15 - 3 =$ _____

|| (11)

$$
\begin{array}{c}
14 \\
-3 \\
\hline
\end{array}
$$ (circled)

$13 - 2 =$ _____ (circled)

$15 - 4 =$ _____ (circled)

$15 - 5 =$ _____

$12 - 1 =$ _____ (circled)

____

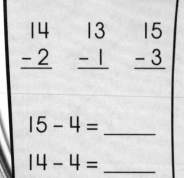

$$
\begin{array}{ccc}
14 & 13 & 15 \\
-2 & -1 & -3 \\
\hline
\end{array}
$$

$15 - 4 =$ _____

$14 - 4 =$ _____

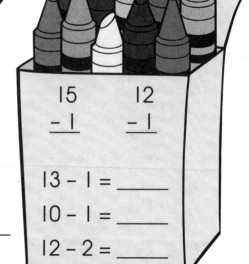

$$
\begin{array}{cc}
15 & 12 \\
-1 & -1 \\
\hline
\end{array}
$$

$13 - 1 =$ _____

$10 - 1 =$ _____

$12 - 2 =$ _____

Week 25 Skills

Subject	Skill	Multi-Sensory Learning Activities
Reading and Language Arts	Understand and write statements, or telling sentences.	• Complete Practice Page 266. • Write 10 sentences. In each sentence, leave off the period. Have your child read each sentence and add the period.
	Understand and write questions, or asking sentences.	• Complete Practice Pages 267–269. • Make a mystery box out of a shoe box decorated with question marks. Secretly hide a familiar object in the box. Have your child ask questions to determine the contents. Write each of your child's questions on a piece of paper. When your child guesses correctly, open the box.
Math	Review addition and subtraction.	• Complete Practice Pages 270–274. • Help your child put one sticker on one card, two stickers on another card, etc., until he or she has cards for 1–15. On three more cards, write +, -, and =. Challenge your child to use the cards to make equations, then solve them. • Put 12 small toys in the cups of an empty egg carton. Take away several toys and ask your child to tell you the subtraction equation. For example, if you remove three toys, your child would say, "12 – 3 = 9." Act out addition problems by adding groups of toys to the empty egg carton.

Telling Sentences

Read the sentences and write them below. Begin each sentence with a capital letter. End each sentence with a period.

1. i like to go to the store with Mom
2. we go on Friday
3. i get to push the cart
4. i get to buy the cookies
5. i like to help Mom

1. _____

2. _____

3. _____

4. _____

5. _____

Asking Sentences

Write the first word of each asking sentence. Be sure to begin each question with a capital letter. End each question with a question mark.

1. _____ you like the zoo   **do**

2. _____ much does it cost   **how**

3. _____ you feed the ducks   **can**

4. _____ you see the monkeys   **will**

5. _____ time will you eat lunch   **what**

Asking Sentences

Read the asking sentences. Write the sentences below. Begin each sentence with a capital letter. End each sentence with a question mark.

1. what game will we play

2. do you like to read

3. how old are you

4. who is your best friend

5. can you tie your shoes

1. _____

2. _____

3. _____

4. _____

5. _____

Review

Look at the picture. In the space below, write one telling sentence about the picture. Then, write one asking sentence about the picture.

Telling sentence:

_____

- -

_____

Asking sentence:

_____

- -

_____

Color Fruit

Use addition or subtraction to solve the problems. Use the code to color the fruit.

3 = yellow	**5 = orange**	**7 = yellow**	**9 = red**
4 = red	**6 = purple**	**8 = green**	**10 = brown**

9
− 4

7
+ 3

6
− 3

1
+ 3

9
− 2

7
+ 2

10
− 4

6
+ 3

8
− 2

Review: Addition and Subtraction

Solve the number problem under each picture. Write **+** or **−** to show if you should add or subtract.

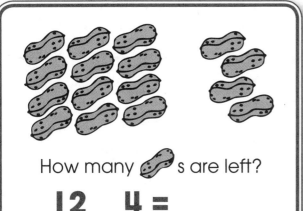

How many s are left?

12   4 = _____

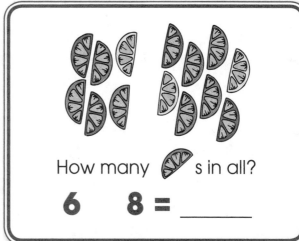

How many s in all?

6   8 = _____

How many s are left?

4   4 = _____

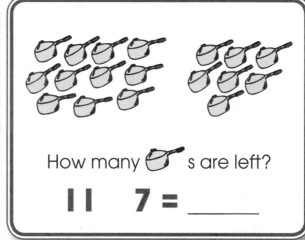

How many s are left?

11   7 = _____

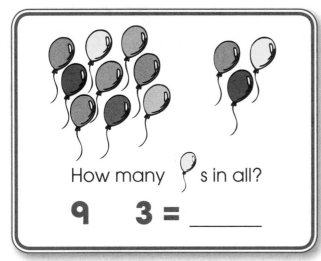

How many s in all?

9   3 = _____

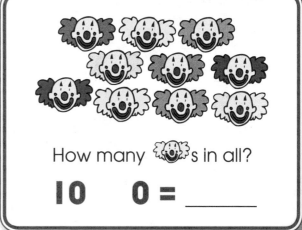

How many s in all?

10   0 = _____

Addition and Subtraction

Solve the problems. Remember, **addition** means "putting together" or adding two or more numbers to find the sum. **Subtraction** means "taking away" or subtracting one number from another.

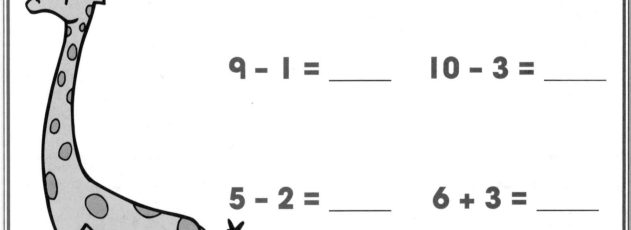

$1 + 3 =$ _____ $4 - 3 =$ _____ $4 + 5 =$ _____

$6 + 1 =$ _____ $7 - 2 =$ _____ $8 - 4 =$ _____

$9 - 1 =$ _____ $10 - 3 =$ _____

$5 - 2 =$ _____ $6 + 3 =$ _____

$8 + 2 =$ _____ $5 + 5 =$ _____

Addition and Subtraction

Remember, **addition** means "putting together" or adding two or more numbers to find the sum. **Subtraction** means "taking away" or subtracting one number from another.

Solve the problems. From your answers, use the code to color the quilt.

Color:

6 = blue
7 = yellow
8 = green
9 = red
10 = orange

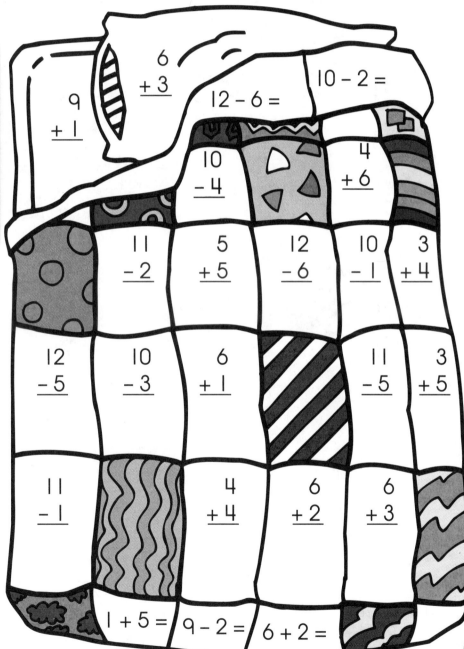

Review

Trace the numbers. Work the problems.

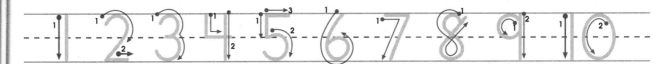

$$
\begin{array}{r}
9 \\
- 3 \\
\hline
\end{array}
\qquad
\begin{array}{r}
6 \\
+ 2 \\
\hline
\end{array}
\qquad
\begin{array}{r}
3 \\
+ 4 \\
\hline
\end{array}
\qquad
\begin{array}{r}
2 \\
- 1 \\
\hline
\end{array}
$$

$$
\begin{array}{r}
5 \\
+ 4 \\
\hline
\end{array}
\qquad
\begin{array}{r}
9 \\
- 5 \\
\hline
\end{array}
\qquad
\begin{array}{r}
7 \\
+ 2 \\
\hline
\end{array}
\qquad
\begin{array}{r}
8 \\
- 6 \\
\hline
\end{array}
$$

$$
\begin{array}{r}
4 \\
- 2 \\
\hline
\end{array}
\qquad
\begin{array}{r}
6 \\
+ 3 \\
\hline
\end{array}
\qquad
\begin{array}{r}
9 \\
- 7 \\
\hline
\end{array}
\qquad
\begin{array}{r}
1 \\
+ 7 \\
\hline
\end{array}
$$

Week 26 Skills

Subject	Skill	Multi-Sensory Learning Activities
Reading and Language Arts	Review statements.	• Complete Practice Pages 276–278. • Write sentences without punctuation or capitalization, such as *the boy has a ball* and *his ball is blue*. Have your child read the sentences and add capitals and punctuation where appropriate.
	Review questions.	• Complete Practice Pages 279 and 280. • Before reading a nonfiction book, encourage your child to think about what he or she would like to know about the topic. Then, work together to write 10 questions. Read the book and discuss the answers. Have your child write statements to answer the questions.
Math	Work with ordinal numbers **first** through **tenth**.	• Complete Practice Pages 281–284. • Plan a scavenger hunt using ordinal numbers in the clues. For example, say "Read the fifth chapter of your book," and place the next clue at the end of the chapter, or "Walk up to the seventh stair. Look under the rug." Hide a treat for the final clue. • Go on an ordinal number field trip. Walk around your neighborhood and count items using ordinal numbers. For example, count fence posts, houses in a row, parked cars, and streetlights. Upon returning, have your child draw a picture of something you counted on your walk and label objects with ordinal numbers.

Telling Sentences

Read the sentences and write them below. Begin each sentence with a capital letter. End each sentence with a period.

1. most children like pets

2. some childen like dogs

3. some children like cats

4. some children like snakes

5. some children like all animals

1. _____

2. _____

3. _____

4. _____

5. _____

Writing Sentences

A **sentence** begins with a capital letter and ends with a period. Read the two sentences on each line. Draw a line between the two sentences. Then, write each sentence correctly.

i have a new bike ———————— it is red

we are twins   we look just alike

i have two tickets   let's go to the movies

the baby is crying   she wants a bottle

Statements

A **statement** is a sentence that tells something. It begins with a capital letter and ends with a period.

Example: The Moon orbits the Earth.

If the sentence is a statement, color the space black. If it is not, color the space yellow.

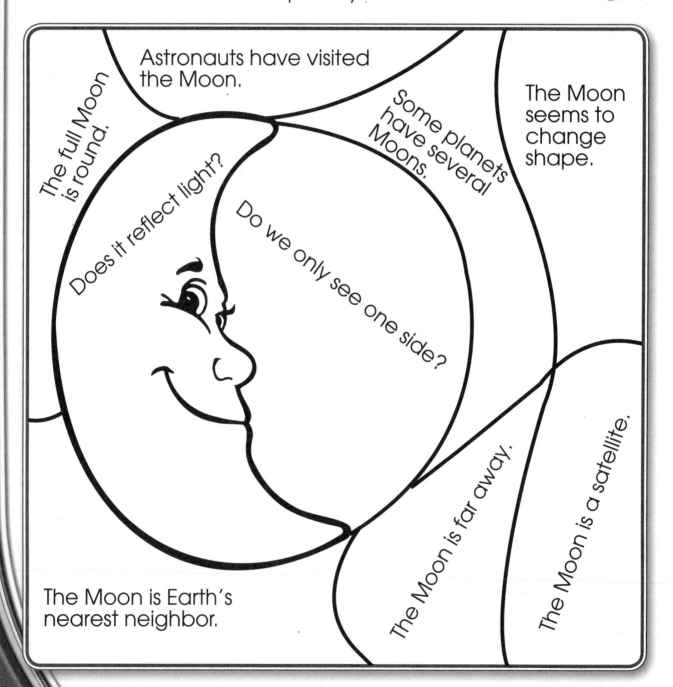

Astronauts have visited the Moon.

The full Moon is round.

Does it reflect light?

Some planets have several Moons.

The Moon seems to change shape.

Do we only see one side?

The Moon is far away.

The Moon is a satellite.

The Moon is Earth's nearest neighbor.

Questions

A **question** is a sentence that asks something. It begins with a capital letter and ends with a question mark.

Example: Have you ever visited a farm? What animals lived on the farm?

If the sentence is a question, put a question mark and color the barn red. If it is not, draw an **X** on the barn.

 1. I'm going to visit my grandma

 2. Would you like to go with me

 3. Will you ask your mother

 4. Did she say you could go

 5. What would you like to do first

 6. Do you want to see the ducks

 7. There are four of them on the pond

 8. We'll see the baby chicks next

 9. Are you glad you came with me

 10. Maybe you can come again

Questions

A **question** begins with a capital letter and ends with a question mark. Look at each picture of Panda. Ask Panda a question to go with each picture.

All in Order

Color the second ball brown.

Color the sixth ball yellow.

Color the fourth ball orange.

Color the first ball black.

Color the fifth ball green.

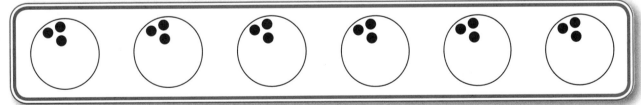

Color the seventh ball purple.

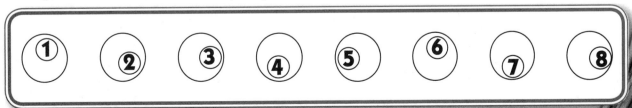

Let's Get Things in Order!

Help Mrs. Brown pick flowers in her garden. The flowers she wants are listed in the chart. Use the descriptions to color the flowers in her garden.

↓	⟶	Color it:
1st row	6th flower	red
2nd row	4th flower	blue
3rd row	1st flower	yellow
4th row	9th flower	pink
5th row	10th flower	orange
6th row	2nd flower	green
7th row	5th flower	black
8th row	7th flower	gray
9th row	8th flower	purple
10th row	3rd flower	brown

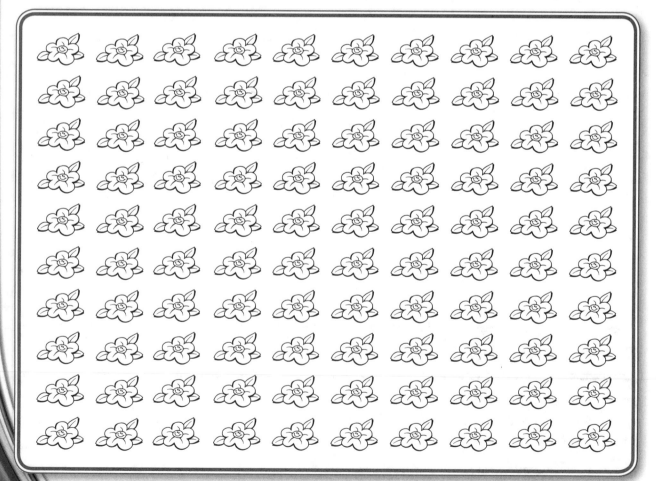

Flags First

Color the ninth flag red.

Write **O** on the second flag.

Color the eighth flag blue.

Write **D** on the fourth flag.

Color the sixth flag yellow.

Write **G** on the first flag.

Color the tenth flag purple.

Write **O** on the third flag.

Color the seventh flag green.

Color the fifth flag orange.

What word did you spell? _____

Ordinal Numbers

Ordinal numbers are used to indicate order in a series, such as **first**, **second** or **third**.

Draw a line to the picture that corresponds to the ordinal number in the left column.

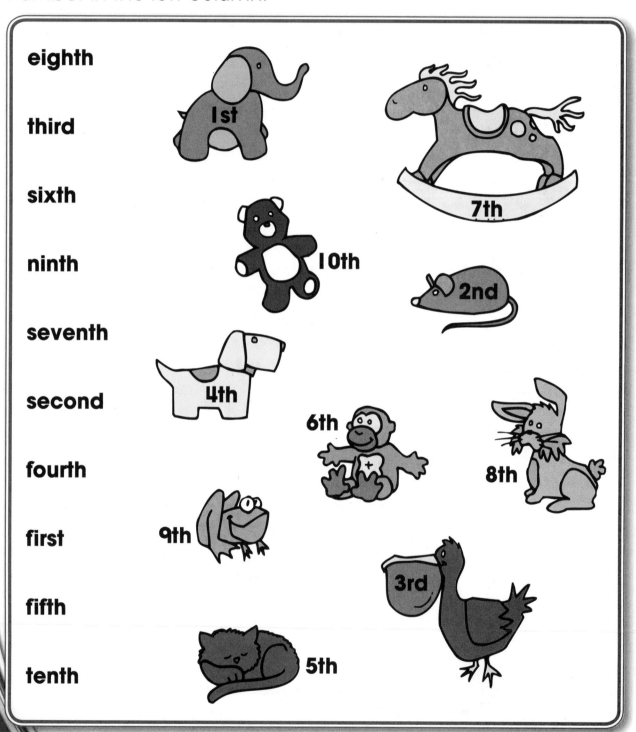

eighth

third

sixth

ninth

seventh

second

fourth

first

fifth

tenth

Week 27 Skills

Subject	Skill	Multi-Sensory Learning Activities
Reading and Language Arts	Understand commas and how to use them in sentences.	• Complete Practice Pages 286 and 287. • Use short lengths of pipe cleaner to make comma shapes. Write a sentence, such as *At the zoo the children saw lions elephants and tigers,* on a large sheet of paper. Invite your child to glue the commas in the appropriate spots.
	Work with the prefix **re**.	• Complete Practice Page 288. • Introduce the prefix **un** to your child. Then, give him or her directions, such as "tie your shoes," or "zip your coat." Write each verb and add the prefix **un** to each word. Then, ask your child to read the new words and perform the tasks.
	Work with suffixes **ing**, **est**, and **ed**.	• Complete Practice Pages 289 and 290. • Read *Roller Coaster* by Marla Frazee. Have your child list the words in the story with **ing**, **est**, or **ed** endings.
Math	Review ordinal numbers.	• Complete Practice Pages 291 and 293. • Look for opportunities to use ordinal numbers in real situations. While in line at the store or waiting for a traffic light in the car, talk about your place in line. Discuss the position of others in line as well.

Commas

Commas are used to separate words in a series of three or more.

My favorite fruits are apples, bananas, and oranges.

Put commas where they are needed in each sentence.

---

1. Please buy milk eggs bread and cheese.

2. I need a folder paper and pencils for school.

3. Some good pets are cats dogs gerbils fish and rabbits.

4. Aaron Mike and Matt went to the baseball game.

5. Major forms of transportation are planes trains and automobiles.

 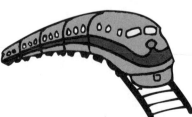 

Commas

We use commas to separate the day from the year.
Example: May 13, 1950

Write the dates in the blanks. Put the commas
in and capitalize the name of each month.

Example: Jack and Dave were born on february 22 2005.

February 22, 2005

1. My father's birthday is may 19 1978.

   _____

2. My sister was fourteen on december 13 2012.

   _____

3. Lauren's seventh birthday was on november 30 2010.

   _____

4. october 13 2013 was the last day I saw my lost cat.

   _____

5. On april 17 2005, we saw the Grand Canyon.

   _____

6. Our vacation lasted from april 2 2002 to april 26 2002.

   _____

7. Molly's baby sister was born on august 14 2011.

   _____

8. My mother was born on june 22 1980.

   _____

Prefixes: The Three Rs

Prefixes are syllables added to the beginning of words that change their meaning. The prefix **re** means "again."

Read the story. Then, follow the instructions.

Kim wants to find ways she can save the Earth. She studies the "three Rs"—reduce, reuse and recycle. Reduce means to make less. Both reuse and recycle mean to use again.

Add **re** to the beginning of each word below. Use the new words to complete the sentences.

_____build   _____fill

_____read   _____tell

_____write   _____run

1. The race was a tie, so Dawn and Kathy had

    to _____ it.

2. The block wall fell down, so Simon had

    to _____ it.

3. The water bottle was empty, so Luna had

    to _____ it.

4. Javier wrote a good story, but he wanted

    to _____ it to make it better.

5. The teacher told us a story, and students had

    to _____ it.

6. Toni didn't understand the directions, so she had to

    _____ them.

Suffixes

Write a word from the word box next to its root word.

coming	visited	running	carried	swimming
lived	hurried	rained	sitting	racing

run _____   come _____

live _____   carry _____

hurry _____   race _____

swim _____   rain _____

visit _____   sit _____

Write a word from the word box to finish each sentence.

1. I _____ my grandmother during vacation.

2. Mary went _____ at the lake with her cousin.

3. Jim _____ the heavy package for his mother.

4. It _____ and stormed all weekend.

5. Cars go very fast when they are _____.

Suffixes

Read the story. Underline the words that end with **est**, **ed** or **ing**. On the lines below, write the root words for each word you underlined.

The funniest book I ever read was about a girl named Nan. Nan did everything backward. She even spelled her name backward. Nan slept in the day and played at night. She dried her hair before washing it. She turned on the light after she finished her book—which she read from the back to the front! When it rained, Nan waited until she was inside before opening her umbrella. She even walked backward. The silliest part: The only thing Nan did forward was back up!

1. _____   6. _____   11. _____

2. _____   7. _____   12. _____

3. _____   8. _____   13. _____

4. _____   9. _____

5. _____   10. _____

Ordinal Numbers

Draw an **X** on the first vegetable, draw a circle around the second vegetable, and draw a square around the third vegetable.

Write the ordinal number below the picture.

✂ **Cut** the children apart. Mix them up. Then, put them back in the correct order.

| first | second | third | fourth | fifth | sixth | seventh | eighth | ninth | tenth |

Sequencing: At the Movies

The children are watching a movie. Read the sentences. Cut out the pictures below. Glue them where they belong in the picture.

1. The first child is eating popcorn.

2. The third child is eating candy.

3. The fourth child has a cup of fruit punch.

4. The second child is eating a big pretzel.

✂ **Cut**

Third Quarter Check-Up

Reading and Language Arts

❑ I can classify and sort objects.

❑ I can understand and identify one- and two-syllable words.

❑ I know synonyms.

❑ I know antonyms.

❑ I can understand and write telling sentences.

❑ I can understand and write asking sentences.

❑ I know how to use commas.

❑ I can work with the prefix **re** and suffixes **ing**, **est**, and **ed**.

Math

❑ I can add through 20.

❑ I can add three numbers.

❑ I can subtract within 15.

❑ I know the commutative property of addition.

❑ I know ordinal numbers **first** through **tenth**.

Final Project

Make an addition mural. Choose a theme, such as seasons, foods, or animals. On a sheet of paper, write six addition problems with a black marker. Then, use different-colored markers to illustrate each problem using pictures of things that fit your theme. Finally, write six telling sentences about the addition problems in your mural.

Fourth Quarter Introduction

As the school year nears its end, many students are feeling confident about the new skills they have learned as first graders. This may be evident in their mastery of grade-appropriate words and spellings, completing addition and subtraction problems with accuracy, and increasing comprehension of what they've read. As the days get warmer and children play outside in the evenings, don't forget to maintain school day routines and continue to support your child's academic growth at home.

Fourth Quarter Skills

Practice pages in this book for Weeks 28–36 will help your child improve the following skills.

Basic Skills
- Use critical thinking to infer meaning

Reading and Language Arts
- Understand homophones
- Use articles appropriately
- Recognize joining words
- Use common prepositions
- Spell common words correctly
- Use context clues to understand missing information
- Put picture stories and sentences in correct sequence
- Demonstrate reading comprehension
- Write sentences and paragraphs on a given topic

Math
- Tell time to the hour, half hour, and five minute intervals
- Know the months of the year
- Recognize pennies, nickels, and dimes
- Work with fractions $\frac{1}{2}$, $\frac{1}{3}$, and $\frac{1}{4}$
- Create, read, and interpret graphs
- Measure familiar objects using inch rulers

Multi-Sensory Learning Activities

Try these fun activities for enhancing your child's learning and development during the fourth quarter of the school year. Be sure to choose activities that include speaking, listening, touching, and active movement.

 Basic Skills

Make up short stories without endings. Have your child predict what will happen next.

Make up realistic situations. Have your child propose how he or she should handle each one. For example, say, "Jack took the ball away from Larry at the playground and would not give it back. What should Larry do?"

 ### Reading and Language Arts

Teach location words, such as **up**, **in**, **over**, **under**, and so on. Have your child brainstorm some of his or her activities of the day and include where the activities were performed. Then, take or find photos of your child in, on, over, next to, behind, and under different objects. Have your child glue one picture per page in a blank book and write a sentence describing where he or she is in each picture.

Cut apart a comic strip. Have your child put the frames back in order and read the comic aloud.

Discuss the beginning, middle, and end of *Where the Wild Things Are* by Maurice Sendak. Have your child draw the sequence of events from the story in a comic strip format. Have him or her write simple dialogue in balloons as in comic strips.

Compose four different short stories and write them on heavy paper using large letters. Cut apart each story so there is one sentence per piece. Mix the sentences from all four stories in a shoebox. Have your child read each sentence, sort the sentences into the four stories, and put the sentences together in a sensible story order.

Change one aspect of a familiar story and ask your child to write how the story might have changed as a result. For example, what if Cinderella never went to the ball, or Red Riding Hood walked on city streets instead of through the woods?

 ### Math

Read *The Grouchy Ladybug* by Eric Carle. Have your child record the times from the book and what the ladybug was doing.

Help your child set up a summer store and price a variety of objects. Your child may practice counting money, adding values, or making change. Encourage your child to use the store all summer, adding new objects as needed.

Cut four circle shapes from construction paper. Cut two in equal halves. Cut the other two in two unequal parts. Let your child play with the pieces. Can he or she find the equal halves that make whole circles?

When your child plays with modeling dough, ask him or her to run a pretend pizza shop. Phone in orders for pizzas and specify whether they should be cut into halves or fourths. The shop might offer rectangular and circular pizza varieties.

Fourth Quarter Introduction, cont.

Make a floor graph by drawing a vertical two-column grid on the sidewalk with chalk. Each square in the grid should be 8 to 12 inches. Gather several shoes and sort them into categories like color, size, type of fastener, or ownership. Choose two categories and label the columns of the floor graph. Have your child place the shoes in the appropriate columns of the graph. Talk about the graph using numbers and comparative language.

Read *Jim and the Beanstalk* by Raymond Briggs. Collect a variety of familiar objects for your child to measure. Provide bottle caps, shoestrings, and other same-sized objects for your child to use as measuring tools.

Gather several twigs of various lengths. Have your child use a ruler, meter stick, yardstick, or a non-standard unit to measure and compare the twig lengths. Then, have your child measure and compare the heights of plants outdoors.

 **Science**

On a sunny day, place a glass jar upside down on the ground, and leave it there for a few hours. Then, have your child draw a picture of the contents of the jar.

Go for a walk and collect a variety of rocks. Using a magnifying glass, observe the rocks. Have your child sort the rocks by color, texture, size, and any other way he or she finds them to be alike. Have your child label each group of rocks and make a list of words that describe the rocks. Then, put several small rocks in a plastic container with a lid. Add water and take turns shaking the container for several minutes. Have your child look at the water in the container. What does he or she observe?

 Seasonal Fun

Conduct an experiment in front of a window on a sunny day to see how a rainbow forms. First, have your child fill a glass baking dish half full with water. Next, have your child set a small mirror in the water. Have your child move the mirror until a rainbow is formed on the wall of the room. The sun reflecting in the water will make the colors. Ask your child to name all the colors he or she sees. Explain that rainbows form when water bends the sunlight.

Have your child find a few different types of flowers in a variety of shapes, sizes, and textures. Then, spread some tempera or acrylic paint into a tray. Ask your child to dip and press a flower into the paint. Then, have your child firmly press the flower onto a piece of construction paper. Remove the flower and repeat.

Week 28 Skills

Subject	Skill	Multi-Sensory Learning Activities
Reading and Language Arts	Recognize homophones, or words that sound the same but are spelled differently.	• Complete Practice Pages 300–302. • Read *The Snowy Day* by Ezra Jack Keats. Help your child find homophones for each of the following words: **new**, **write**, **hi**, **maid**, **son**, and **haul**.
	Understand the articles **a**, **an**, and **the**.	• Complete Practice Pages 303 and 304. • Give your child a topic starter, such as "When I was little…" and ask him or her to write a short paragraph. Then, ask your child to circle all of the articles **a**, **an**, and **the** he or she used in the paragraph, tallying which of the three articles was used the most.
Math	Tell time to the hour and half hour.	• Complete Practice Pages 305 and 306. • Help your child make a learning clock with movable hands. To attach the hands, push a paper fastener through the hands and the clock face, then fold the ends back. Have your child practice telling time to the hour and half hour.
	Become familiar with the months of the year and time duration.	• Complete Practice Pages 307 and 308. • Make a calendar for the current month. Ask your child to label important dates, holidays, and events going on this month.

Different Meanings

Circle the word that matches the picture. Then, write the other word in the blank to complete the sentence.

This is a present _____ your birthday.

four   for

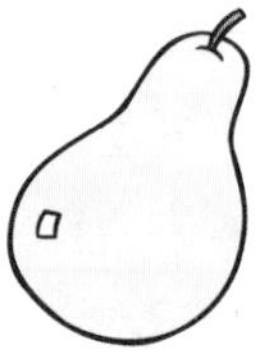

Jane lost a _____ of new shoes.

pair   pear

We _____ in the car for two hours.

road   rode

The boys will either swim _____ go to the ball game.

oar   or

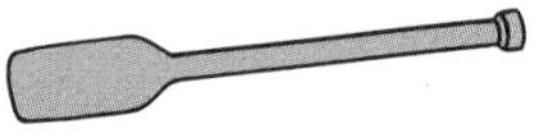

Let's _____ at eight o'clock.

meet   meat

The scrape on his knee causes a lot of _____.

pane   pain

Old Mother Hubbard's cupboard was _____.

bear   bare

Homophones

Homophones are words that sound the same but are spelled differently and mean something different. **Blew** and **blue** are homophones.

Look at the word pairs. Choose the word that describes the picture. Write the word on the line next to the picture.

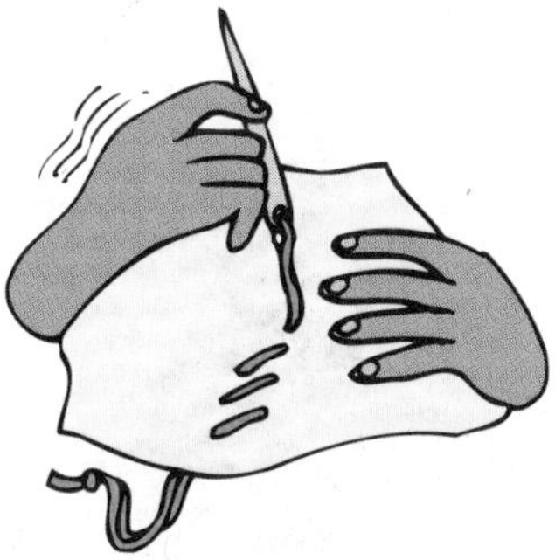

1. sew   so   _____

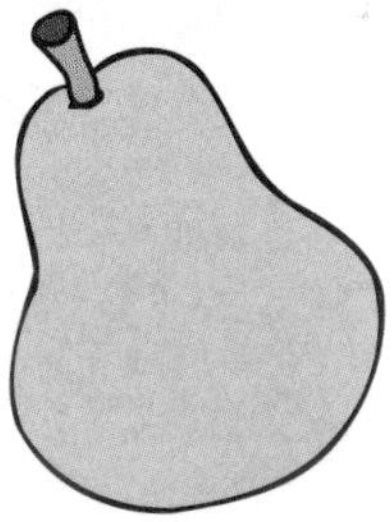

2. pair   pear   _____

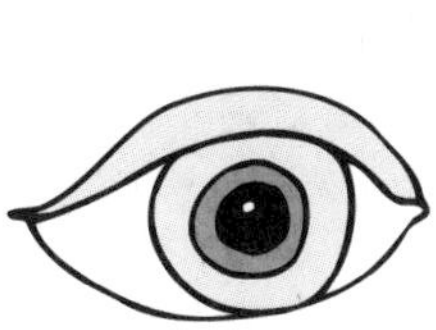

3. eye   I   _____

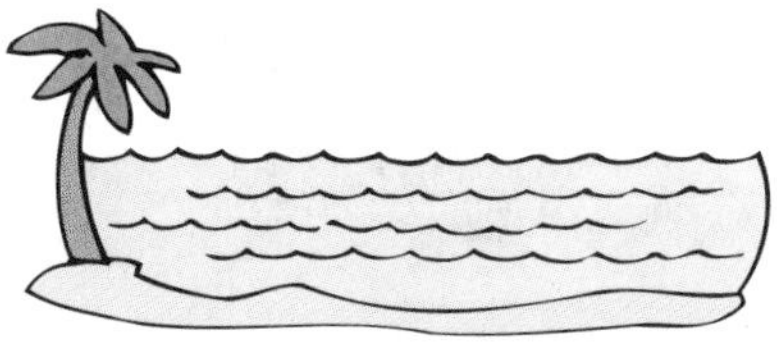

4. see   sea   _____

Homophones

Read each sentence. Underline the two words that sound the same but are spelled differently and mean something different.

1. Tom ate eight grapes.

2. Becky read *Little Red Riding Hood*.

3. I went to buy two dolls.

4. Five blue feathers blew in the wind.

5. Would you get wood for the fire?

Articles

Articles are small words that help us to better understand nouns. **A** and **an** are articles. We use **an** before a word that begins with a vowel. We use **a** before a word that begins with a consonant.

Example: We looked in **a** nest. It had **an** eagle in it.

Read the sentences. Write **a** or **an** in the blank.

1. I found _____ book.

2. It had a story about _____ ant in it.

3. In the story, _____ lion gave three wishes to _____ ant.

4. The ant's first wish was to ride _____ elephant.

5. The second wish was to ride _____ alligator.

6. The last wish was _____ wish for three more wishes.

Articles

Articles are words used before nouns. **A**, **an** and **the** are articles. We use **a** before words that begin with a consonant. We use **an** before words that begin with a vowel.

Example: **a peach**   **an apple**

Write **a** or **an** in the sentences below.

Example: My bike had _____a_____ flat tire.

1. They brought _____ goat to the farm.

2. My mom wears _____ old pair of shoes to mow the lawn.

3. We had _____ party for my grandfather.

4. Everybody had _____ ice-cream cone after the game.

5. We bought _____ picnic table for our backyard.

6. We saw _____ lion sleeping in the shade.

7. It was _____ evening to be remembered.

8. He brought _____ blanket to the game.

9. _____ exit sign was above the door.

10. They went to _____ orchard to pick apples.

11. He ate _____ orange for lunch.

Who "Nose" These Times?

Write the time under each clock.

Example:

4:00   4:30

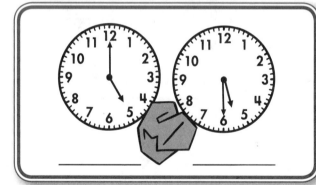

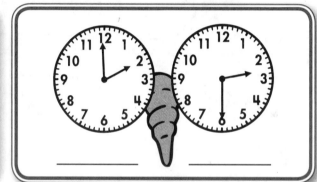

_____   _____

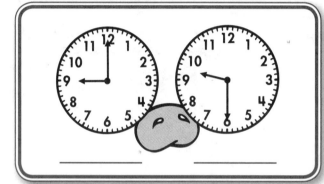

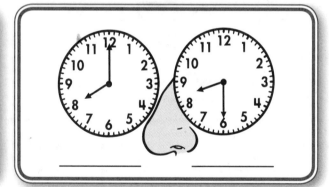

_____   _____

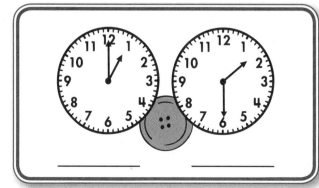

_____   _____

Sock Clocks

Draw the hands on the sock clocks.

1:30

7:00

4:30

10:00

3:30

9:30

4:00

2:30

6:00

How Long Does It Take?

Look at the activity in each picture. How long do you think each thing will take? Circle the best estimate for each.

I minute   I hour

I minute   I hour

I minute   I hour

I minute   I hour

I minute   I hour

I minute   I hour

Hmm, What Month Is It?

There are 12 months in a year. The first month is January. The last month is December. Some months have 31 days. Some months have 30 days. February is the shortest month with 28 days.

Write **1** to **12** in the boxes to put the months in order. The first one is done for you.

☐ April	☐ February	☐ May
☐ October	☐ July	☐ August
☐ December	☐1 January	☐ March
☐ September	☐ June	☐ November

Write the correct answer.

_____   _____
first month   last month

Circle the correct answer.

Some months have 30 days.	Yes	No
Some months have 31 days.	Yes	No
February is the longest month.	Yes	No
February has 28 days.	Yes	No

COMPLETE YEAR GRADE 1

Week 29 Skills

Subject	Skill	Multi-Sensory Learning Activities
Reading and Language Arts	Understand the joining words **and**, **but**, and **or**.	• Complete Practice Pages 310–312. • Give your child two sheets of construction paper. Help your child cut one sheet into long strips. Give your child a topic and ask him or her to write a simple sentence about it on each strip. With the other sheet of paper, cut three shorter strips and write the words **and**, **but**, and **or**. Then, ask your child to choose two sentence strips and a conjunction to create compound sentences.
	Recognize common prepositions.	• Complete Practice Pages 313 and 314. • Fold a sheet of paper into fourths. Open the paper, and in each box write a preposition that indicates location (**under**, **over**, **up**, **in**, **on**, **next to**, **through**, etc.). Then, have your child draw him or herself in each position in relation to another object.
Math	Review time to the hour and half hour.	• Complete Practice Pages 315–318. • Brainstorm a list of words related to time. Discuss the number of hours in a day, days in a week, and months in a year. Explain that hours are made up of minutes and that minutes are made up of seconds.

Compound Predicates

A **compound predicate** is made by joining two sentences that have the same subject. The predicates are joined together by the word **and**.

Example: Tom can jump.
Tom can run.

Tom can <u>run</u> **and** <u>jump</u>.

Combine the sentences. Write the new sentence on the line.

1. The dog can roll over.
    The dog can bark.

    _____

2. My mom plays with me.
    My mom reads with me.

    _____

3. Tara is tall.
    Tara is smart.

    _____

Joining Words

Joining words join two ideas to make one long sentence. Three words help do this:

and — if both sentences are much the same.
Example: I took my dog for a walk, **and** I played with my cat.

but — if the second sentence says something different than the first sentence. Sometimes the second sentence tells why you can't do the first sentence.
Example: I want to play outside, **but** it is raining.

or — if each sentence names a different thing you could do.
Example: You could eat your cookie, **or** you could give it to me.

Use the word given to join the two short sentences into one longer sentence. The first one is done for you.

1. **(but)** My aunt lives far away. She calls me often.

My aunt lives far away, but she calls me often.

2. **(and)** My sister had a birthday. She got a new bike.

3. **(or)** We can play outside. We can play inside.

Joining Words

Read each pair of sentences. Then, join them with **and**, **but** or **or**.

1. My uncle likes popcorn.
   He does not like peanuts.

   _____

   _____

2. He could read a book.
   He could tell me his own story.

   _____

   _____

3. My little brother is sleepy.
   He wants to go to bed.

   _____

   _____

Correctly Positioned

Read the sentences. Use the words to complete the sentences.

after	last	right	before	first	left	now	next

1. Buck will read the _____ story.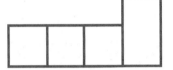

2. We must go to the bus stop _____.

3. We must get some logs _____ we can build a fire.

4. That is the _____ slice of pizza.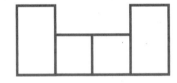

5. Plant the flowers to the _____ of the tree.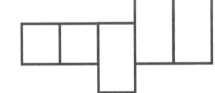

6. This was the _____ time she sang by herself.

7. Go to the _____, not the right.

8. She will go to bed _____ she brushes her teeth.

Prepositions

Prepositions show relationships between the noun or pronoun and another noun in the sentence. The preposition comes before that noun.

Example: The <u>book</u> is on the table.

Common Prepositions

above	behind	by	near	over
across	below	in	off	through
around	beside	inside	on	under

Circle the preposition in each sentence.

1. The dog ran fast around the house.

2. The plates in the cupboard were clean.

3. Put the card inside the envelope.

4. The towel on the sink was wet.

5. I planted flowers in my garden.

6. My kite flew high above the trees.

7. The chair near the counter was sticky.

8. Under the ground, worms lived in their homes.

9. I put the bow around the box.

10. Beside the pond, there was a playground.

Time

Write the time that is on each clock.

Example:

_____2_____ **o'clock**

_____ **o'clock**

_____ **o'clock**

_____ **o'clock**

Time

Write the time that is on each clock.

_____ o'clock

_____ o'clock

_____ o'clock

_____ o'clock

Time: Hour

The short hand of the clock tells the hour. The long hand tells how many minutes after the hour. When the minute hand is on the 12, it is the beginning of the hour.

Look at each clock. Write the time.

Example:

__3__ o'clock

___ o'clock   ___ o'clock   ___ o'clock   ___ o'clock

___ o'clock   ___ o'clock   ___ o'clock   ___ o'clock

Time: Hour, Half-Hour

The short hand of the clock tells the hour. The long hand tells how many minutes after the hour. When the minute hand is on the **6**, it is on the half-hour. A half-hour is thirty minutes. It is written **:30**, such as **5:30**.

Look at each clock. Write the time.

Example:

hour half-hour

$\underline{1}$:$\underline{30}$

___ : ___   ___ : ___   ___ : ___   ___ : ___

___ : ___   ___ : ___   ___ : ___   ___ : ___

Week 30 Skills

Subject	Skill	Multi-Sensory Learning Activities
Reading and Language Arts	Practice spelling strategies for grade-level words.	• Complete Practice Pages 320–323. • Test your child with short spelling words. Have your child use finger paints to write each spelling word on a large poster. • Give a spelling test using riddles. For example, say, "I am both a color and a fruit. What am I?" Encourage your child to say the answer to the riddle and then spell the word aloud.
Math	Review time to the hour and half-hour; tell time to intervals of five minutes.	• Complete Practice Pages 324–328. • Move the hands on your child's learning clock (see page 299) through the hours of the day, discussing what your child would be doing at each time. • Have your child look at the clock frequently throughout the day. State what time it is and talk about your child's schedule, such as, "We'll be eating dinner in one hour." • Have your child draw pictures showing activities for each hour of the day between 8 a.m. and 8 p.m. Include a clock face in each picture.
Bonus: Science		• Collect several objects with different textures. Put each one in a separate paper bag. Ask your child to touch each object without looking at it and describe what he or she feels (rough, cold, hard, prickly, etc.).

Extensions

Read the clues. Look at the pictures. Write the words.

| mean | rake | way | team | mail | beak | save |

If you can spell **take**, then you can spell

_____

- - - - - - - - - - - - - - - - - - -

_____

If you can spell **gave**, then you can spell

_____

- - - - - - - - - - - - - - - - - - -

_____

If you can spell **may**, then you can spell

_____

- - - - - - - - - - - - - - - - - - -

_____

This ___

If you can spell **nail**, then you can spell

_____

- - - - - - - - - - - - - - - - - - -

_____

Read each sentence. Write the words in the boxes.

1. That bird has a very big ___.

2. It is not nice to be ___ to anyone.

3. Pete plays on the baseball ___.

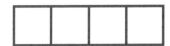

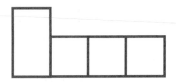

My World

Fill in the missing letters for each word.

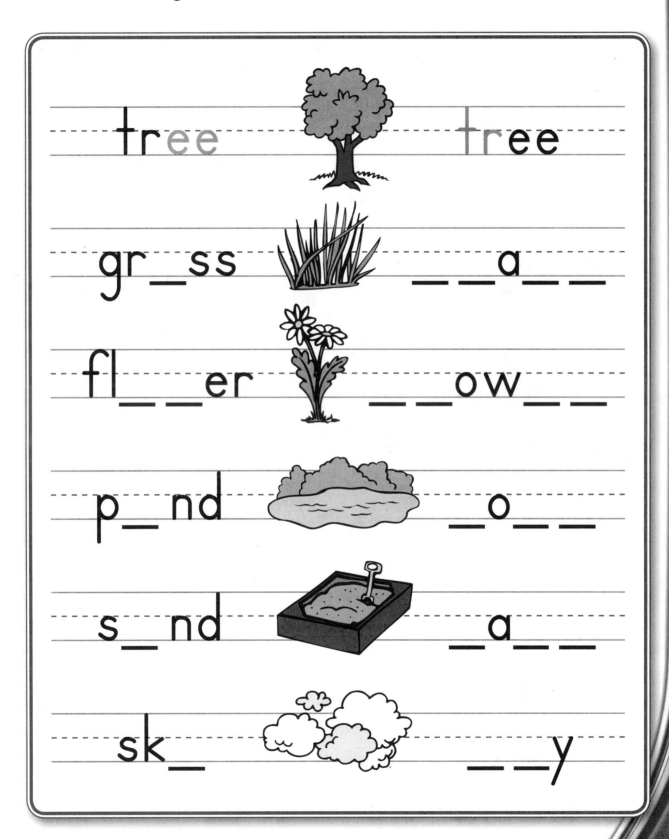

tree   tree

gr_ss   __a__

fl__er   __ow__

p_nd   _o__

s_nd   _a__

sk_   __y

Action Words

Circle the word that is spelled correctly. Then, write the correct spelling in the blank.

Example:

seep
(sleep)
slep

sleep

paly
pay
play

seee
cee
see

rum
run
runn

jump
jumb
junp

mack
maek
make

Sense Words

Circle the word that is spelled correctly. Then, write the correct spelling in the blank.

Example:

tast
(taste)
tste

touch
tuch
touh

smel
smll
smell

her
hear
har

see
se
sea

Time: Hour, Half-Hour

Draw the hands on each clock to show the correct time.

 2:30

 9:00

 7:00

 4:30

3:00

 1:30

Time: Counting by Fives

Fill in the numbers on the clock face. Count by fives around the clock. There are 60 minutes in one hour.

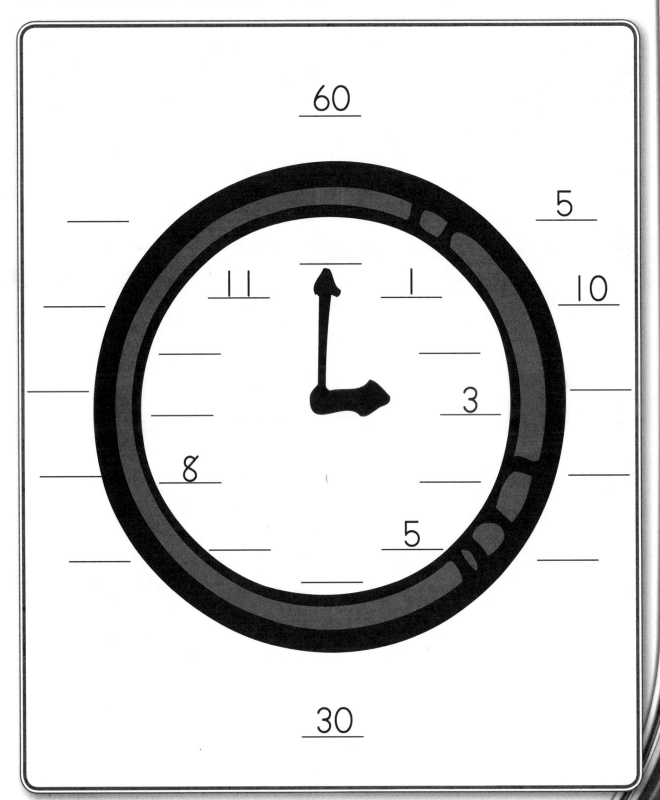

Review: Time

Look at the time on the digital clocks and draw the hands on the clocks.

Look at each clock. Write the time.

_____ o'clock   _____ o'clock

Look at each clock. Write the time.

____ : ____   ____ : ____   ____ : ____

Review: Time

Tell what time it is on the clocks.

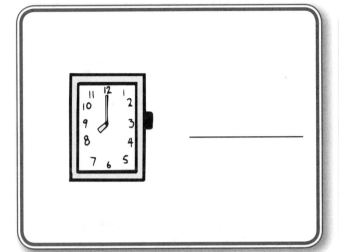 _____

 _____

 _____

 _____

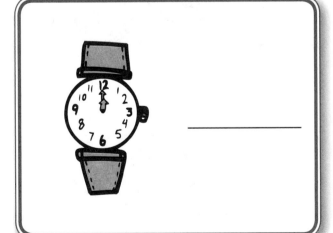 _____

 _____

Review: Time

Match the time on the clock with the digital time.

10:00

5:00

3:00

9:00

2:00

COMPLETE YEAR GRADE 1

Week 31 Skills

Subject	Skill	Multi-Sensory Learning Activities
Reading and Language Arts	Use context clues to understand missing content.	• Complete Practice Pages 330–333. • Make an activity sheet of sentences, leaving blanks where words have been omitted. Leave out singular and plural nouns or verbs. Provide word choices for your child. Have your child write the correct word on the blank in each sentence.
Math	Work with pennies, nickels, and dimes.	• Complete Practice Pages 334–337. • Provide your child with pennies, nickels, and dimes to explore. Observe how he or she "plays" with the coins. You might encourage sorting, patterning, counting, or identifying the coins. • Write a different amount (1–15¢) on each of several index cards. Put several nickels and pennies in a box with the cards. Instruct your child to make the amount written on each card as many ways as possible using only nickels and pennies.
	Review time, money, addition, and subtraction.	• Complete Practice Page 338. • Tell your child real-life money story problems involving addition and subtraction. Have your child use dimes, nickels, and pennies to build each problem and solve for the answer.

Sentences: Things That Go

Finish writing the names of the things that go. Draw a line from the first part of the sentence to the part that completes it. Put a period at the end of each sentence.

Example:

The blue _____bike_____   is in the bike rack [.]

1. The _____c_____   climbed up the hill ☐

2. Bob's _____t_____   is in the garage ☐

3. The _____t_____   was in the field ☐

4. My dad's _____p_____   is full ☐

Sentences: Color Names

Some of these sentences tell a whole idea. Others have something missing. If something is missing, draw a line to the word that completes the sentence. Put a period at the end of each sentence.

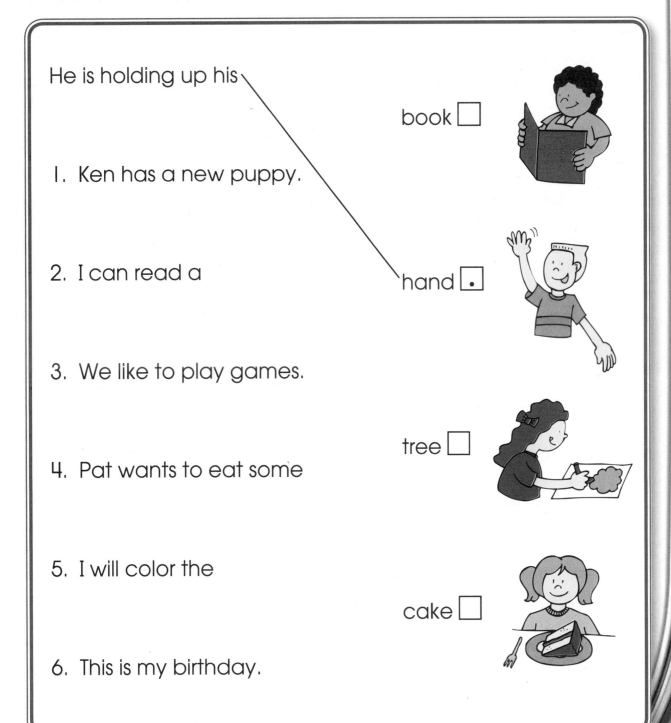

He is holding up his

book ☐

1. Ken has a new puppy.

2. I can read a

hand ⊡

3. We like to play games.

tree ☐

4. Pat wants to eat some

5. I will color the

cake ☐

6. This is my birthday.

Sentences: Animal Names

Finish writing the name of each animal on the line. Draw a line from the first part of the sentence to the part that completes it. Put a period at the end of each sentence.

Example:

A green _____ frog _____ jumps in the water [.]

1. Ken's _____ c _____   barks a lot ☐

2. My friend's _____ d _____   climbs trees ☐

3. Pat's _____ f _____   sits on his finger ☐

4. My little _____ b _____   swims in the water ☐

Sentences: Things That Go

Draw a line from the first part of each sentence to the part that completes it. Put a period at the end of each sentence.

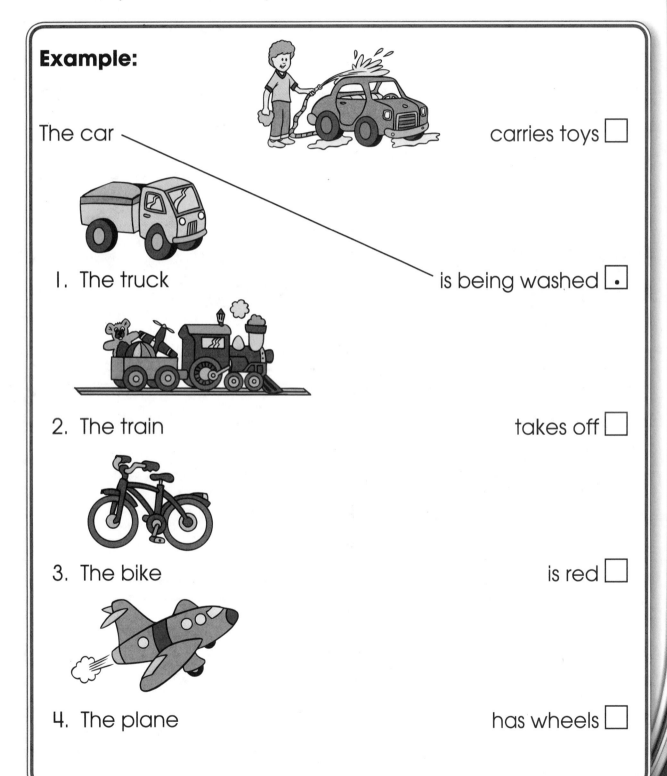

Example:

The car   carries toys ☐

1. The truck   is being washed ⊡

2. The train   takes off ☐

3. The bike   is red ☐

4. The plane   has wheels ☐

Money: Penny and Nickel

A penny is worth one cent. It is written **1¢** or **$.01**. A nickel is worth five cents. It is written **5¢** or **$.05**.

Count the money and write the answers.

 penny   1 penny = 1¢

 nickel   1 nickel = 5¢

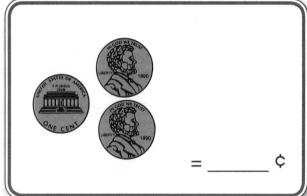

= _____ ¢

= _____ ¢

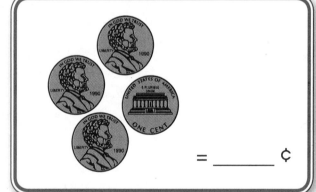

= _____ ¢

= _____ ¢

= _____ ¢

= _____ ¢

Money: Penny, Nickel, Dime

A penny is worth one cent. It is written **1¢** or **$.01**. A nickel is worth five cents. It is written **5¢** or **$.05**. A dime is worth ten cents. It is written **10¢** or **$.10**.

Add the coins pictured and write the total amounts in the blanks.

dime		**nickel**		**nickel**		**pennies**
10¢	=	5¢	+	5¢	=	10¢

10¢   +   1¢   =   _____ ¢

10¢   +   _____ ¢   =   _____ ¢

_____ ¢   +   _____ ¢   +   _____ ¢   =   _____ ¢

_____ ¢   +   _____ ¢   =   _____ ¢

Money

Match the amounts in each purse to the price tags.

Money: Penny, Nickel, Dime

Match the correct amount of money with the price
of the object.

Review

What time is it?

_____ **o'clock**

Draw the hands on each clock.

2:30   7:30   11:00

How much money?

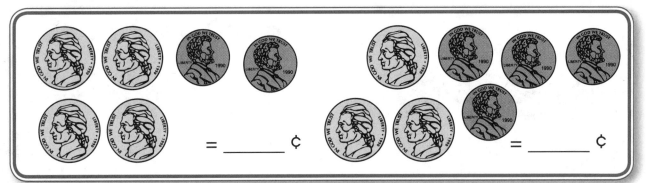

= _____ ¢   = _____ ¢

Add or subtract.

9 + 3 = _____   6 + 8 = _____   15 − 9 = _____

12 − 8 = _____   12 + 2 = _____   7 + 6 = _____

Week 32 Skills

Subject	Skill	Multi-Sensory Learning Activities
Reading and Language Arts	Review context clues.	• Complete Practice Pages 340–344. • Find a comic strip. Cut out one of the frames in the middle. Glue the comic to a sheet of paper, leaving space for your child to draw what he or she thinks happened in the missing frame. • Copy and enlarge a comic strip and remove the words. Glue the comic onto a larger piece of paper and cut it into sections. Have your child dictate new dialogue for the comic strip based on the drawings.
Math	Understand fractions $\frac{1}{2}$, $\frac{1}{3}$, and $\frac{1}{4}$.	• Complete Practice Pages 345–348. • Use sidewalk chalk and a yardstick to draw geometric shapes. Draw lines dividing the shapes into equal parts and have your child shade in fractional parts such as one-half or one-third. • Cut out a circle from a piece of paper and divide it into fourths. Have your child put a name of a season in each section and illustrate it with drawings or magazine clippings. Then, have your child recite the months and sort the months by seasons, writing the names in the appropriate quadrant of the circle. • Read *Fraction Action* by Loreen Leedy. Look around for familiar things that come in halves, thirds, and fourths.

Which Word?

Write the words in alphabetical order. The first one has been done for you.

| bath | bang | teeth | rang | path | hang | math | sang |

1. bang 2. _____ 3. _____ 4. _____

5. _____ 6. _____ 7. _____ 8. _____

Complete the sentences below.

1. The hammer struck the nail with a loud _____.

2. At 7:00, Casie's alarm _____.

3. Joseph likes to help _____ the laundry on the clothesline.

4. My brother _____ in the choir.

5. Renee's favorite subject in school is _____.

6. Ron lost his first two baby _____.

7. My friends like to go hiking on a _____ through the forest.

8. Sara takes a _____ on Saturday night.

Which Word?

Write each word next to its picture.

ant	cost	desk	left	milk	land	wasp	pest

Write the missing words.

1. How much does this toy _____ ?

2. My little sister sometimes acts like a _____ .

3. I'd like a glass of _____ with my cookies.

4. I was stung by a _____ .

On Your Mark

Write the word that ends with each letter.

| park | car | march | barn | arm | scarf | cart | star |

T _____   **K** _____

R _____   **F** _____

N _____   **M** _____

R _____   **CH** _____

Write a word to complete each sentence.

1. The animals on the farm sleep in the _____.

2. Father drove the _____ to the _____.

3. When I am in the band, I would like to _____ in the parade.

4. A black and white horse pulled a red _____.

5. We searched the night sky for the brightest _____.

6. Jane wore a red _____ around her neck.

7. Tommy fell and broke his _____.

Which Word?

Write the words that rhyme with the pictures below.

| thorn | born | pork | north | sport | porch | stork |

Complete the sentences below with the words.

1. Ryan's baby sister was _____ last night.

2. The lion has a _____ in its paw.

3. At night, the family likes to swing on the _____.

4. My house is on the _____ side of the street.

5. Baseball is Francisco's favorite _____.

The Angr-r-ry Dog

Sort the words in the columns according to the **r** spellings.

| curl | turn | bird | fern | girl | dirt | her | church |

er words	ir words	ur words

Complete the sentences below with words from the list.

1. The _____'s dress got _____ on it when she fell.

2. The _____ landed on the bell outside the _____.

3. The farmer told Zach to go in the barn and _____ left.

4. The leaves on the _____ plant are large and green.

5. Maria's father asked _____ to dry the dishes.

Fractions: Halves $\frac{1}{2}$

Color only the shapes that show halves.

$\frac{1}{2}$ $\dfrac{\text{Part shaded or divided}}{\text{Number of equal parts}}$

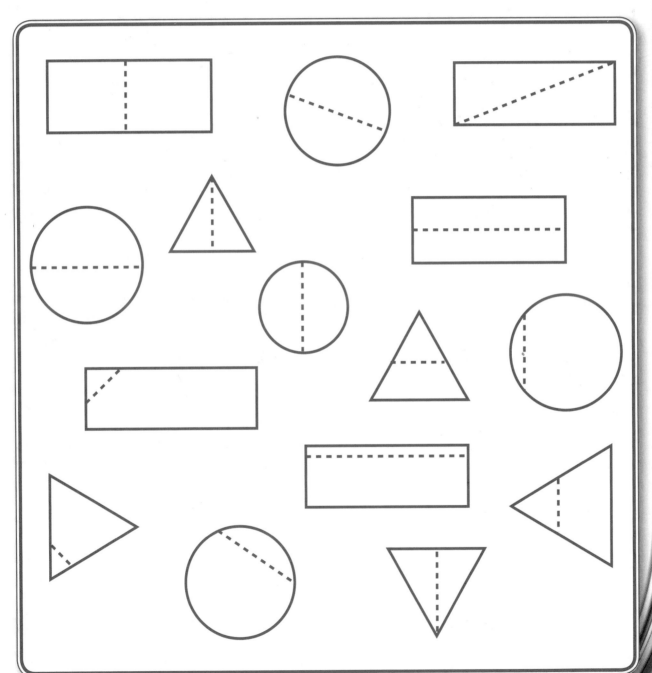

Fractions: Thirds $\frac{1}{3}$

Circle the objects that have 3 equal parts.

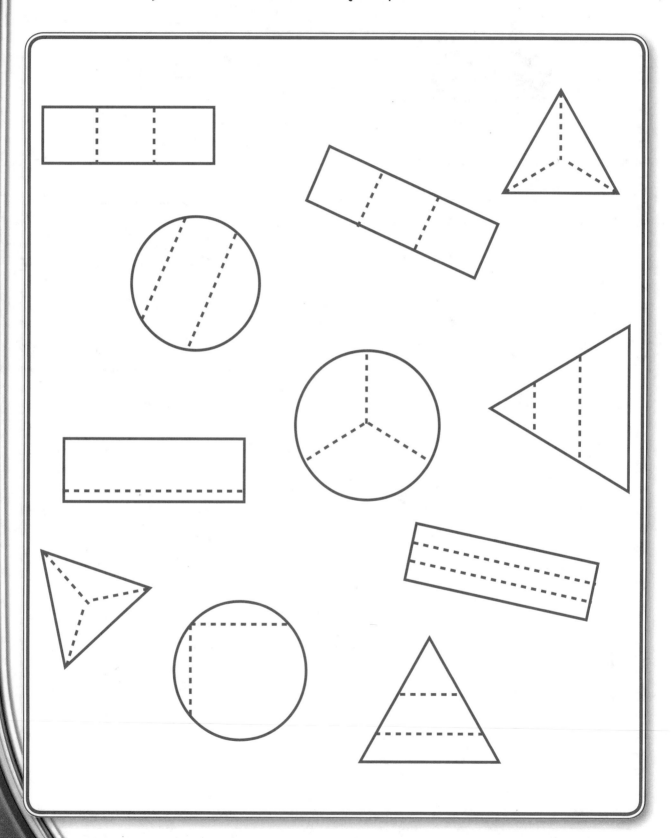

Fractions: Fourths $\frac{1}{4}$

Circle the objects that have 4 equal parts.

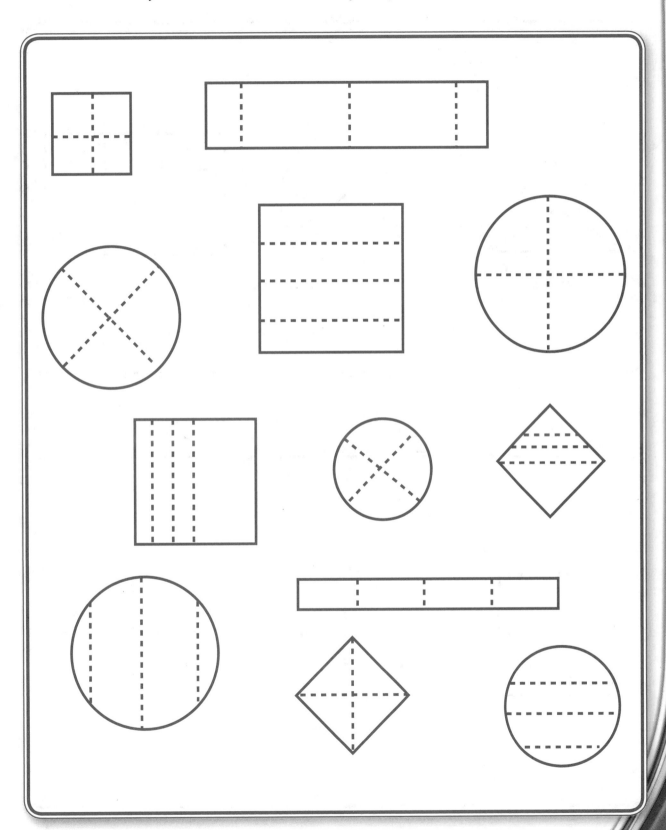

Fractions: Thirds and Fourths

Each object has 3 equal parts. Color one section.

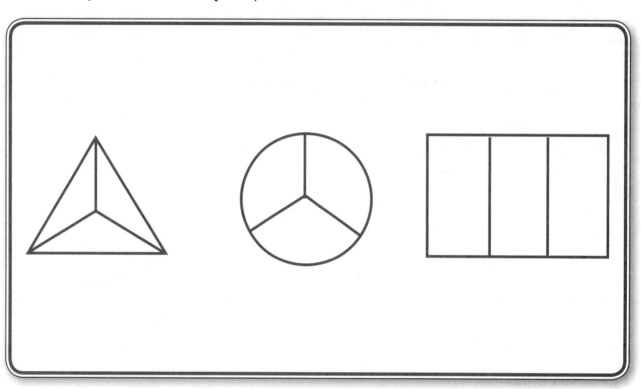

Each object has 4 equal parts. Color one section.

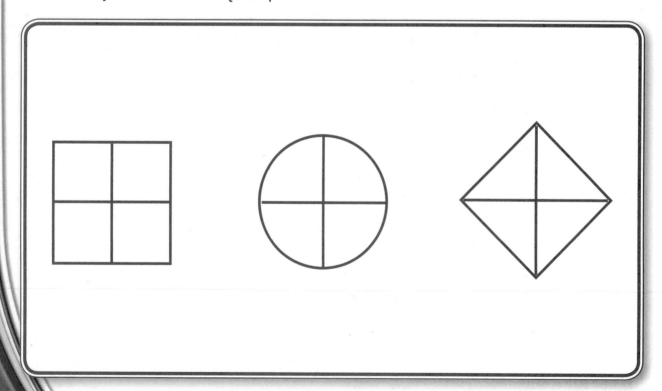

Week 33 Skills

Subject	Skill	Multi-Sensory Learning Activities
Reading and Language Arts	Put picture stories and sentences in correct sequence.	• Complete Practice Pages 350–354. • Write a short story on a piece of paper. Cut each sentence apart and shuffle them. Ask your child to read the sentences and put them in the correct order. • Have your child describe a familiar routine, such as getting ready for bed or getting ready for school, in sequential steps. Write the steps he or she describes in order.
Math	Review fractions.	• Complete Practice Pages 355–357. • Cut construction paper into different shapes. Ask your child to divide each into two parts. Ask your child if the two parts are the same. Teach your child to fold the shape, carefully matching the corners to create two parts that are the same. Repeat this activity with three or four other shapes. • Read *Eating Fractions* by Bruce McMillan. Teach your child about fair sharing. Split a cookie in half. Cut a bagel into thirds. Cut an apple into fourths. Have your child analyze whether the foods were split carefully enough to call them equal.

Sequencing: Pig Gets Ready

Number the pictures of Pig getting ready for the party to show the order of the story.

What kind of party do you think Pig is going to? _____

Sequencing: Raking Leaves

Write a number in each box to show the order of the story.

Sequencing: Make an Ice-Cream Cone

Number the boxes in order to show how to make an ice-cream cone.

Sequencing: How Flowers Grow

Read the story. Then, write the steps to grow a flower.

> First, find a sunny spot. Then, plant the seed. Water it. The flower will start to grow. Pull the weeds around it. Remember to keep giving the flower water. Enjoy your flower.

1. _____

2. _____

3. _____

4. _____

5. _____

Sequencing: Eating a Cone

What if a person never ate an ice-cream cone? Could you explain how to eat it? Think about what you do when you eat an ice-cream cone?

Write directions to teach someone how to eat an ice-cream cone.

How to Eat an Ice-Cream Cone

1. _____

_____

2. _____

_____

3. _____

_____

4. _____

Review: Fractions

Count the equal parts, then write the fraction.

Example:

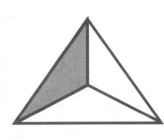

Shaded part = __1__ Write

Equal parts = __3__

$\dfrac{1}{3}$

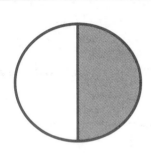

Shaded part = __1__ Write

Equal parts = _____

____

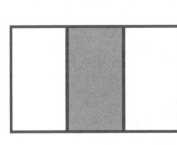

Shaded part = __1__ Write

Equal parts = _____

____

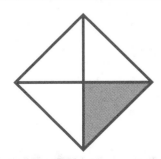

Shaded part = __1__ Write

Equal parts = _____

____

Review

Color the object with thirds red. Color the object with halves blue. Color the object with fourths green.

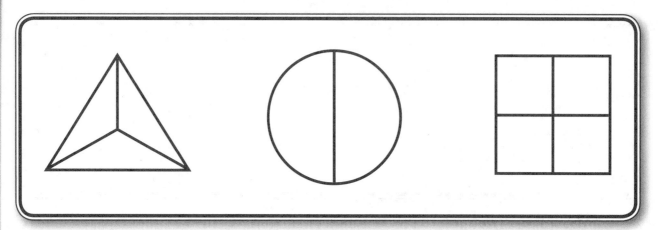

Draw a line to the correct equal part.

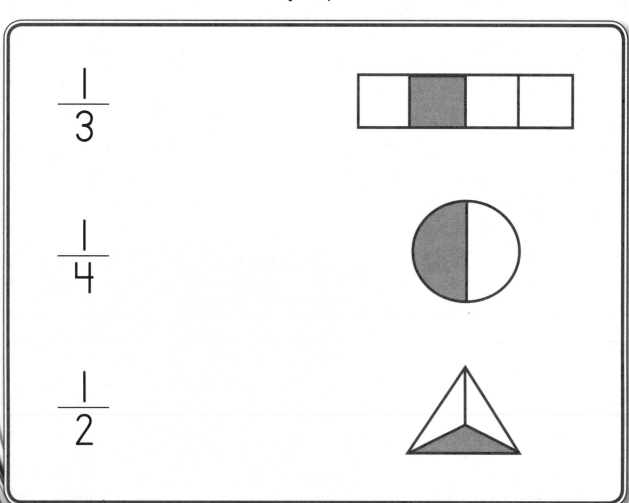

$\frac{1}{3}$

$\frac{1}{4}$

$\frac{1}{2}$

Equal and Unequal Parts

Cut out each shape below along the solid lines. Then, fold the shape on the dotted lines. Do you have equal or unequal parts? Sort the shapes by equal and unequal parts.

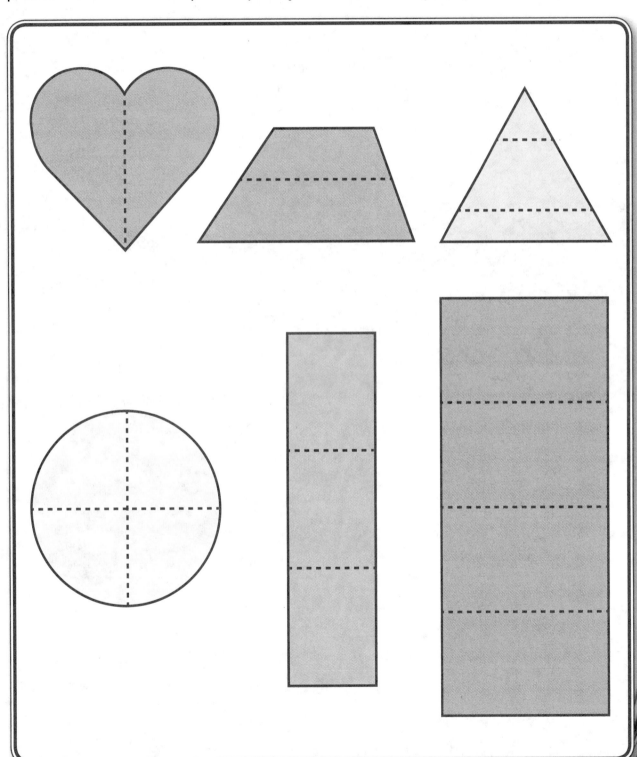

Week 34 Skills

Subject	Skill	Multi-Sensory Learning Activities
Reading and Language Arts	Answer questions about texts to demonstrate reading comprehension.	• Complete Practice Pages 360–363. • Read *Blueberries for Sal* by Robert McCloskey. After reading, ask comprehension questions to test your child's understanding of the story, such as "How old might Sal be?" • Read passages from a book as dialogue. Have your child read one part while you read another.
Math	Review fractions.	• Complete Practice Pages 364 and 365. • Draw two circles, two squares, and two triangles. Cut out one of each shape. Cut each matching shape into two, three, or four equal parts. Instruct your child to mix up the pieces, then reassemble the parts on top of each whole shape. Have your child name the fractions.
	Create, read, and interpret graphs.	• Complete Practice Pages 366–368. • Have your child sort the items in a small bag of snack mix, such as cereal, peanuts, and raisins. Create a graph illustrating the number of each item that the bag contained.

Comprehension: Cats

Look at the pictures and read about four cats. Then, write the correct name beside each cat.

Fluffy, Blackie and Tiger are playing. Tom is sleeping. Blackie has spots. Tiger has stripes.

Same and Different: Cats

Compare the picture of the cats on page 360 to this picture.
Write a word from the box to tell what is different about
each cat.

| purple ball | green bow | blue brush | red collar |

1. Tom is wearing a _____ .

2. Blackie has a _____ .

3. Fluffy is wearing a _____ .

4. Tiger has a _____ .

Comprehension: Babies

Read about babies. Then, write the answers.

Babies are small. Some babies cry a lot. They cry when they are wet. They cry when they are hungry. They smile when they are dry. They smile when they are fed.

1. Name two reasons babies cry.

    ----------------------------   ----------------------------

2. Name two reasons babies smile.

    ----------------------------   ----------------------------

3. Write a baby's name you like.

Comprehension: Babies

Read each sentence. Draw a picture of a baby's face in the box to show if she would cry or smile.

1. The baby needs to have her diaper changed.

2. The baby has not eaten for awhile.

3. Dad put a dry diaper on the baby.

4. The baby is going to finish her bottle.

5. The baby finished her food but is still hungry.

Fraction Food

Count the equal parts. Circle the fraction that names one of the parts.

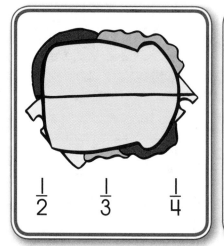

$\dfrac{1}{2}$ $\dfrac{1}{3}$ $\dfrac{1}{4}$

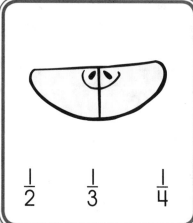

$\dfrac{1}{2}$ $\dfrac{1}{3}$ $\dfrac{1}{4}$

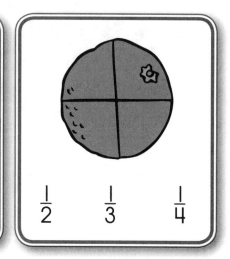

$\dfrac{1}{2}$ $\dfrac{1}{3}$ $\dfrac{1}{4}$

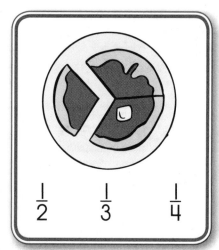

$\dfrac{1}{2}$ $\dfrac{1}{3}$ $\dfrac{1}{4}$

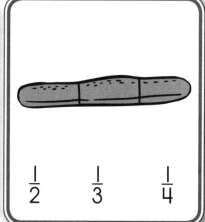

$\dfrac{1}{2}$ $\dfrac{1}{3}$ $\dfrac{1}{4}$

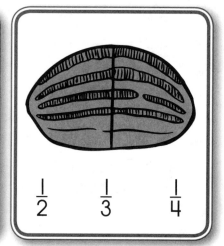

$\dfrac{1}{2}$ $\dfrac{1}{3}$ $\dfrac{1}{4}$

$\dfrac{1}{2}$ $\dfrac{1}{3}$ $\dfrac{1}{4}$

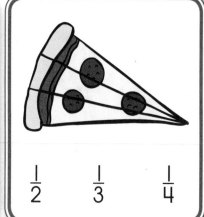

$\dfrac{1}{2}$ $\dfrac{1}{3}$ $\dfrac{1}{4}$

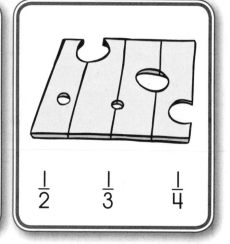

$\dfrac{1}{2}$ $\dfrac{1}{3}$ $\dfrac{1}{4}$

Fraction Review

How many equal parts?

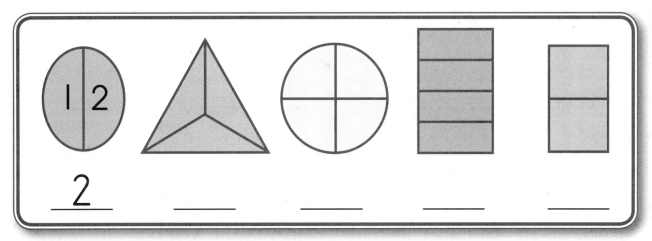

Color shapes with 2 equal parts red. Color shapes with 3 equal parts blue. Color shapes with 4 equal parts green.

Graphing

Look at the graph below. Then, answer the questions on page 367.

10				
9				
8				
7				
6				
5				
4				
3				
2				
1				

hot dog   **hamburger**   **pizza**   **chicken**

Graphing

Answer the questions about the graph on page 366.

- How many people like hot dogs best? _____

- How many people like pizza best? _____

- How many people like chicken best? _____

- Which food do most people like best? _____

- Which two foods do the same number of people like best?

  _____ and _____

- Which food do the fewest number of people like best?

  _____

Living or Not Living?

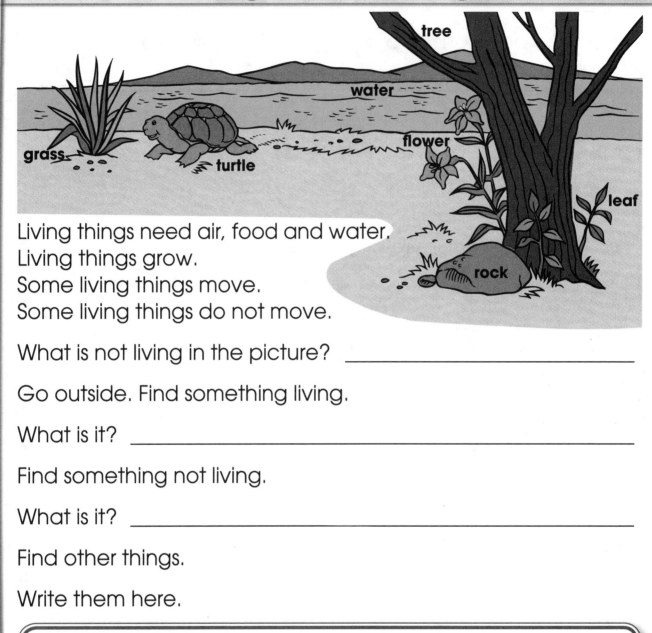

Living things need air, food and water.
Living things grow.
Some living things move.
Some living things do not move.

What is not living in the picture? _____

Go outside. Find something living.

What is it? _____

Find something not living.

What is it? _____

Find other things.

Write them here.

Living	Not Living
_____	_____
_____	_____
_____	_____

Week 35 Skills

Subject	Skill	Multi-Sensory Learning Activities
Reading and Language Arts	Review reading comprehension.	• Complete Practice Pages 370–374. • Sing and do the "Hokey Pokey." Once your child is familiar with the song, change the order of the commands. • Give a series of oral directions to create a picture. For example, say, "Fold a sheet of paper in fourths. Number the boxes left to right, starting at the top left. Draw a blue butterfly in box number three, an orange sun with a red face in box one," and so on.
Math	Measure familiar objects using inch rulers.	• Complete Practice Pages 375–377. • Tell your child to look around the room and guess how many steps long he or she thinks the room is. Record his or her guess on a piece of paper, then have your child walk across the room, counting steps along the way. Instruct your child to write down the result on a piece of paper. How close was the guess to the correct measurement? Next, measure the room in feet and inches.
Bonus: Science		• Help your child start a plant from a seed. Have him or her plant the seed in a pot of dirt. He or she should water the plant as needed and place it in a sunny spot. Encourage your child to measure its growth on a weekly basis.

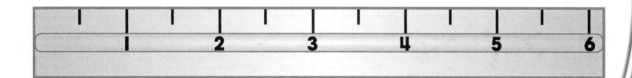

A Falling Star

Have you ever seen a falling star? Falling stars are not really stars. They are small pieces of rock. As falling stars fall, they get hot and burn. They look big because they give off so much light. That is why they are so bright in the night sky. Did you know that **meteor** is another name for a falling star?

Circle the correct answer.

A falling star is really a star.	Yes	No
Falling stars are pieces of rock.	Yes	No
Falling stars burn as they fall.	Yes	No

Unscramble the answer.

Another name for a falling star is _____ .

ermote
2 6 1 5 3 4

Draw two yellow falling stars in the picture.

Comprehension: An Animal Party

Use the picture for clues. Write words from the box to answer the questions.

bear

dog

giraffe

pig

cat

elephant

hippo

tiger

1. Which animals have bow ties?

   _____   _____

   - - - - - - - - - - - -   - - - - - - - - - - - -

   _____   _____

2. Which animal has a striped shirt?

   _____

   - - - - - - - - - - - -

   _____

3. Which animal has a hat?

   _____

   - - - - - - - - - - - -

   _____

Comprehension: Play Simon Says

Read how to play Simon Says. Then, answer the questions.

Simon Says

Here is how to play Simon Says: One kid is Simon. Simon is the leader. Everyone must do what Simon says and does but only if the leader says, "Simon says" first. Let's try it.

SIMON SAYS, CLAP YOUR HANDS!

"Simon says, 'Pat your head.'" "Simon says, 'Pat your nose. Pat your toes.'" Oops! Did you pat your toes? I did not say, "Simon says" first. If you patted your toes, you are out!

1. Who is the leader in this game?

   _____

   -

   _____

2. What must the leader say first each time?

   _____

   -

   _____

3. What happens if you do something and the leader did not say, "Simon says?"

   _____

   -

   _____

Comprehension: How We Eat

Read the story. Use words from the box to answer
the questions.

| fork | ice cream | knife | soup |

People eat with spoons and forks. They use a spoon to
eat soup and ice cream. They use a fork to eat potatoes.
They use a knife to cut their meat. They say, "Thank you. It
was good!" when they finish.

1. What do we use to cut food?

   _____

2. What are two things you can eat with a spoon?

   _____   _____

3. What do we use to eat meat and potatoes?

   _____

Comprehension: Write a Party Invitation

Read about the party. Then, complete the invitation.

   The party will be at Dog's house. The party will start at 1:00 P.M. It will last 2 hours. Write your birthday for the date of the party.

Party Invitation

_____

- - - - - - - - - - - - - - - - - - -

Where: _____

_____

- - - - - - - - - - - - - - - - - - -

Date: _____

_____

- - - - - - - - - - - - - - - - - - -

Time It Begins: _____

_____

- - - - - - - - - - - - - - - - - - -

Time It Ends: _____

_____

- - - - - - - - - - - - - - - - - - -

_____

On the last line, write something else about the party.

COMPLETE YEAR GRADE I

A String Activity

Cut a piece of string as long as your pencil. Use the string to measure things. List the things you measure below.

Longer	Same	Shorter

Length

Use a penny to measure each object.

 is _____ penny long.

 is _____ pennies long.

 is _____ pennies long.

 is _____ pennies long.

 is _____ pennies long.

 is _____ pennies long.

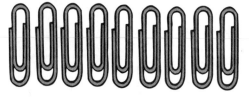 is _____ pennies long.

Measurement

A ruler has 12 inches. 12 inches equal 1 foot.

Cut out the ruler at the bottom of the page. Measure the objects to the nearest inch.

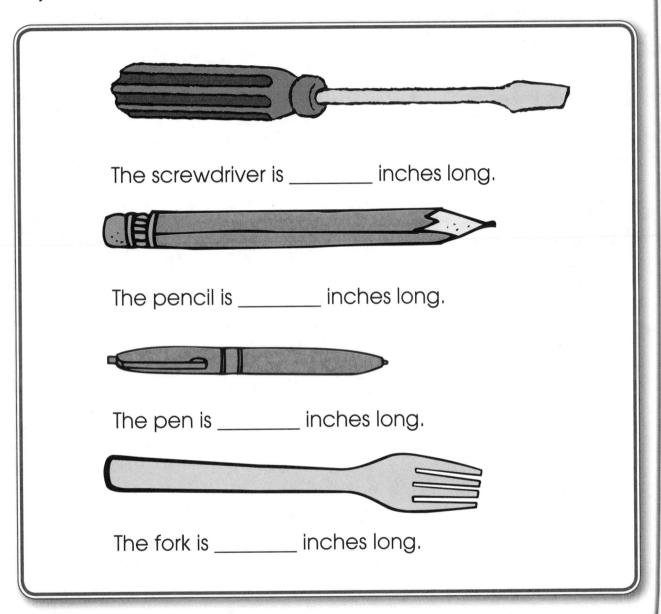

The screwdriver is _____ inches long.

The pencil is _____ inches long.

The pen is _____ inches long.

The fork is _____ inches long.

✂ **Cut** -

Week 36 Skills

Subject	Skill	Multi-Sensory Learning Activities
Reading and Language Arts	Write sentences and paragraphs about a given topic.	• Complete Practice Pages 380–384. • Brainstorm a list of words that could be used to replace the word **said** in your child's writing. Look in books for ideas. Have your child invent a dialogue between an animal and its mother. Encourage him or her to use words other than **said** in the animals' conversation.
Basic Skills	Use critical thinking to infer meaning that is not overtly stated.	• Complete Practice Pages 385 and 387. • Give your child a scenario and ask him or her to infer its meaning. For example, say, "Mother bundled Maria in two thick sweaters and three pairs of socks, and also made her wear two pairs of mittens and a scarf. Maria could hardly walk when she went out to play." Then, ask, "What season is it? How did you know?"
Bonus: Math		• Put a cup, pint, quart, half-gallon, and gallon container on a table. Have your child find out which container is equal to two cups. Remove the cup container. Tell your child to find out how many cups each of the other containers holds (without using the cup measure).

Traveling the World Through Maps

Pretend that you are an explorer traveling around the world. What is one of the first things you will need? A map of the Earth, of course! A map is a group of carefully drawn pictures. It can be of the world, your city or your neighborhood. Maps have been used for a long time by people all over the world. The very first maps were made from dirt, sand or clay. The Chinese painted maps on silk. Why do you think people need maps?

Write on the lines below.

All About You!

Write a story telling what you like to do. Then, draw a picture to go with your story on another sheet of paper.

Sentence Sequence

Sentences can tell a story. Write **1**, **2** and **3** in the circles to tell what happened first, second and third. Write a sentence to tell about each picture.

1. _____

2. _____

3. _____

Writing: My Snake Story

Write a fictional (make-believe) story about a snake. Make sure to include details and a title.

_____ title

_____

- -

_____

- -

_____

- -

_____

- -

_____

- -

_____

- -

_____

- -

_____

A Friendly Letter

Write a letter to a friend about what you did today. Be sure to use proper capitalization, commas, and ending punctuation.

date

Dear _____,

Your friend,

Family Portraits

Families may be big or small. No matter how many people are in a family, each person is important to the others.

Cut out the pictures at the bottom of the page. Read the clues. Glue the pictures of the members of this family in the frame where they belong.

Our Family

- Grandfather is in the middle.
- The girl is on the right end.
- The boy is on the left end.
- Mother is between Grandmother and the boy.
- Father is beside the girl.

✂ **Cut** -

Everyone Is Welcome

Cut out the pictures of the people at the bottom of the page. Read the clues carefully. Glue the people where they belong at the table.

- Robert already has his hamburger.
- Kioko will pass the plate of hamburgers to the others at the table.
- Mike asks Teresa to please pass the pitcher of lemonade so that he may fill his glass.
- Pablo likes sitting between his friends Kioko and Teresa.
- Sue likes hot dogs better than hamburgers.

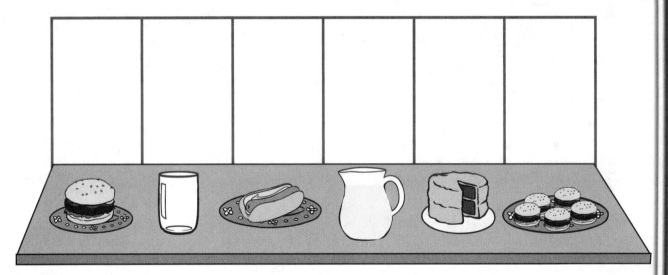

Cut -

| Kioko | Pablo | Sue | Robert | Teresa | Mike |

Fourth Quarter Check-Up

Basic Skills

❑ I can use critical thinking to infer meaning that is not overtly stated.

Reading and Language Arts

❑ I recognize and understand homophones.

❑ I can use articles appropriately.

❑ I can use joining words correctly.

❑ I know common prepositions.

❑ I know spelling strategies for common words.

❑ I can use context clues to understand missing information.

❑ I can put picture stories and sentences in correct sequence.

❑ I can answer questions correctly about a text I have read.

❑ I can write sentences and paragraphs about a given topic.

Math

❑ I can tell time to the hour, half-hour, and five minute intervals.

❑ I am familiar with the months of the year.

❑ I recognize pennies, nickels, and dimes.

❑ I understand the fractions $\frac{1}{2}$, $\frac{1}{3}$, and $\frac{1}{4}$.

❑ I can create, read, and interpret graphs.

❑ I can measure familiar objects using inch rulers.

Final Project

Read *The Doorbell Rang* by Pat Hutchins and act out the story. How did the feelings of the two main characters change over the course of the story? With an adult, bake cookies and divide each cookie into four equal parts.

Colors

Red   Orange   Yellow   Green   Blue   Purple

Brown   Black   White   Gray   Pink

Two-Dimensional Shapes

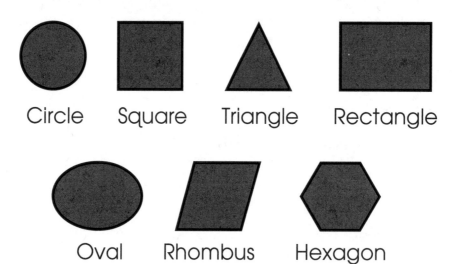

Circle   Square   Triangle   Rectangle

Oval   Rhombus   Hexagon

Three-Dimensional Shapes

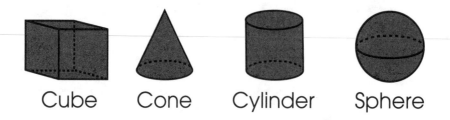

Cube   Cone   Cylinder   Sphere

Common Consonant Blends

bl	cr	sl
cl	dr	sm
fl	fr	sn
gl	pr	sp
sl	tr	st
br	sk	sw

Digraphs

ch	th
sh	wh

Ordinal Numbers

first

second

third

fourth

fifth

sixth

seventh

eighth

ninth

tenth

Numbers 1–100

1	2	3	4	5	6	7	8	9	10
11	12	13	14	15	16	17	18	19	20
21	22	23	24	25	26	27	28	29	30
31	32	33	34	35	36	37	38	39	40
41	42	43	44	45	46	47	48	49	50
51	52	53	54	55	56	57	58	59	60
61	62	63	64	65	66	67	68	69	70
71	72	73	74	75	76	77	78	79	80
81	82	83	84	85	86	87	88	89	90
91	92	93	94	95	96	97	98	99	100

Money

penny = 1¢

nickel = 5¢

dime = 10¢

Fractions

$\frac{1}{2}$

$\frac{1}{3}$

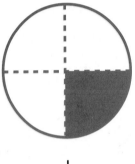

$\frac{1}{4}$

Measurement

Inches

First Grade Sight Words

about	day	keep	their
after	find	long	them
again	first	man	then
ask	from	now	where
ate	had	old	which
back	hers	only	word
because	how	or	would
by	if	rain	write
could	jump	right	you

Recommended Read-Alouds for Grade 1

- ☐ *Old Black Fly* by Jim Ayelsworth
- ☐ *Max's Words* by Kate Banks
- ☐ *Stone Soup* by Marcia Brown
- ☐ *Diary of a Wombat* by Jackie French
- ☐ *There's a Monster Under My Bed* by James Howe
- ☐ *Swimmy* by Leo Lionni
- ☐ *Frog and Toad Are Friends* by Arnold Lobel
- ☐ *Little Bear* by Elsie H. Minarik
- ☐ *Fancy Nancy* by Jane O'Connor
- ☐ *Henry and Mudge* by Cynthia Rylant
- ☐ *The Relatives Came* by Cynthia Rylant
- ☐ *The Boy Who Loved Words* by Roni Schotter
- ☐ *The Stinky Cheese Man and Other Fairly Stupid Stories* by Jon Scieska
- ☐ *Horton Hears a Who* by Dr. Seuss
- ☐ *It Looked Like Spilt Milk* by Charles G. Shaw
- ☐ *Heckedy Peg* by Audrey Wood

Answer Key

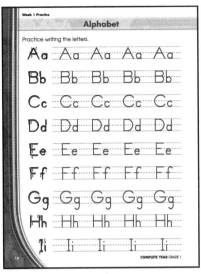

18

20

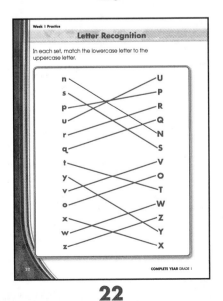

22

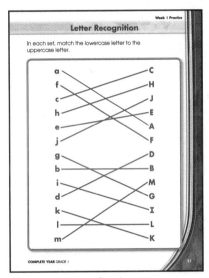

19

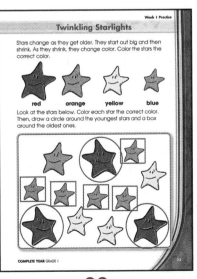

21

23

Answer Key

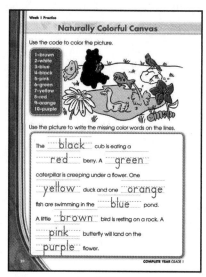

24

25

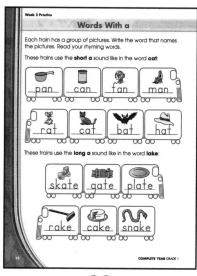

28

29

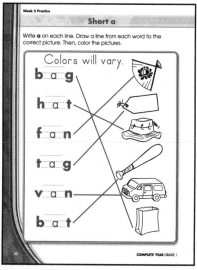

30

31

Answer Key

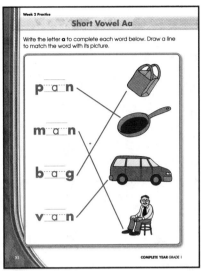

32

33

34

35

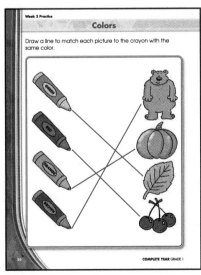

36

38

Answer Key

39

40

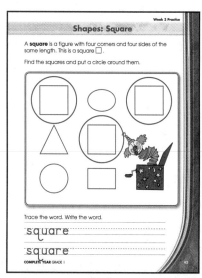

41

42

43

44

Answer Key

Shapes: Square and Circle

Practice drawing squares. Trace the samples and make four of your own.

Practice drawing circles. Trace the samples and make four of your own.

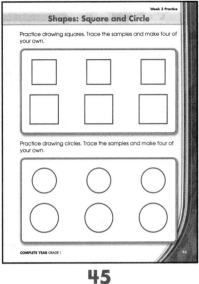

COMPLETE YEAR GRADE 1

45

Shapes: Triangle

A **triangle** is a figure with three corners and three sides. This is a triangle △.

Find the triangles and put a circle around them.

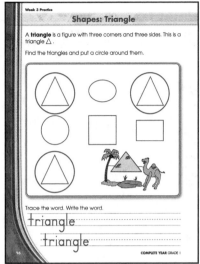

Trace the word. Write the word.

triangle

triangle

COMPLETE YEAR GRADE 1

46

Words With i

Short i sounds like the **i** in **pig**. **Long i** sounds like the **i** in **kite**. Draw a circle around the words with the **short i** sound. Draw an **X** on the words with the **long i** sound.

COMPLETE YEAR GRADE 1

48

Short and Long Ii

Say the name of each picture. If it has the **short i** sound, color it yellow. If it has the **long i** sound, color it red.

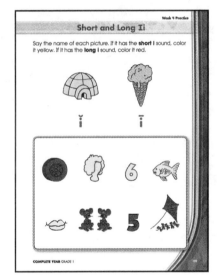

COMPLETE YEAR GRADE 1

49

Short i

Write **i** on each line. Color the correct picture for each word.

p i g   l i d

s i x   m i lk

w i g   g i ft

COMPLETE YEAR GRADE 1

50

Picky Pigs

Write the missing word in each sentence.

pig   sit   pin   fin   dig   win   hit   lid

1. The dog can **dig** a hole.

2. Put the **lid** on the pan.

3. He will **sit** on the bench.

4. Tom **hit** the ball into the stands.

5. The **pig** sits in the mud.

6. A **fin** helps a fish swim.

7. Will he **win** the prize?

8. Mom can **pin** the diaper on the baby.

COMPLETE YEAR GRADE 1

51

Answer Key

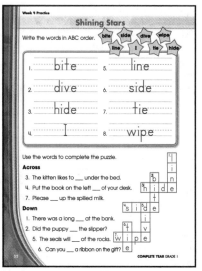

52

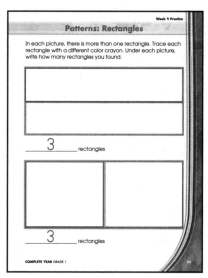

53

54

55

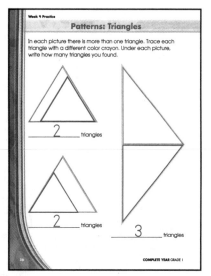

56

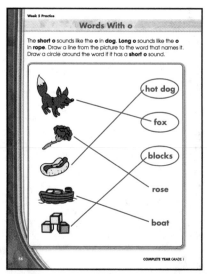

58

Answer Key

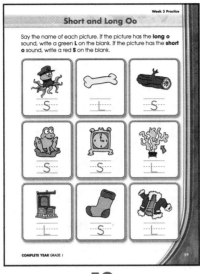

59

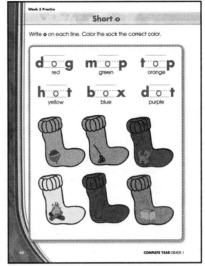

60

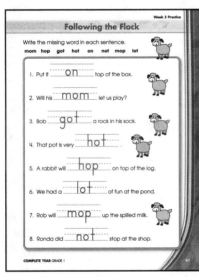

61

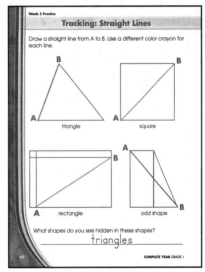

62

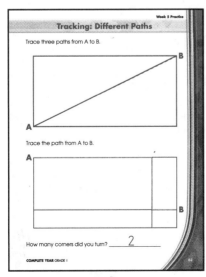

63

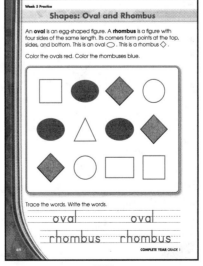

64

Answer Key

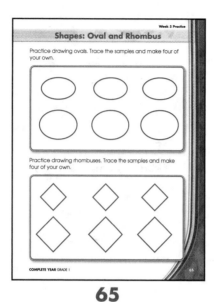

65

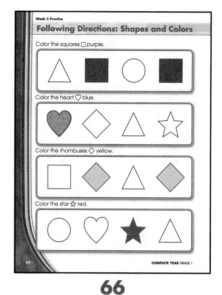

66

68

Short and Long Uu

69

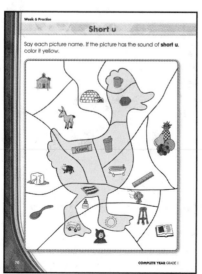

70

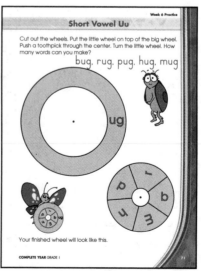

71

Answer Key

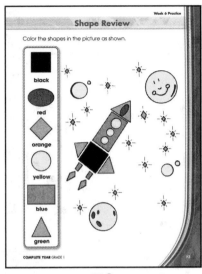

73

Shape Review

Trace the circles in red.

Trace the squares in blue.

Trace the rectangles in yellow.

Trace the triangles in green.

Trace the ovals in purple.

Trace the rhombuses in orange.

74

75

Classifying: Shapes

Mary and Rudy are taking a trip into space. Help them find the stars, moons, circles and diamonds.

Color the shapes. Use yellow for the ☆s. Use red for the ◯s. Use blue for the ☾s. Use purple for the ◇s.

How many stars? 5   How many moons? 5
How many circles? 4   How many rhombuses? 4

76

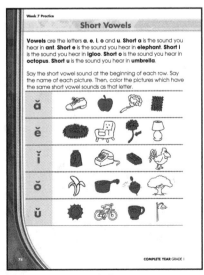

78

Short Vowel Sounds

In each box are three pictures. The words that name the pictures have missing letters. Write **a**, **e**, **i**, **o** or **u** to finish the words.

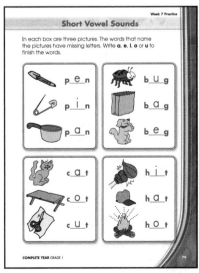

79

403

Answer Key

80

81

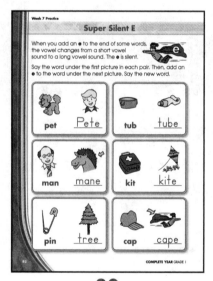

82

83

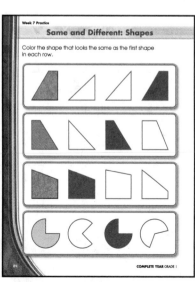

84

85

Answer Key

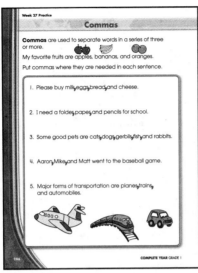

86

88

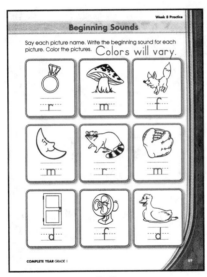

89

90

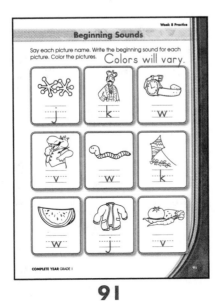

91

92

Answer Key

93

95

98

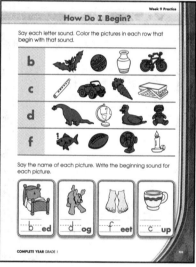

99

100

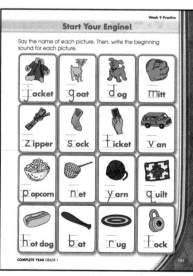

101

Answer Key

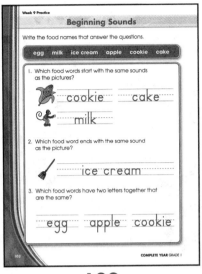

102

103

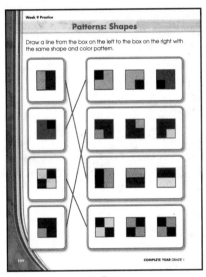

104

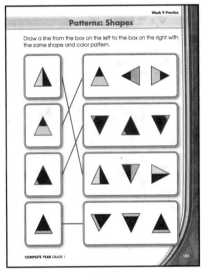

105

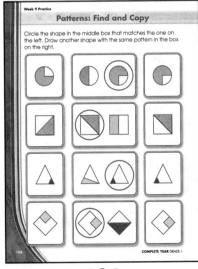

106

112

Answer Key

113

114

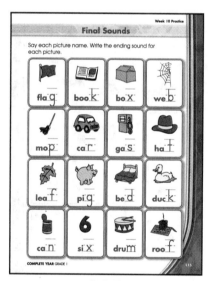

115

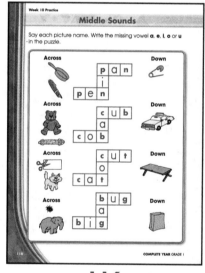

116

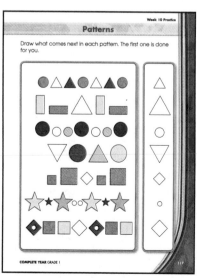

117

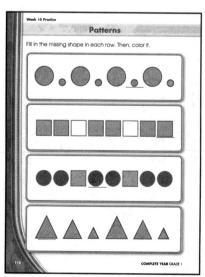

118

Answer Key

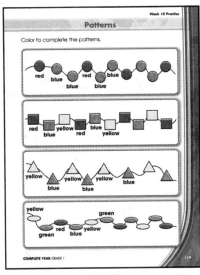

119

120

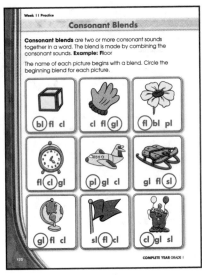

122

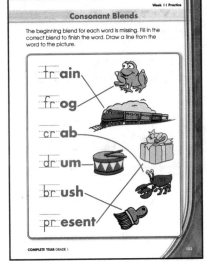

123

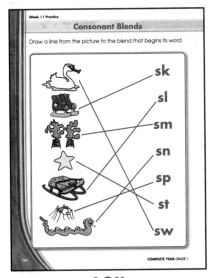

124

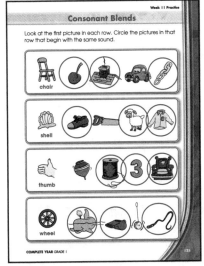

125

Answer Key

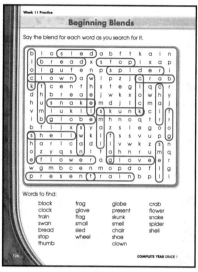

126

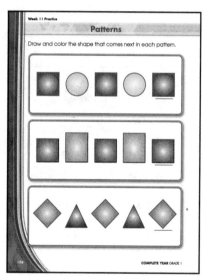

128

130

127

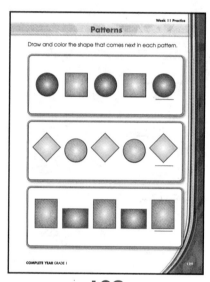

129

132

Answer Key

133

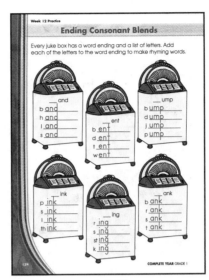

134

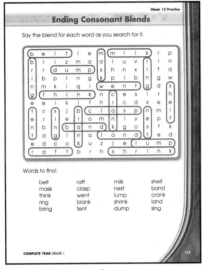

135

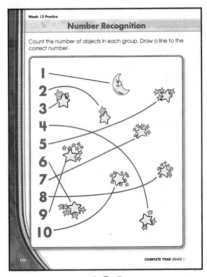

136

137

138

Answer Key

139

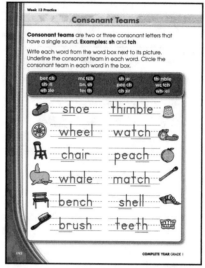

142

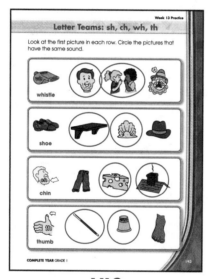

143

144

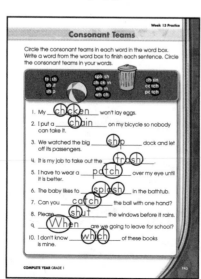

145

Consonant Teams (146)

Look at the words in the word box. Write all of the words that end with the **ng** sound under the picture of the **ring**. Write all of the words that end with the **nk** sound under the picture of the **sink**. Finish the sentences with words from the word box.

| strong | rank | bring | bank | honk | hang | thank |
| long | hunk | song | stung | bunk | song | junk |

ng		**nk**	
strong		rank	
long		hunk	
bring		bank	
song		honk	
stung		bunk	
hang		thank	
sang		junk	

1. **Honk** your horn when you get to my house.
2. He was **stung** by a bumblebee.
3. We are going to put our money in a **bank**.
4. I want to **thank** you for the birthday present.
5. My brother and I sleep in **bunk** beds.

146

Answer Key

147

Number Word Find

Find the number words hidden in the box.

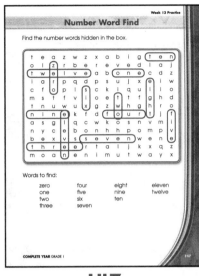

Words to find:

zero	four	eight	eleven
one	five	nine	twelve
two	six	ten	
three	seven		

COMPLETE YEAR GRADE 1

148

Number Words

Number the buildings from one to six.

Draw a line from the word to the number.

two — 1
five — 3
six — 5
four — 6
one — 2
three — 4

COMPLETE YEAR GRADE 1

149

Number Words

Number the buildings from **5** to **10**.

Draw a line from the word to the number.

nine — 8
seven — 10
five — 7
eight — 5
six — 9
ten — 6

COMPLETE YEAR GRADE 1

150

Number Recognition Review

Match the correct number of objects with the number. Then, match the number with the word.

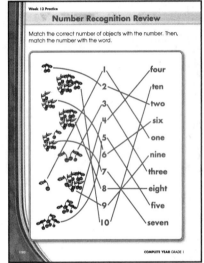

1 — four
2 — ten
3 — two
4 — six
5 — one
6 — nine
7 — three
8 — eight
9 — five
10 — seven

COMPLETE YEAR GRADE 1

152

Digraphs

Circle the correct digraph for each picture. Color the pictures.

Colors will vary.

sh (ch)	(wh) th	ch (sh)
wh (th)	(sh) ch	(tch) sh
(sh) ch	(ch) sh	(wh) th
(sh) ch	(ch) sh	wh (th)

COMPLETE YEAR GRADE 1

153

Cheer Up!

Say the name of each picture. Write the word that rhymes with it. Read the sentences. Use the words to complete the puzzle.

chop chin cheek check chain children child chase

chase   chain
chop   chin

Across

3. They will use a ___ to pull the car.

5. Many ___ like to go to the circus.

6. Write a ___ mark in the correct box.

Down

1. The baby spilled food on his ___.

2. Only one ___ is on the slide.

4. They like to run and ___ each other.

6. Dad will ___ the stump into logs.

7. The kitten licked the girl's ___.

COMPLETE YEAR GRADE 1

413

Answer Key

154

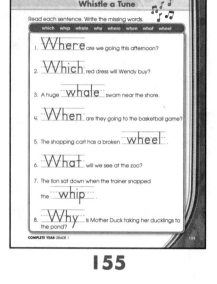

155

156

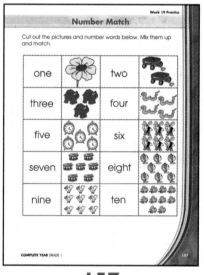

157

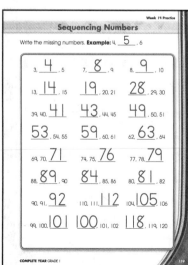

159

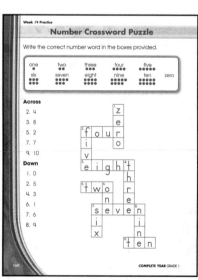

160

Answer Key

Nouns

A **noun** is a word that names a person, place or thing. When you read a sentence, the noun is what the sentence is about.

Complete each sentence with a noun.

The **cat** is fat.

My **house** is blue.

The **tree** has apples.

The **sun** is hot.

COMPLETE YEAR GRADE 1

162

Nouns

Write these naming words in the correct box.

store	zoo	child	baby	teacher	table
cat	park	gym	woman	sock	horse

Person
child woman
baby teacher

Place
store park
zoo gym

Thing
cat table
sock horse

COMPLETE YEAR GRADE 1

163

Proper Nouns

A **proper noun** is a special name for a person, place or thing. It always begins with a capital letter. Write a proper noun to name each person and pet. Use the word box.

Rover	Sarah	Pedro	Jack and Jill	Piggy	Fluffy

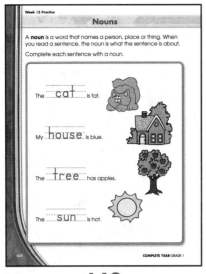

Sarah

Rover

Fluffy

Piggy

Jack and Jill

Pedro

COMPLETE YEAR GRADE 1

164

Proper Nouns

Proper nouns are the names of specific people, places and pets. Proper nouns begin with a capital letter.

Write the proper nouns on the lines below. Use a capital letter at the beginning of each word.

logan, utah
Logan, Utah

mike smith
Mike Smith

lynn cramer
Lynn Cramer

buster
Buster

fluffy
Fluffy

chicago, illinois
Chicago, Illinois

COMPLETE YEAR GRADE 1

165

Pronouns

A **pronoun** is a word that can take the place of a noun in a sentence.

Example: My dad is a pilot. **He** flies airplanes.
My dad loves to fly. **He** is a good pilot.

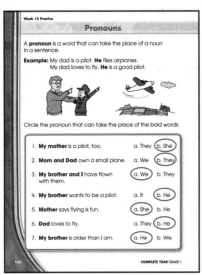

Circle the pronoun that can take the place of the bold words.

1. **My mother** is a pilot, too.   a. They   (b. She)
2. **Mom and Dad** own a small plane.   a. We   (b. They)
3. **My brother and I** have flown with them.   (a. We)   b. They
4. **My brother** wants to be a pilot.   a. It   (b. He)
5. **Mother** says flying is fun.   (a. She)   b. He
6. **Dad** loves to fly.   a. They   (b. He)
7. **My brother** is older than I am.   (a. He)   b. We

COMPLETE YEAR GRADE 1

166

Number Review

Count the objects and write the number word.

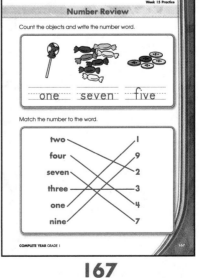

one   seven   five

Match the number to the word.

two — 2
four — 4
seven — 7
three — 3
one — 1
nine — 9

COMPLETE YEAR GRADE 1

167

415

Answer Key

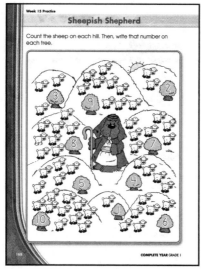

168

169

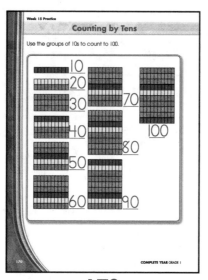

170

172

173

174

Answer Key

175

Week 16 Practice

Verbs

A **verb** tells what a person, animal or thing does. Color the spaces with verbs yellow. Color the other spaces green.

COMPLETE YEAR GRADE 1

Week 16 Practice

Past-Tense Verbs

A **past-tense verb** tells about something that has already happened. Add **ed** to most verbs to show the past tense. Write the past tense of each verb.

Examples: pass**ed** play**ed** walk**ed** crawl**ed**

1. push pushed
2. want wanted
3. help helped
4. heat heated
5. color colored
6. pull pulled

Write the past tense of each verb on the blank.

1. I handed Mom a gift. (hand)
2. She opened it quickly. (open)
3. Mom looked surprised. (look)

COMPLETE YEAR GRADE 1

176

Week 16 Practice

Counting by Fives

Count by fives to draw the path to the playground.

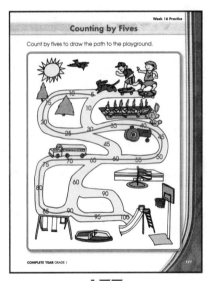

COMPLETE YEAR GRADE 1

177

Week 16 Practice

Counting by Fives

Use tally marks to count by fives. Write the number next to the tallies. **Example:** A tally mark stands for one = 1. Five tally marks look like this = ||||

Tally	Number	Tally	Number
					5														
									10														35
									15														40
													20														45
													25														
													30														50

178

Week 16 Practice

Caterpillar Count

Count by 5s. Draw triangles around each number in the box.

1	2	3	4	5	6	7	8	9	10
11	12	13	14	15	16	17	18	19	20
21	22	23	24	25	26	27	28	29	30
31	32	33	34	35	36	37	38	39	40
41	42	43	44	45	46	47	48	49	50

Count by 5s.
5 10 15 20 25
30 35 40 45 50

Count by 10s. Draw boxes around each number in the box.

1	2	3	4	5	6	7	8	9	10
11	12	13	14	15	16	17	18	19	20
21	22	23	24	25	26	27	28	29	30
31	32	33	34	35	36	37	38	39	40
41	42	43	44	45	46	47	48	49	50

Count by 10s.
10 20 30 40 50

COMPLETE YEAR GRADE 1

179

Week 16 Practice

Less Than, Greater Than

The open mouth points to the larger number. The small point goes to the smaller number. Draw the symbol < or > to the correct number.

Example: 5 > 3 This means that 5 is greater than 3, and 3 is less than 5.

12 > 2   16 > 6

16 > 15   1 < 2

7 > 1   19 > 5

9 > 6   11 < 13

COMPLETE YEAR GRADE 1

180

417

Answer Key

Past-Tense Verbs

Some verbs tell what happened in the past. Verbs that end with **ed** tell about the past. **Examples:** Jill bak**ed** a cake for the bake sale. It tast**ed** delicious.

Write the verb that tells what happened in the past. Write it in the blank.

1. First, Jill **measured** the flour.
   (measured, measures)

2. She **added** some baking powder and salt.
   (adds, added)

3. Next, she **mixed** the sugar and the butter.
   (mixed, mixes)

4. She **cracked** an egg into the bowl.
   (cracked, cracks)

5. She **poured** in a little milk and vanilla.
   (pours, poured)

6. Jill **spooned** the batter into a cake pan.
   (spooned, spoons)

7. She **baked** it for 35 minutes.
   (bakes, baked)

COMPLETE YEAR GRADE 1

182

Past-Tense Verbs

A **past-tense verb** tells about action that has already happened. Add **ed** to most verbs to show the past tense. **Example:** We paint**ed** in art class yesterday. I finish**ed** my picture on time.

Write the past tense of the verb in the blank.

1. Ms. Lewis **passed** out the papers.
   (passes, passed)

2. I **printed** my name.
   (printed, print)

3. We **listened** to the directions.
   (listen, listened)

4. We **added** water to the paint.
   (added, add)

5. I **mixed** yellow and blue.
   (mixed, mix)

6. I **painted** a stem.
   (painted, paint)

7. I **cleaned** my brush.
   (clean, cleaned)

COMPLETE YEAR GRADE 1

183

Circus Action

Circle the verb in each sentence below.

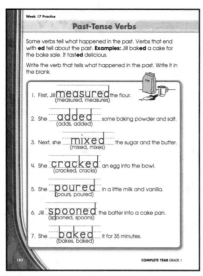

1. The bear (climbs) a ladder.

2. Two tiny dogs (dance).

3. A boy (eats) popcorn.

4. A woman (swings) on a trapeze.

5. The clown (falls) down.

6. A tiger (jumps) through a ring.

COMPLETE YEAR GRADE 1

184

Nouns and Verbs

A **noun** is a person or thing a sentence tells about. A verb tells what the person or thing does.

Circle the noun in each sentence. Underline the verb.
Example: The (cat) sleeps.

1. (Jill) plays a game on the computer.

2. (Children) swim in the pool.

3. The (car) raced around the track.

4. (Mike) throws the ball to his friend.

5. (Monkeys) swing in the trees.

6. (Terry) laughed at the clown.

COMPLETE YEAR GRADE 1

185

Review

Read the sentences below. Draw a red circle around the nouns. Draw a blue line under the verbs.

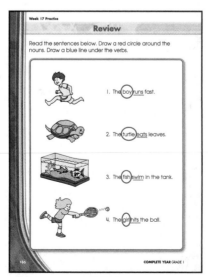

1. The (boy) runs fast.

2. The (turtle) eats leaves.

3. The (fish) swim in the tank.

4. The (girl) hits the ball.

COMPLETE YEAR GRADE 1

186

Place Value

Write the value of each number below.

35	3	tens	5	ones
19	1	ten	9	ones
8	0	tens	8	ones
26	2	tens	6	ones
49	4	tens	9	ones
10	1	ten	0	ones

Write the number below.

4 tens 6 ones	46	3 tens 2 ones	32
2 tens 9 ones	29	4 tens 0 ones	40
1 ten 4 ones	14	0 tens 6 ones	6
2 tens 1 one	21	4 tens 7 ones	47
3 tens 3 ones	33	1 ten 1 one	11

COMPLETE YEAR GRADE 1

187

Answer Key

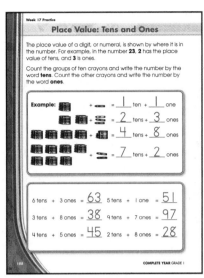

188

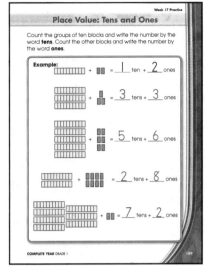

189

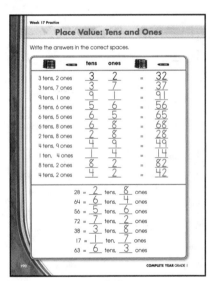

190

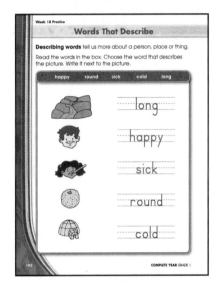

192

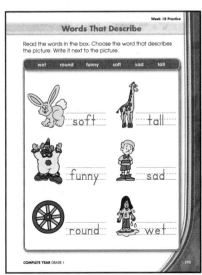

193

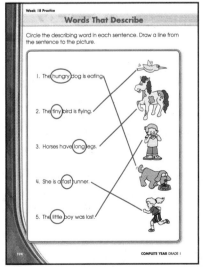

194

Answer Key

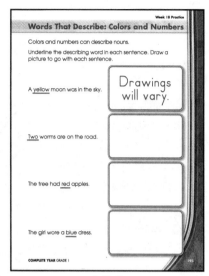

195

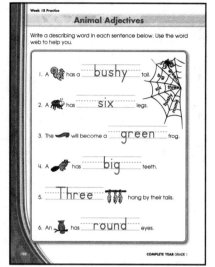

196

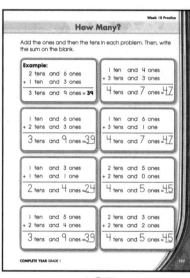

197

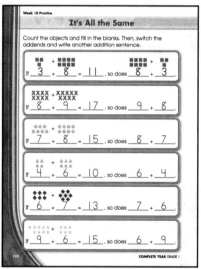

198

199

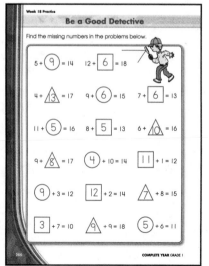

200

Answer Key

206

What's What?

Write the words from the word box in the correct place.

car	house	boat	plane	cow	window
girl	hen	bird	dog	tree	rocks

Living
1. girl
2. hen
3. bird
4. dog
5. cow
6. tree

Non-Living
1. car
2. house
3. boat
4. plane
5. window
6. rocks

COMPLETE YEAR GRADE 1

207

Food Fun

Read the names of each food in the box. Write the words where they belong.

carrots	cherries	chicken	cheese	fish	ham
cake	lettuce	bagel	oranges	pears	rolls
beans	milk	toast	pie	candy bar	yogurt

GRAINS: bagel, toast, rolls

VEGETABLE: carrots, lettuce, beans

DAIRY: milk, cheese, yogurt

FRUITS: cherries, oranges, pears

SWEETS: cake, candy bar, pie

MEATS: fish, chicken, ham

COMPLETE YEAR GRADE 1

208

Classifying

Classifying is putting similar things into groups.
Write each word from the word box on the correct line.

baby	donkey	whale	family	fox
uncle	goose	grandfather	kangaroo	policeman

People
- baby
- family
- grandfather
- policeman
- uncle

Animals
- goose
- whale
- fox
- kangaroo
- donkey

COMPLETE YEAR GRADE 1

209

Classifying

Read the sentences. Write the words from the word box where they belong.

bush	rocket	cake	thunder	bicycle	Danger
airplane	wind	candy	rain	car	grass
Stop	truck	Poison	flower	pie	bird

1. These things taste sweet.
   cake   candy   pie
2. These things come when it storms.
   wind   thunder   rain
3. These things have wheels.
   truck   bicycle   car
4. These are words you see on signs.
   Stop   Poison   Danger
5. These things can fly.
   airplane   rocket   bird
6. These things grow in the ground.
   bush   flower   grass

COMPLETE YEAR GRADE 1

210

Classifying

The words in each box form a group. Choose the word from the word box that describes each group and write it on the line.

clothes	animals	colors
fruits	noises	toys
family	coins	flowers

rose buttercup tulip daisy	crash bang ring pop	mother father sister brother
flowers	noises	family

puzzle wagon blocks doll	green purple blue red	grapes orange apple plum
toys	colors	fruits

shirt socks dress coat	dime penny nickel quarter	dog horse elephant moose
clothes	coins	animals

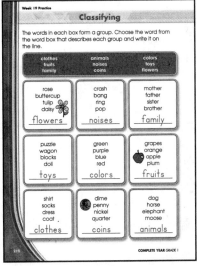

COMPLETE YEAR GRADE 1

211

Addition 1-5

Count the tools in each toolbox. Write your answers in the blanks. Circle the problem that matches your answer.

2 + 2   2 + 1   4
5 + 0   4 + 2   6

6 + 2   4 + 3   8
3 + 1   2 + 3   5

COMPLETE YEAR GRADE 1

Answer Key

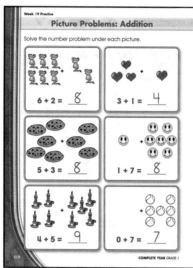

212

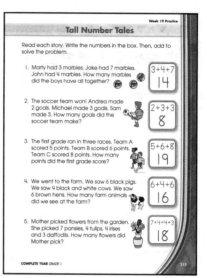

213

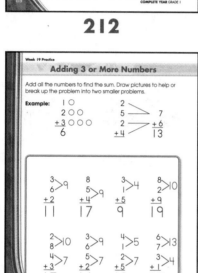

214

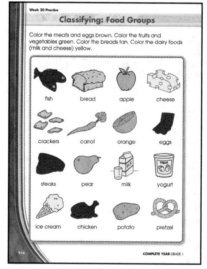

216

217

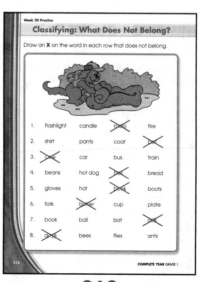

218

Answer Key

219

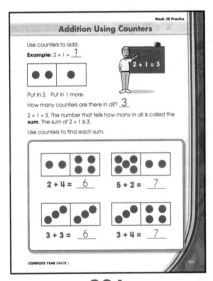

221

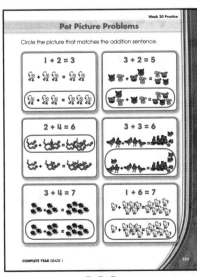

223

220

222

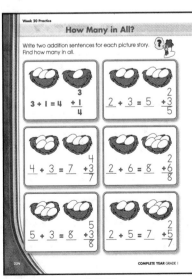

224

Answer Key

226

227

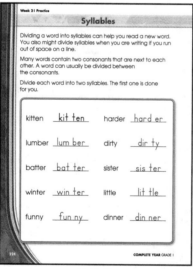

228

229

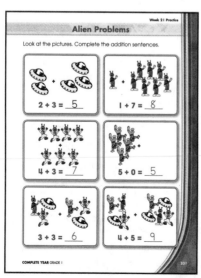

231

232

Answer Key

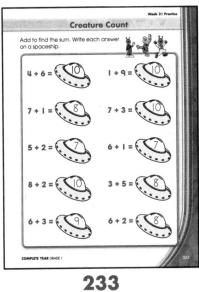

233

234

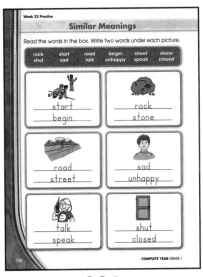

236

237

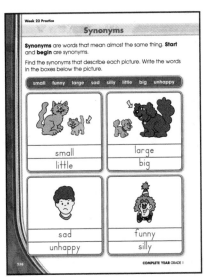

238

239

Answer Key

240

Synonyms

Synonyms are words that have the same meaning.

Read each sentence and look at the underlined word. Circle the word that means the same thing. Write the new words.

1. The little dog ran. — tall   funny   (small)
2. The happy girl smiled. — (glad)   sad   good
3. The bird is in the big tree. — green   pretty   (tall)
4. He was nice to me. — (kind)   mad   bad
5. The baby is tired. — (sleepy)   sad   little

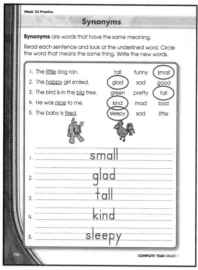

1. small
2. glad
3. tall
4. kind
5. sleepy

COMPLETE YEAR GRADE 1

241

How Many in All?

Count the number in each group and write the number on the line. Then, add the groups together and write the sum.

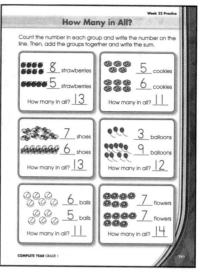

- 8 strawberries
- 5 strawberries
- How many in all? 13

- 5 cookies
- 6 cookies
- How many in all? 11

- 7 shoes
- 6 shoes
- How many in all? 13

- 3 balloons
- 9 balloons
- How many in all? 12

- 6 balls
- 5 balls
- How many in all? 11

- 7 flowers
- 7 flowers
- How many in all? 14

COMPLETE YEAR GRADE 1

242

Addition Grid

Write the sums where the columns and rows meet. The first one shows you what to do.

+	1	2	3	4	5	6	7	8	9
1	2	3	4	5	6	7	8	9	10
2	3	4	5	6	7	8	9	10	11
3	4	5	6	7	8	9	10	11	12
4	5	6	7	8	9	10	11	12	13
5	6	7	8	9	10	11	12	13	14
6	7	8	9	10	11	12	13	14	15
7	8	9	10	11	12	13	14	15	16
8	9	10	11	12	13	14	15	16	17
9	10	11	12	13	14	15	16	17	18

COMPLETE YEAR GRADE 1

243

Now, on the Count of . . .

Trace each number and write its number word next to it.

1 one   2 two   3 three
4 four   5 five   6 six
7 seven   8 eight
9 nine   10 ten

Solve the problems. Write the answers on the lines. Then, write the answers using the correct number words in the puzzle.

Across
1. 3 + 2 = 5
2. 4 + 2 = 6
3. 2 + 1 = 3
4. 1 + 0 = 1
5. 5 + 3 = 8
7. 2 + 7 = 9

Down
1. 2 + 2 = 4
2. 4 + 3 = 7
3. 0 + 2 = 2
6. 4 + 6 = 10

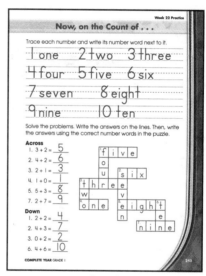

COMPLETE YEAR GRADE 1

244

Addition: Commutative Property

The **commutative property of addition** states that even if the order of the numbers is changed in an addition sentence, the sum will stay the same.

Example: 2 + 3 = 5
                3 + 2 = 5

Look at the addition sentences below. Complete the addition sentences by writing the missing numerals.

5 + 4 = 9   3 + 1 = 4   2 + 6 = 8
4 + 5 = 9   1 + 3 = 4   6 + 2 = 8

6 + 1 = 7   4 + 3 = 7   1 + 9 = 10
1 + 6 = 7   3 + 4 = 7   9 + 1 = 10

Now try these:

6 + 3 = 9   10 + 2 = 12   8 + 3 = 11
3 + 6 = 9   2 + 10 = 12   3 + 8 = 11

Look at these sums. Can you think of two number sentences that would show the commutative property of addition?

___ + ___ = 9   Answers will vary.   ___ + ___ = 9

COMPLETE YEAR GRADE 1

246

Synonyms

Read each sentence and look at the underlined word. Circle the word that means the same thing. Write the new words.

1. The boy was mad. — happy   (angry)   pup
2. The dog is brown. — (pup)   cat   rat
3. I like to scream. — soar   mad   (shout)
4. The bird can fly. — (soar)   jog   warm
5. The girl can run. — sleep   (jog)   shout
6. I am hot. — (warm)   cold   soar

1. angry
2. pup
3. shout
4. soar
5. jog
6. warm

COMPLETE YEAR GRADE 1

Answer Key

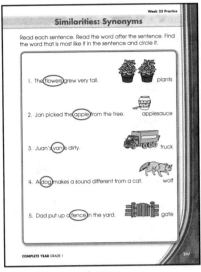

247

248

249

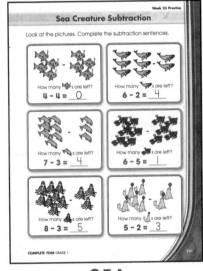

251

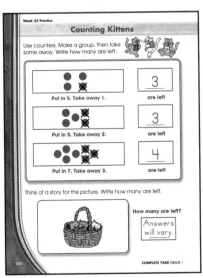

252

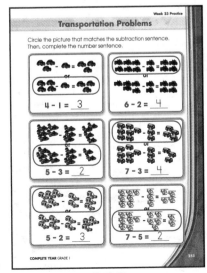

253

Answer Key

254

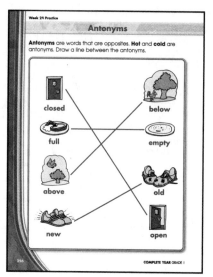

256

257

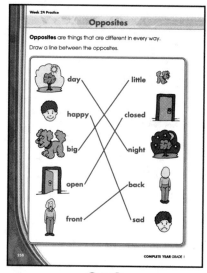

258

259

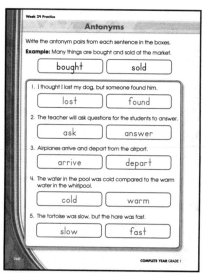

260

Answer Key

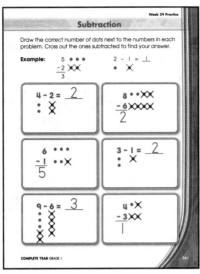

261

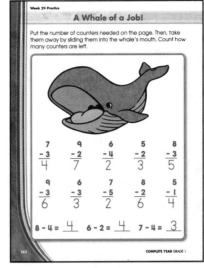

262

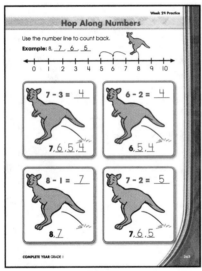

263

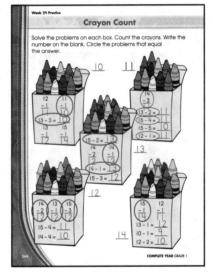

264

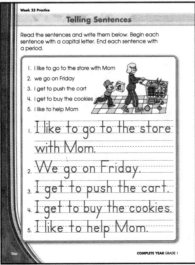

266

Asking Sentences

Write the first word of each asking sentence. Be sure to begin each question with a capital letter. End each question with a question mark.

1. Do you like the zoo? do
2. How much does it cost? how
3. Can you feed the ducks? can
4. Will you see the monkeys? will
5. What time will you eat lunch? what

COMPLETE YEAR GRADE 1

267

Answer Key

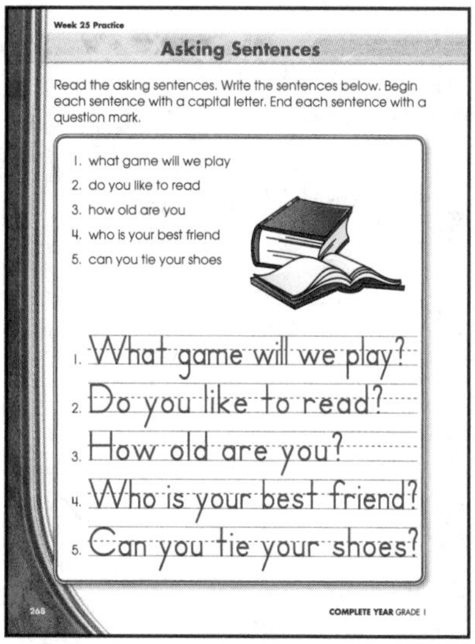
Week 25 Practice

Asking Sentences

Read the asking sentences. Write the sentences below. Begin each sentence with a capital letter. End each sentence with a question mark.

1. what game will we play
2. do you like to read
3. how old are you
4. who is your best friend
5. can you tie your shoes

1. What game will we play?
2. Do you like to read?
3. How old are you?
4. Who is your best friend?
5. Can you tie your shoes?

268 COMPLETE YEAR GRADE 1

268

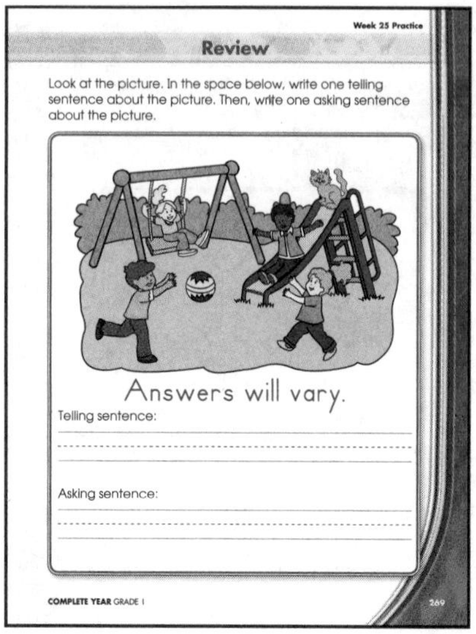
Week 25 Practice

Review

Look at the picture. In the space below, write one telling sentence about the picture. Then, write one asking sentence about the picture.

Answers will vary.

Telling sentence:

Asking sentence:

COMPLETE YEAR GRADE 1 269

269

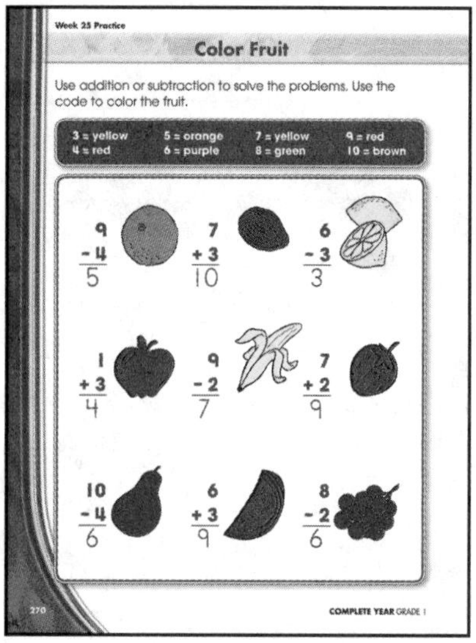
Week 25 Practice

Color Fruit

Use addition or subtraction to solve the problems. Use the code to color the fruit.

3 = yellow 4 = red 5 = orange 6 = purple 7 = yellow 8 = green 9 = red 10 = brown

9 − 4 = 5 7 + 3 = 10 6 − 3 = 3

1 + 3 = 4 9 − 2 = 7 7 + 2 = 9

10 − 4 = 6 6 + 3 = 9 8 − 2 = 6

270 COMPLETE YEAR GRADE 1

270

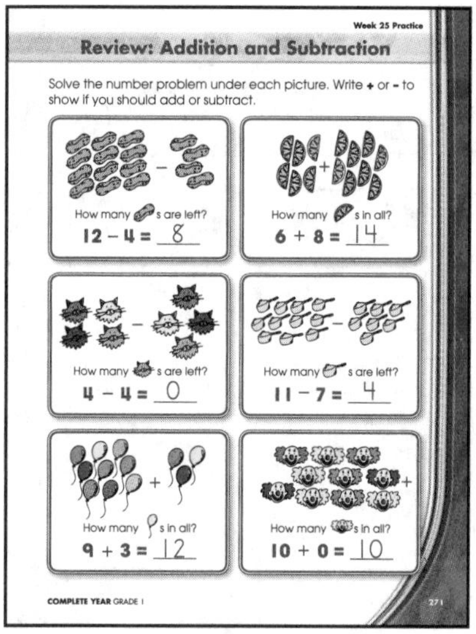
Week 25 Practice

Review: Addition and Subtraction

Solve the number problem under each picture. Write + or − to show if you should add or subtract.

How many are left? 12 − 4 = 8

How many in all? 6 + 8 = 14

How many are left? 4 − 4 = 0

How many are left? 11 − 7 = 4

How many in all? 9 + 3 = 12

How many in all? 10 + 0 = 10

COMPLETE YEAR GRADE 1 271

271

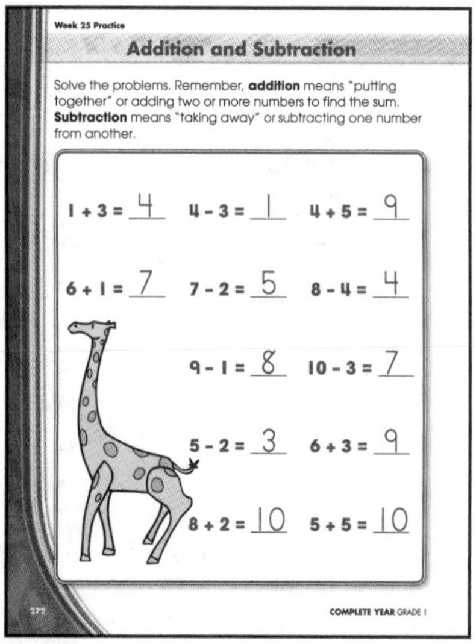
Week 25 Practice

Addition and Subtraction

Solve the problems. Remember, **addition** means "putting together" or adding two or more numbers to find the sum. **Subtraction** means "taking away" or subtracting one number from another.

1 + 3 = 4 4 − 3 = 1 4 + 5 = 9

6 + 1 = 7 7 − 2 = 5 8 − 4 = 4

9 − 1 = 8 10 − 3 = 7

5 − 2 = 3 6 + 3 = 9

8 + 2 = 10 5 + 5 = 10

272 COMPLETE YEAR GRADE 1

272

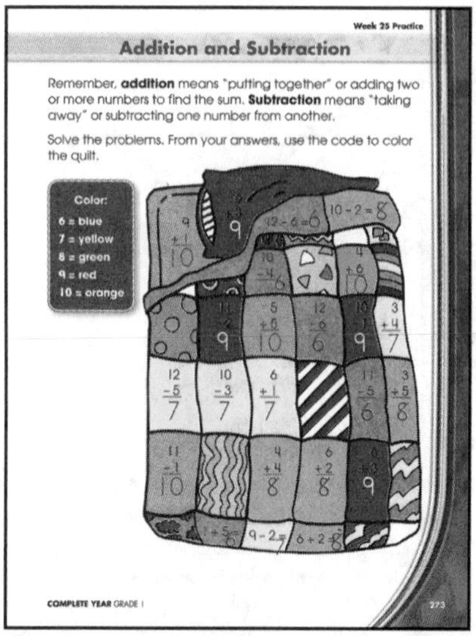
Week 25 Practice

Addition and Subtraction

Remember, **addition** means "putting together" or adding two or more numbers to find the sum. **Subtraction** means "taking away" or subtracting one number from another.

Solve the problems. From your answers, use the code to color the quilt.

Color:
6 = blue
7 = yellow
8 = green
9 = red
10 = orange

COMPLETE YEAR GRADE 1 273

273

Answer Key

274

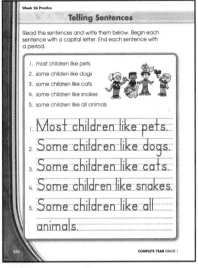

276

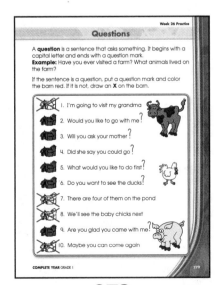

277

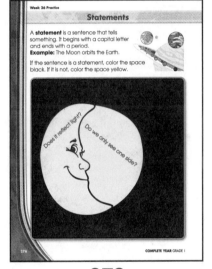

278

279

280

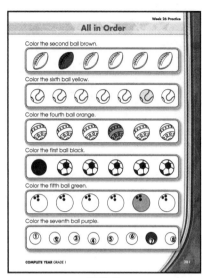

281

All in Order

Color the second ball brown.

Color the sixth ball yellow.

Color the fourth ball orange.

Color the first ball black.

Color the fifth ball green.

Color the seventh ball purple.

282

Let's Get Things in Order!

Help Mrs. Brown pick flowers in her garden. The flowers she wants are listed in the chart. Use the descriptions to color the flowers in her garden.

↓	→	Color it:
1st row	6th flower	red
2nd row	4th flower	blue
3rd row	1st flower	yellow
4th row	9th flower	pink
5th row	10th flower	orange
6th row	2nd flower	green
7th row	5th flower	black
8th row	7th flower	gray
9th row	8th flower	purple
10th row	3rd flower	brown

283

Flags First

Color the ninth flag red.
Write **O** on the second flag.
Color the eighth flag blue.
Write **D** on the fourth flag.
Color the sixth flag yellow.
Write **G** on the first flag.
Color the tenth flag purple.
Write **O** on the third flag.
Color the seventh flag green.
Color the fifth flag orange.
What word did you spell? GOOD

284

Ordinal Numbers

Ordinal numbers are used to indicate order in a series, such as **first**, **second** or **third**.

Draw a line to the picture that corresponds to the ordinal number in the left column.

eighth
third
sixth
ninth
seventh
second
fourth
first
fifth
tenth

286

Commas

Commas are used to separate words in a series of three or more.

My favorite fruits are apples, bananas, and oranges.

Put commas where they are needed in each sentence.

1. Please buy milk, eggs, bread, and cheese.

2. I need a folder, paper, and pencils for school.

3. Some good pets are cats, dogs, gerbils, fish, and rabbits.

4. Aaron, Mike, and Matt went to the baseball game.

5. Major forms of transportation are planes, trains, and automobiles.

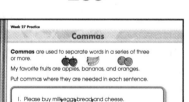

287

Commas

We use commas to separate the day from the year.
Example: May 13, 1950

Write the dates in the blanks. Put the commas in and capitalize the name of each month.
Example: Jack and Dave were born on february 22 2005.
February 22, 2005

1. My father's birthday is may 19 1978.
May 19, 1978

2. My sister was fourteen on december 13 2012.
December 13, 2012

3. Lauren's seventh birthday was on november 30 2010.
November 30, 2010

4. october 13 2013 was the last day I saw my lost cat.
October 13, 2013

5. On april 17 2005, we saw the Grand Canyon.
April 17, 2005

6. Our vacation lasted from april 2 2002 to april 26 2002.
April 2, 2002 to April 26, 2002

7. Molly's baby sister was born on august 14 2011.
August 14, 2011

8. My mother was born on june 22 1980.
June 22, 1980

Answer Key

Prefixes: The Three Rs

Prefixes are syllables added to the beginning of words that change their meaning. The prefix **re** means "again."

Read the story. Then, follow the instructions.

Kim wants to find ways she can save the Earth. She studies the "three Rs"—reduce, reuse and recycle. Reduce means to make less. Both reuse and recycle mean to use again.

Add **re** to the beginning of each word below. Use the new words to complete the sentences.

re build   re fill
re read   re tell
re write   re run

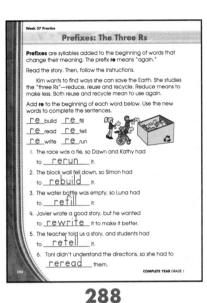

1. The race was a tie, so Dawn and Kathy had to __rerun__ it.

2. The block wall fell down, so Simon had to __rebuild__ it.

3. The water bottle was empty, so Luna had to __refill__ it.

4. Javier wrote a good story, but he wanted to __rewrite__ it to make it better.

5. The teacher told us a story, and students had to __retell__ it.

6. Toni didn't understand the directions, so she had to __reread__ them.

COMPLETE YEAR GRADE 1

288

Suffixes

Write a word from the word box next to its root word.

| coming | visited | running | carried | swimming |
| lived | hurried | rained | sitting | racing |

run __running__   come __coming__
live __lived__   carry __carried__
hurry __hurried__   race __racing__
swim __swimming__   rain __rained__
visit __visited__   sit __sitting__

Write a word from the word box to finish each sentence.

1. I __visited__ my grandmother during vacation.

2. Mary went __swimming__ at the lake with her cousin.

3. Jim __carried__ the heavy package for his mother.

4. It __rained__ and stormed all weekend.

5. Cars go very fast when they are __racing__.

COMPLETE YEAR GRADE 1

289

Suffixes

Read the story. Underline the words that end with **est**, **ed** or **ing**. On the lines below, write the root words for each word you underlined.

The funniest book I ever read was about a girl named Nan. Nan did everything backward. She even spelled her name backward. Nan slept in the day and played at night. She dried her hair before washing it. She turned on the light after she finished her book—which she read from the back to the front! When it rained, Nan waited until she was inside before opening her umbrella. She even walked backward. The silliest part: The only thing Nan did forward was back up!

1. funny
2. name
3. spell
4. play
5. dry
6. wash
7. turn
8. finish
9. rain
10. wait
11. open
12. walk
13. silly

COMPLETE YEAR GRADE 1

290

Ordinal Numbers

Draw an **X** on the first vegetable, draw a circle around the second vegetable, and draw a square around the third vegetable.

Write the ordinal number below the picture.

first second third fourth fifth sixth seventh eighth ninth tenth

✂ **Cut** the children apart. Mix them up. Then, put them back in the correct order.

| first | second | third | fourth | fifth | sixth | seventh | eighth | ninth | tenth |

COMPLETE YEAR GRADE 1

291

Sequencing: At the Movies

The children are watching a movie. Read the sentences. Cut out the pictures below. Glue them where they belong in the picture.

1. The first child is eating popcorn.
2. The third child is eating candy.
3. The fourth child has a cup of fruit punch.
4. The second child is eating a big pretzel.

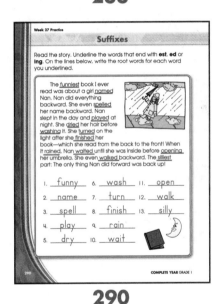

COMPLETE YEAR GRADE 1

293

Different Meanings

Circle the word that matches the picture. Then, write the other word in the blank to complete the sentence.

This is a present __for__ your birthday. (four / for)

Jane lost a __pair__ of new shoes. (pair / pear)

We __rode__ in the car for two hours. (road / rode)

The boys will either swim __or__ go to the ball game. (oar / or)

Let's __meet__ at eight o'clock. (meet / meat)

The scrape on his knee causes a lot of __pain__. (pane / pain)

Old Mother Hubbard's cupboard was __bare__. (bear / bare)

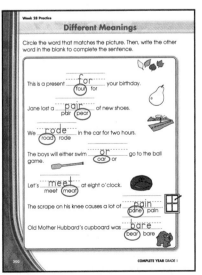

COMPLETE YEAR GRADE 1

300

Answer Key

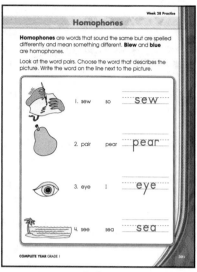

301

302

303

304

305

306

Answer Key

307

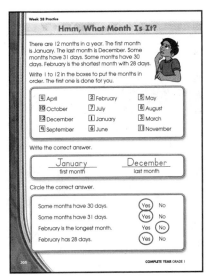

308

310

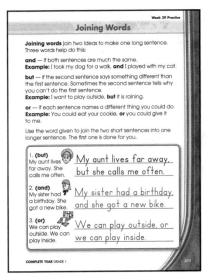

311

312

Correctly Positioned

Week 29 Practice

Read the sentences. Use the words to complete the sentences.

| after | last | right | before | first | left | now | next |

1. Buck will read the _____ story. → n e x t

2. We must go to the bus stop _____. → n o w

3. We must get some logs _____ we can build a fire. → b e f o r e

4. That is the _____ slice of pizza. → l a s t

5. Plant the flowers to the _____ of the tree. → r i g h t

6. This was the _____ time she sang by herself. → f i r s t

7. Go to the _____, not the right. → l e f t

8. She will go to bed _____ she brushes her teeth. → a f t e r

COMPLETE YEAR GRADE 1

313

Answer Key

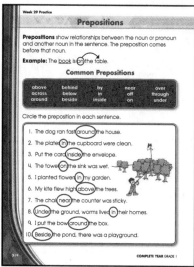

314

315

316

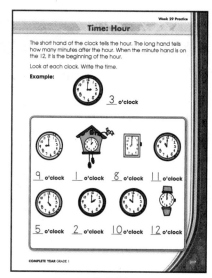

317

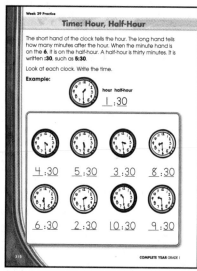

318

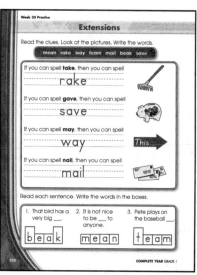

320

Answer Key

My World

321

322

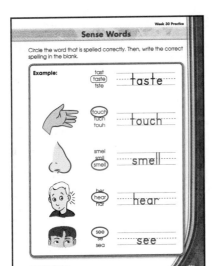

323

Time: Hour, Half-Hour

324

325

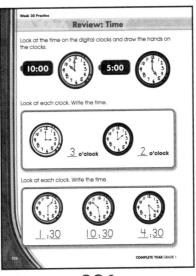

326

Answer Key

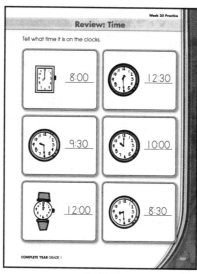

327

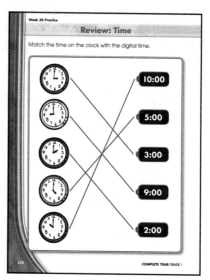

328

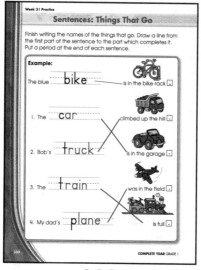

330

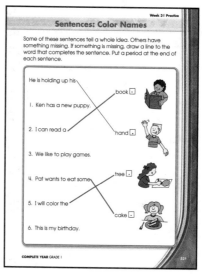

331

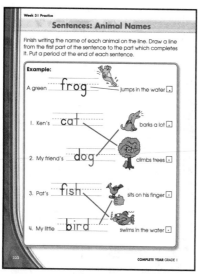

332

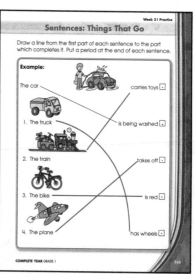

333

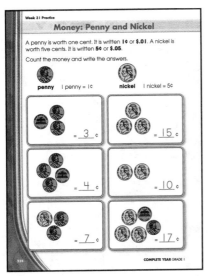

334

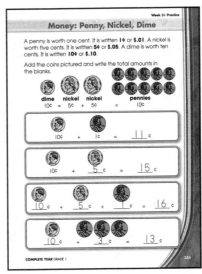

335

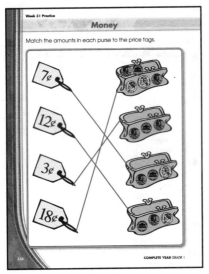

336

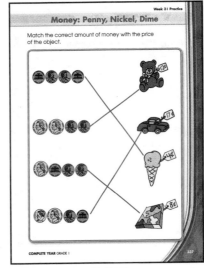

337

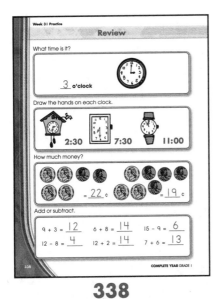

338

Which Word?

Write the words in alphabetical order. The first one has been done for you.

| bath | bang | teeth | rang | path | hang | math | sang |

1. bang 2. bath 3. hang 4. math
5. path 6. rang 7. sang 8. teeth

Complete the sentences below.

1. The hammer struck the nail with a loud __bang__.
2. At 7:00, Casie's alarm __rang__.
3. Joseph likes to help __hang__ the laundry on the clothesline.
4. My brother __sang__ in the choir.
5. Renee's favorite subject in school is __math__.
6. Ron lost his first two baby __teeth__.
7. My friends like to go hiking on a __path__ through the forest.
8. Sara takes a __bath__ on Saturday night.

340

Answer Key

341

342

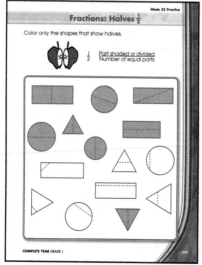

343

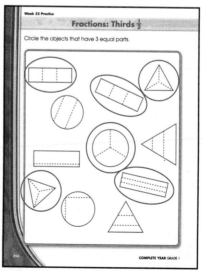

344

345

346

Answer Key

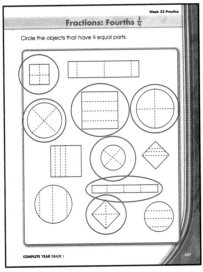

347

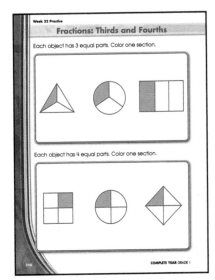

348

350

351

352

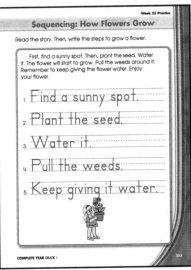

353

Answer Key

Sequencing: Eating a Cone

What if a person never ate an ice-cream cone? Could you explain how to eat it? Think about what you do when you eat an ice-cream cone.

Write directions to teach someone how to eat an ice-cream cone.

How to Eat an Ice-Cream Cone

1. _____
2. _____
   Answers will vary.
3. _____
4. _____

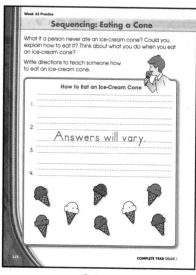

354

Review: Fractions

Count the equal parts, then write the fraction.

Example:

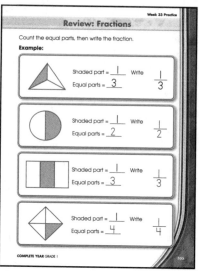

Shaded part = 1   Equal parts = 3   Write $\frac{1}{3}$

Shaded part = 1   Equal parts = 2   Write $\frac{1}{2}$

Shaded part = 1   Equal parts = 3   Write $\frac{1}{3}$

Shaded part = 1   Equal parts = 4   Write $\frac{1}{4}$

355

Review

Color the object with thirds red. Color the object with halves blue. Color the object with fourths green.

Draw a line to the correct equal part.

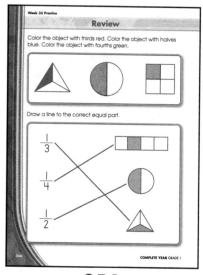

$\frac{1}{3}$

$\frac{1}{4}$

$\frac{1}{2}$

356

Equal and Unequal Parts

Cut out each shape below along the solid lines. Then, fold the shape on the dotted lines. Do you have equal or unequal parts? Sort the shapes by equal and unequal parts.

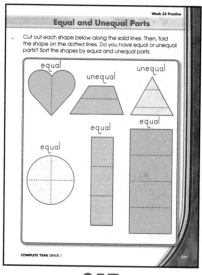

equal   unequal   unequal   equal   equal   equal

357

Comprehension: Cats

Look at the pictures and read about four cats. Then, write the correct name beside each cat.

Fluffy, Blackie and Tiger are playing. Tom is sleeping. Blackie has spots. Tiger has stripes.

Fluffy

Tiger

Blackie

Tom

360

Same and Different: Cats

Compare the picture of the cats on page 360 to this picture. Write a word from the box to tell what is different about each cat.

| purple ball | green bow | blue brush | red collar |

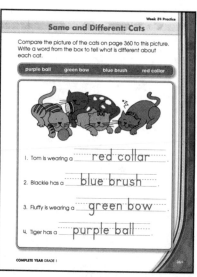

1. Tom is wearing a   red collar
2. Blackie has a   blue brush
3. Fluffy is wearing a   green bow
4. Tiger has a   purple ball

361

442

COMPLETE YEAR GRADE 1

Answer Key

Comprehension: Babies

Read about babies. Then, write the answers.

Babies are small. Some babies cry a lot. They cry when they are wet. They cry when they are hungry. They smile when they are dry. They smile when they are fed.

1. Name two reasons babies cry.

   wet   hungry

2. Name two reasons babies smile.

   dry   fed

3. Write a baby's name you like.

   Answers will vary.

362

Comprehension: Babies

Read each sentence. Draw a picture of a baby's face in the box to show if she would cry or smile.

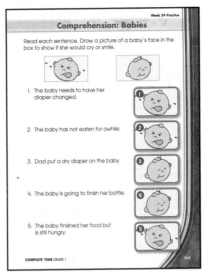

1. The baby needs to have her diaper changed.

2. The baby has not eaten for awhile.

3. Dad put a dry diaper on the baby.

4. The baby is going to finish her bottle.

5. The baby finished her food but is still hungry.

363

Fraction Food

Count the equal parts. Circle the fraction that names one of the parts.

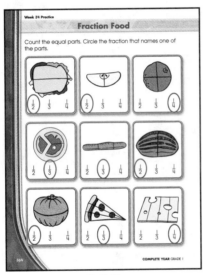

364

Fraction Review

How many equal parts?

2   3   4   4   2

Color shapes with 2 equal parts red. Color shapes with 3 equal parts blue. Color shapes with 4 equal parts green.

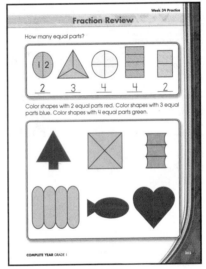

365

Graphing

Answer the questions about the graph on page 366.

- How many people like hot dogs best?   6

- How many people like pizza best?   8

- How many people like chicken best?   6

- Which food do most people like best?   pizza

- Which two foods do the same number of people like best?

   hot dog and chicken

- Which food do the fewest number of people like best?

   hamburger

367

Living or Not Living?

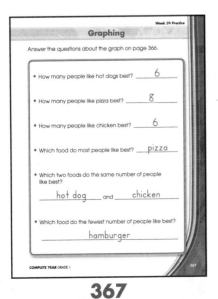

Living things need air, food and water.
Living things grow.
Some living things move.
Some living things do not move.

What is not living in the picture? water and rock

Go outside. Find something living.

What is it?   Answers will vary.

Find something not living.

What is it?   Answers will vary.

Find other things.

Write them here.

Living	Not Living
Answers will vary.	

368

443

Answer Key

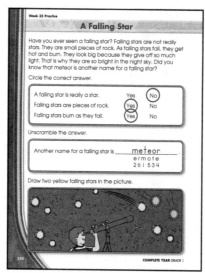

370

371

372

373

374

375

Length

Use a penny to measure each object.

is __1__ penny long.

is __3__ pennies long.

is __4__ pennies long.

is __3__ pennies long.

is __3__ pennies long.

is __3__ pennies long.

is __3__ pennies long.

376

COMPLETE YEAR GRADE 1

376

Measurement

A ruler has 12 inches. 12 inches equal 1 foot.

Cut out the ruler at the bottom of the page. Measure the objects to the nearest inch.

The screwdriver is __5__ inches long.

The pencil is __4__ inches long.

The pen is __3__ inches long.

The fork is __4__ inches long.

✂ Cut -

COMPLETE YEAR GRADE 1

377

377

Traveling the World Through Maps

Pretend that you are an explorer traveling around the world. What is one of the first things you will need? A map of the Earth, of course! A map is a group of carefully drawn pictures. It can be of the world, your city or your neighborhood. Maps have been used for a long time by people all over the world. The very first maps were made from dirt, sand or clay. The Chinese painted maps on silk. Why do you think people need maps?

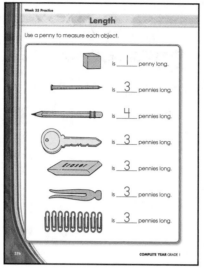

Write on the lines below.

Answers will vary.

380

COMPLETE YEAR GRADE 1

380

Answer Key

All About You!

Write a story telling what you like to do. Then, draw a picture to go with your story on another sheet of paper.

Answers will vary.

COMPLETE YEAR GRADE 1

381

Sentence Sequence

Sentences can tell a story. Write **1**, **2** and **3** in the circles to tell what happened first, second and third. Write a sentence to tell about each picture.

1.
2. Answers will vary.
3.

COMPLETE YEAR GRADE 1

382

Writing: My Snake Story

Write a fictional (make-believe) story about a snake. Make sure to include details and a title.

title

Answers will vary.

COMPLETE YEAR GRADE 1

383

384

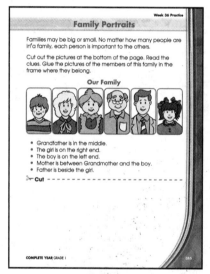

385

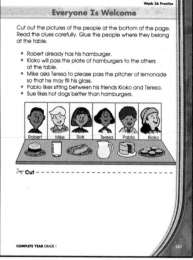

387